OCR Religious Ethics for AS and A2

Third Edition

JILL OLIPHANT

EDITED BY JON MAYLED

Routledge
Taylor & Francis Group

LONDON AND NEW YORK

First edition published in 2007
Second edition published in 2008

This third edition published in 2014
by Routledge
2 Park Square, Milton Park, Abingdon, Oxon OX14 4RN

and by Routledge
711 Third Avenue, New York, NY 10017

Routledge is an imprint of the Taylor & Francis Group, an informa business

British Library Cataloguing in Publication Data
A catalogue record for this book is available from the British Library

Library of Congress Cataloging in Publication Data
Oliphant, Jill, 1949–
    OCR religious ethics for AS and A2 / Jill Oliphant ; edited by
    Jon Mayled. – Third Edition.
        pages cm
    Includes bibliographical references and index.
    1. Religious ethics–Textbooks. I. Mayled, Jon, editor of compilation.
    II. Oliphant, Jill, 1949– Religious ethics for AS and A2. III. Title.
    BJ1188.O45 2014
    205–dc23   2014005765

ISBN: 978-0-415-52357-8 (pbk)
ISBN: 978-1-315-76647-8 (ebk)

Typeset in CharterITC
by Keystroke, Station Road, Codsall, Wolverhampton
Printed and bound by CPI Group (UK) Ltd, Croydon, CR0 4YY

This book is dedicated to Hannah, Lucinda and Miranda

Contents

Illustrations

Acknowledgements

I am very grateful to the many people who have helped me prepare this book, particularly to Lesley Riddle of Taylor & Francis for commissioning me to write this text. I much appreciate the support I have received from Taylor & Francis staff. I also wish to thank greatly the people who have read drafts of the book and made so many helpful suggestions, for all their assistance and support, not to mention their patience while waiting for parts of the text.

I am also very grateful to the friends and family members who have supported and encouraged this project. I would like to thank in particular the sixth-form students of Angley School who read early drafts of the book, especially Emma Whittall who did the drawings for the chapter on genetic engineering.

The scripture quotations contained herein are from The New Revised Standard Version of the Bible, Anglicised Edition, copyright © 1989, 1995 by the Division of Christian Education of the National Council of the Churches of Christ in the United States of America, and are used by permission. All rights reserved.

Extracts from examination papers and specification details are produced by the kind permission of OCR.

Every effort has been made to trace copyright-holders. Any omissions brought to our attention will be remedied in future editions.

How to Use this Book

This book has been written for OCR students but it will be of use to all AS and A2 level Religious Studies students, as well as students taking the Ethics section of AS/A2 Philosophy and Scottish National Examinations at Higher Level.

The book is designed for students to use in class and at home. Every chapter provides an overview of the major themes and issues of Religious Ethics on the OCR specification for Religious Studies. The following six features are designed to help you make the most effective use of the book:

1 **What you will learn about in this chapter**
   This highlights the key issue or issues you should think about while studying each chapter.
2 **OCR checklist**
   The box in each chapter about the OCR specification tells you which topics from the AS/A2 Religious Studies course are covered.
3 **Essential terminology box**
   At the beginning of every chapter there is a box listing the key terminology for the chapter. You should be able to use this terminology accurately in examinations.
4 **Review questions**
   The review questions in every chapter are designed to test your understanding of topics discussed in the chapter. Make use of this section as a way to assess your learning about and from the issues in the chapter.
5 **Examination questions practice**
   At the end of every chapter there is a section about answering examination questions on the topic, with an exam style question.
6 **Further reading**
   The reading suggested at the end of each chapter suggests ways of exploring topics in greater depth.

Answering Examination Questions

To be successful in Advanced Level Religious Studies you must learn examination techniques. Some advice to guide you is given below, but there is no substitute for practising writing examination questions. There are example questions at the end of the chapters in this book, and your teacher will give you plenty of other questions with which to practise.

Some important aspects to answering examination questions are explained below.

Your work will be assessed on how well you meet the following two Assessment Objectives (AO):

AO1 Demonstrate Knowledge and Understanding

- select and demonstrate clearly relevant knowledge and understanding through the use of evidence, examples and correct language and terminology appropriate to the course of study. In addition, for synoptic assessment, A Level candidates should demonstrate knowledge and understanding of the connections between different elements of their course of study.

AO2 Analysis, Evaluation and Application

- critically evaluate and justify a point of view through the use of evidence and reasoned argument. In addition, for synoptic assessment, A Level candidates should relate elements of their course of study to their broader context and to aspects of human experience.

All AS questions are in two parts (a) and (b). Part (a) assesses AO1 and Part (b) assesses AO2. These are weighted at 70% for AO1 and 30% for AO2.

All A2 questions are in one part. This combines both AO1 and AO2. The AOs are weighted at 70% for AO1 and 30% for AO2.

All questions are marked according to the OCR Levels of Response. See: http://www.ocr.org.uk/qualifications/as-a-level-gce-religious-studies-h172-h572/.

Practise writing answers

It is very important that you practise answering questions for Religious Studies examinations by handwriting answers. In an examination you have very little time to write answers and you have to write not type. This takes practice; try to avoid typing answers when you practise doing examination questions at home.

SUBJECT KNOWLEDGE

At both AS and A2 level the majority of marks are given for your demonstration of a good understanding of the topic the question is examining. It is important not only that you learn the work you have studied, but also that you are able to select the knowledge that is relevant to an answer. For example, if the question is (AS level): *Explain how a follower of Natural Law might approach the issue of abortion*, your answer should be focused on the Natural Law approach to abortion, not writing everything you know about Natural Law or abortion.

When preparing for examination questions, it is a good idea to think about not only what a question is asking, but also what material you have studied that is relevant to the question.

Selecting the correct information

Think about how you would answer the two questions below. Make a list of the topics and information you need to include in any answer. Be specific – for example, do not just say 'Utilitarianism' for question 1.

1   *Explain Mill's approach to Utilitarianism.*
2   *Explain the main strengths of Utilitarianism.*

TIMING

It is very important that you learn how to complete questions in the time available. In an examination the time available is very limited. It is a good idea to practise timing yourself writing answers to examination-style questions. You will get a low mark if a question is incomplete, as this limits the maximum level your answer can reach.

Always try to spend equal amounts of time on each whole question you answer, as each question is worth the same number of marks. However, at AS level there are two parts within a question. In this case you may be expected to spend slightly longer completing the section of each question for which the higher mark is awarded.

UNDERSTANDING THE QUESTIONS

It is very important that you think carefully about what a question is asking you. The table below focuses on some of the common instruction words used in OCR questions and what they mean.

Instruction word	Explanation
Explain as in: '**Explain** Kant's theory of duty.'	When a question uses the word **Explain**, it is telling you to demonstrate your knowledge of the topic in the question, and your ability to select and show understanding of relevant information and to use technical terms accurately. Thus, in the example question, you would need to demonstrate what you know about Kant's theory of duty, such as the categorical imperative, universalisability and the importance of good will.
Discuss as in: 'People are not free to make moral decisions.' **Discuss.**	The word **Discuss** in a question is telling you that you should examine the strengths and weaknesses of arguments for and against the statement in the question. You need to consider whether arguments in favour of and against the statement are successful. To do this, you will need to demonstrate an accurate understanding of one or more philosophers' views and the strengths and w-akness of these views.
'Kant's ethical theory is too inflexible.' **Discuss.**	At **AS level**, you would need to state (not explain in detail) one or more arguments in agreement with the statement, such as Kant's lack of consideration for consequences, the conflict of maxims, and the importance of universal and unchanging principles, and present reasons for and/or against the claim. At **A2 level** if a question uses the word **Discuss**, as well as considering arguments for and against the statement in the question, you need to explain accurately and in detail the philosophers' views and ideas to which the statement is referring. At **AS level** you need only to state the views briefly in a **Discuss** question.
Assess as in: '**Assess** a Utilitarian approach to the environment.'	**Assess** is normally used as an **A2 level** instruction word. By **Assess** the examiner means that you should first **explain** the issue you are being asked to assess and second you should present arguments for and against the issue you have been asked to assess. Part of your assessment should present reasons analysing the strengths and weaknesses of arguments supporting or disagreeing with the issue. You should finish your answer with a conclusion which presents the result of your assessment.

In the case of the example question, you would need to explain clearly and precisely the anthropomorphism of Utilitarianism and the application of the principle of utility. Second, you should present philosophers' and theologians' arguments for and against a Utilitarian approach. You should analyse the strengths and weaknesses of the philosophers' and theologians' arguments concerning a Utilitarian approach to the environment.

Remember that at A2 the two AOs are combined and that you need to demonstrate both in your answer.

To what extent as in:
'*To what extent* can conscience be considered to be the voice of God?'

The instruction *to what extent* commonly appears in the Ethics A2 paper, such as 'To what extent can conscience be considered to be the voice of God?' The question asks why some philosophers and theologians might hold this view. Next, you need to assess the strengths and weaknesses of reasons for holding these views and compare the strengths of the different reasons for holding this view with each other. The *extent* will be limited or defined by the strongest view you have considered.

In the example question you need to explain the strengths and weaknesses of reasons philosophers and theologians give when discussing the ways conscience comes from God. The extent of the role of God in forming conscience will be decided by comparing the different reasons and arguments you present and deciding which one is strongest.

Remember that at A2 the two AOs are combined and that you need to demonstrate both in your answer.

How fair as in:
'*How fair* is the claim that moral language is meaningful, even if religious language is not?'

How fair is another instruction phrase which commonly appears in the Ethics A2 paper, such as 'How fair is the view that Religious Ethics are absolute?' To complete a task beginning with *how fair* you need to explain reasons why philosophers and theologians support this view and then even if Religious Ethics are absolute *assess* the strengths and weaknesses of these reasons. The *fairness* of the view in the question is decided by comparing the strengths of reasons for and against the view in the question and deciding which reasoning is strongest. The view in the question is only fair if you can demonstrate that the reasoning of the philosophers and theologians in agreement with the view in the question is stronger than that of those who disagree.

In the case of the example question above, you would need to explain the reasons why philosophers and theologians might believe Religious Ethics are absolute, and consider the strengths and weaknesses of these reasons when compared to the views of people who disagree. The *fairness* of the view in the question is decided by considering whether arguments that *moral language is meaningful even if religious language is not* are stronger than views which disagree.

Remember that at A2 the two AOs are combined and that you need to demonstrate both in your answer.

Timeline

Scientists, Ethicists and Thinkers

This timeline gives the names and dates of people whose great ideas are discussed within the book. This list is not a comprehensive list of every important or significant ethicist of Western civilisation.

Protagoras (c.480–c.411 BCE)	480 BCE
Socrates (c.470–c.399 BCE)	
Plato (428–347 BCE)	
Aristotle (384–322 BCE)	
Epicurus (341–270 BCE)	
Cicero (106–43 BCE)	
Jesus of Nazareth (c.3 BCE–30)	
Saul of Tarsus/Paul (9–67)	0
Eusebius (c.260–c.340)	
Ambrose of Milan (c.340–397)	
St Jerome (c.347–420)	
Augustine of Hippo (354–430)	
Pelagius (c.360–c.420)	
St Francis of Assisi (1182–1226)	1100
Thomas Aquinas (1225–1274)	1200
John Duns Scotus (c.1266–1308)	
William of Ockham (1280–1349)	
Francisco de Vitoria (1480–1546)	1400
John Calvin (1509–1564)	1500
Francisco Suárez (1548–1617)	
Francis Bacon (1561–1626)	
Hugo Grotius (1583–1645)	
René Descartes (1596–1650)	
Baruch Spinoza (1632–1677)	1600
John Locke (1632–1704)	
Isaac Newton (1642–1727)	
Gottfried Wilhelm Leibniz (1646–1716)	

Joseph Butler (1692–1752)

David Hume (1711–1776)   1700

Emerich de Vattal (1714–1767)

Paul-Henri Thiry (Baron) d'Holbach
(1723–1789)

Immanuel Kant (1724–1804)   1800

Jeremy Bentham (1748–1832)

Pierre Laplace (1749–1827)

John Henry Newman (1801–1890)

John Stuart Mill (1806–1873)

Charles Robert Darwin (1809–1882)

Søren Kierkegaard (1813–1855)

Henry Sidgwick (1838–1900)

Ivan Pavlov (1849–1936)

Sigmund Freud (1856–1939)

Clarence Darrow (1857–1938)

Pope Pius XI (1857–1939)

Mohandas 'Mahatma' Ghandi (1869–1948)

H.A. Prichard (1871–1947)

Bertrand Russell (1872–1970)

G.E. Moore (1873–1958)

W.D. Ross (1877–1971)

John B. Watson (1878–1958)

Albert Einstein (1879–1955)

Karl Barth (1886–1968)

Aldo Leopold (1887–1948)

Reinhold Niebuhr (1892–1971)

Jean Piaget (1896–1980)

Pope Paul VI (1897–1978)

Erich Fromm (1900–1980)   1900

Werner Heisenberg (1901–1976)

Alan Marshall (1902–1984)

Karl Popper (1902–1994)

B.F. Skinner (1904–1990)

Jean-Paul Sartre (1905–1980)

Joseph Fletcher(1905–1991)

Dietrich Bonhoeffer (1906–1945)

Rachel Carson (1907–1964)

C.L. Stevenson (1908–1979)

A.J. Ayer (1910–1989)

Richard Brandt (1910–1997)

Aarne Naess (1912–2009)

Thomas Merton (1915–1968)

J.L. Mackie (1917–1981)
John Hospers (1918–2011)
G.E.M Anscombe (1919–2001)
R.M. Hare (1919–2002)
James Lovelock (1919–)
Philippa Foot (1920–2010)
John Rawls (1921–2002)
Lawrence Kohlberg (1927–1987)
Annette Baier (1929–2012)
Germain Grisez (1929–)
Martin Luther King, Jr. (1929–1968)
Alasdair MacIntyre (1929–)
Judith Jarvis Thomson (1929–)
Bernard Williams (1929–2003)
Enda McDonagh (1930–)
Daniel Macguire (1931–)
Richard Holloway (1933–)
Ted Honderich (1933–)
Richard Sylvan (Routley) (1935–1996)
Walter Wink (1935–2012)
Keith Ward (1938–)
Helga Kuhse (1940–)
James Rachels (1941–2003)
J. Baird Callicott (1941–)
Richard Dawkins (1941–)
Jonathan Glover (1941–)
Michael Slote (1941–)
Joseph Boyle (1942–)
Peter Van Inwagen (1942–)
Rosalind Hursthouse (1943–)
Roger Scruton (1944–)
Mary Anne Warren (1946–2010)
Julia Annas (1946–)
Peter Singer (1946–)
Richard Gula (1947–)
Robert Louden (1953–)
Steven Pinker (1954–)
Robert Song (1962–)   1962

AS ETHICS

PART I

1 What Is Ethics?

Essential terminology

Deduction
Definition
Factual statement
Fallacy
Logic

Ethics is the philosophical study of good and bad, right and wrong. It is commonly used interchangeably with the word 'morality', and is also known as moral philosophy. The study of ethics requires you to look at moral issues such as abortion, euthanasia and cloning, and to examine views that are quite different from your own. You need to be open-minded, you need to use your critical powers, and above all learn from the way different ethical theories approach the issues you study for AS and A2.

Ethics needs to be applied with logic so that we can end up with a set of moral beliefs that are supported with reasons, are consistent and reflect the way we see and act in the world. Ethical theories are constructed logically, but give different weights to different concepts.

However, it is not enough to prove that the theory you agree with is true and reasonable; you must also show where and how other philosophers went wrong.

FALLACIES

With the possible exception of you and me, people usually do not have logical reasons for what they believe. This is especially true for ethical issues. Here are some examples of how not to arrive at a belief. We call them *fallacies*.

Here are some common beliefs; you may recognise your own reasons for holding a particular view:

- A belief based on the mistaken idea that a rule which is generally true is without exceptions; for example: 'Suicide is killing oneself – killing is murder – I'm opposed to euthanasia.'
- A belief based on peer pressure, appeal to herd mentality or xenophobia; for example: 'Most people don't believe in euthanasia, so it's probably wrong.'
- A belief in fact or obligation simply based on sympathy; for example: 'It's horrible to use those poor apes to test drugs, so I'm opposed to it.'

- An argument based on the assumption that there are fewer alternatives than actually exist; for example: 'It's either euthanasia or long, painful suffering.'
- An argument based on only the positive half of the story; for example: 'Animal research has produced loads of benefits – that's why I support it.'
- Hasty generalisation: concluding that a population has some quality based on a misrepresentative sample; for example: 'My grandparents are in favour of euthanasia, and I would think that most old people would agree with it.'
- An argument based on an exaggeration; for example: 'We owe all of our advances in medicine to animal research, and that's why I'm for it.'
- The slippery slope argument: the belief that a first step in a certain direction amounts to going far in that direction; for example: 'If we legalise euthanasia this will inevitably lead to killing the elderly, so I'm opposed to it.'
- A subjective argument that truth varies according to personal opinion; for example: 'Euthanasia may be right for you, but it's wrong for me.'
- An argument based on tradition: the belief that X is justified simply because X has been done in the past; for example: 'We've done well without euthanasia for thousands of years, we shouldn't change now.'

Is–ought fallacy

David Hume (1711–1776) observed that often when people are debating a moral issue they begin with facts and slide into conclusions that are normative; that is, conclusions about how things ought to be. He argued that no amount of facts taken alone can ever be sufficient to imply a normative conclusion: the is–ought fallacy. For example, it is a fact that slavery still exists in some form or other in many countries – that is an 'is'. However, this fact is morally neutral, and it is only when we say we 'ought' to abolish slavery that we are making a moral judgement. The fallacy is saying that the 'ought' statement follows logically from the 'is', but this does not need to be the case. Another example is to say that humans possess reason and this distinguishes us from other animals – it does not logically follow that we ought to exercise our reason to live a fulfilled life.

AREAS OF ETHICS

Ethics looks at what you *ought* to do as distinct from what you may in fact do. Ethics is usually divided into three areas: *meta-ethics, normative ethics* and *applied ethics*.

1   *Meta-ethics* looks at the meaning of the language used in ethics, and
    includes questions such as: are ethical claims capable of being true or
    false, or are they expressions of emotion? If true, is that truth only
    relative to some individual, society or culture? What does it mean to say
    something is good or bad, and what do the words 'good' and 'bad' mean?
    (This is studied at A2.)

2   *Normative ethics* asks the question 'what ought I to do?' and attempts
    to arrive at practical moral standards (or norms) that tell us right from
    wrong, and how to live moral lives. These are what we call ethical
    theories. This may involve explaining the good habits we should
    acquire, looking at whether there are duties we should follow, or
    whether our actions should be guided by their consequences for
    ourselves and/or others. There are various ethical theories that are
    described as normative:

    • **Teleological** or **consequential** ethics, where ethical decisions
      are based on the consequences of an action
    • **Deontological** ethics, which is based on duty and obligation
    • **Virtue Ethics**, which is based on the good character of the moral
      agent (this is studied at A2)
    • Ethics based on **God-given laws (Divine Command)** – see
      Chapter 6 on Religious Ethics.

3   *Applied ethics* is the application of theories of right and wrong and
    theories of value to specific issues such as abortion, euthanasia, cloning,
    foetal research, and lying and honesty.

Ethics is not just giving your own opinion, and the way it is studied at
AS and A2 is very like philosophy: it is limited to facts, logic and definition.
Ideally, a philosopher is able to prove that a theory is true and reasonable
based on accurate definitions and verifiable facts. Once these definitions and
facts have been established, a philosopher can develop the theory through a
process of deduction, by showing what logically follows from the definitions
and facts. The theory may then be applied to controversial moral issues. It is
a bit like baking a cake.

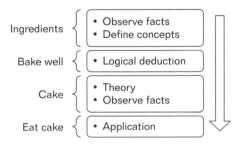

THE DEFINITIONS OF THE MAIN THEORIES IN NORMATIVE ETHICS

Deontological ethics – certain actions are right or wrong in themselves. Deontological ethics is concerned with the acts that are right or wrong in themselves (**intrinsically** right or wrong). This may be because these acts go against some duty or obligation or they break some **absolute** law; for example a deontologist may say that killing is wrong as the actual act of killing another human being is always wrong. Deontologists are always certain in their moral decisions and can take strong moral positions, such as being totally against war. On the other hand they do not take into account the circumstances, or different cultures or different religious views.

Teleological ethics is concerned with the ends, results or consequences of an action. Followers of teleological ethics consider the consequence of an ethical decision before they act. The action is not intrinsically good (good in itself) but is only good if the results are good – the action produces happiness and love. However, the main problem with teleological ethics is that it can never be sure what the result or consequence of an action might be – it is possible to make an educated guess but not to be absolutely sure, and sometimes we can only tell if the consequences of an action are right with hindsight. Another problem with teleological ethics is that some actions are always wrong, rape for example, and can never be justified by the consequence.

Moral objectivism claims that there are certain universal and absolute values. Modern moral objectivists do not believe that these universal values hold for ever, but they hold until they are proven to be false.

Moral subjectivism claims that moral statements are simply a matter of personal opinion. We simply make our own morality according to our own experiences and see our moral views as true for ourselves or our society and not necessarily applying to others.

Intrinsic good – something is good in itself: it has value simply because it exists without any references to the consequences. This applies to deontological ethics.

Instrumental good – something that is good because of the effects or consequences it has, or as a means to some other end or purpose. To explain this **Peter Singer** (*Practical Ethics*, 2011, p. 246) uses the example of money – it has value because of the things we can buy with it, but if we were marooned on a desert island we would not want it.

ETHICAL THEORIES

If we are to have valid ethical arguments then we must have some normative premises to begin with. These normative premises are either statements of ethical theories themselves or statements implied by ethical theories.

The ethical theories that will be examined in this book are:

Utilitarianism:	An action is right if it maximises the overall happiness of all people.
Kantian Ethics:	Treat other people the way you wish they would treat you, and never treat other people as if they were merely objects.
Cultural relativism:	What is right or wrong varies according to the beliefs of each culture.
Divine Command:	Do as the creator tells you.
Natural Law:	Everything is created for a purpose, and when this is examined by human reason a person should be able to judge how to act in order to find ultimate happiness.
Situation Ethics:	Based on agape which wills the good of others.
Virtue Ethics:	Agent-centred not act-centred. Practising virtuous behaviour will lead to becoming a virtuous person and contribute to a virtuous society.

Essential terminology

Absolute
Consequentialism
Cultural relativism
Descriptive relativism
Moral absolutism
Moral objectivism
Moral relativism
Subjectivism

2 Moral Absolutism and Moral Relativism

This chapter introduces some of the main ethical theories that are looked at in more detail in later chapters. You should read this chapter again once you have studied them. You will need absolute and relative morality for the AS Ethics paper.

Examination questions on absolute and relative morality may be approached in more than one way:

- looking at normative ethical theories, both absolute and relative
- looking at Cultural relativism
- looking at relative meta-ethical theories.

WHAT YOU WILL LEARN ABOUT IN THIS CHAPTER

- What is meant in ethics to call a system relativist.
- Moral relativism as distinct from Cultural relativism.
- Situation Ethics as an example of relative ethical systems.
- What is meant by moral absolutism.
- Absolute and relative ways of understanding 'right' and 'wrong'.
- The skills to decide whether there are any moral absolutes, or whether morality is completely relative, or whether there is an in-between position.
- The strengths and weaknesses of moral absolutism.
- The strengths and weaknesses of moral relativism.

KEY SCHOLARS

- Protagoras (c.480–c.411 BCE)
- Socrates (c.470–c.399 BCE)
- Plato (428–347 BCE)
- Aristotle (384–322 BCE)
- Joseph Fletcher (1905–1991)

THE OCR CHECKLIST

Candidates should be able to demonstrate knowledge and understanding of:

- the concepts of absolutist and relativist morality;
- what it means to call an ethical theory absolutist and objective;
- what it means to call an ethical theory relativist and subjective;
- the terms deontological and teleological.

Candidates should be able to discuss critically these concepts and their strengths and weaknesses.

From OCR A Level Religious Studies Specification H172.

WHAT IS ETHICAL RELATIVISM?

We all make ethical judgements about what we consider to be right and wrong, and we often have different views about ethical issues. We make judgements about actions or behaviour as being absolutely wrong in all circumstances – this is absolute ethics, which takes a deontological approach. An ethical relativist, on the other hand, believes that there are circumstances and situations in which actions or behaviour that are usually considered to be 'wrong' can be considered to be 'right'.

There are basically two sorts of ethical relativism: Cultural relativism, which says that right and wrong, good and evil are relative to a culture, to a way of life that is practised by a whole group of people; and individual relativism, which says that right and wrong, good and evil are relative to the preferences of an individual. Both cultural and individual relativism hold that there are no universally valid moral principles. All principles and values are relative to a particular culture or age. Ethical relativism means that there is no such thing as good 'in itself', but if an action seems good to you and bad to me, that is it, and there is no objective basis for us to discover the truth.

The problem today is that relativism tends to lead people into thinking that truth depends on who holds it, or that there is only one truth – their own. We often hear people say, 'Well that's your point of view, but it's not mine', and this can actually be a way of stopping thinking. Truth then no longer matters, as everything depends on the community to which one belongs, or one's own perspective. Where there is no agreed set of values, relativism can seem very attractive.

Moral relativism
There are no universally valid moral principles and so there is no one true morality.

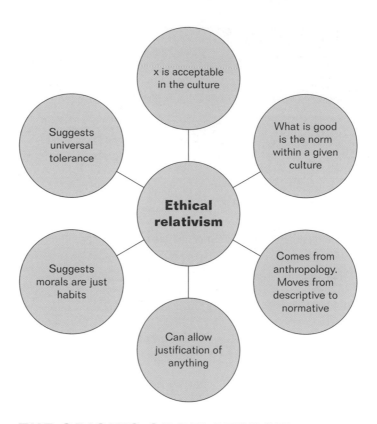

Subjectivism

Each person's values are relative to that person and so cannot be judged objectively.

THE ORIGINS OF RELATIVISM

We can trace the origins of Western ethical thinking to the city states of ancient Greece. At the time of Homer (c. eighth century BCE), being good meant being a heroic warrior, and the type of person you were – noble, courageous, strong – was the most important thing. This became further developed in the ethical theories of Socrates, Plato and Aristotle, who looked at the ideas of character and virtue.

However, everything began to change, and by the sixth century BCE there was no longer any moral certainty. **Alasdair MacIntyre** in his book *A Short History of Ethics* (1985) says this was due to the discovery of other civilisations with different ideas of what it meant to be good and changes within Greek society itself. The discovery of these different cultures led the Greeks to question the absoluteness of their own moral ideas; also, as the city states expanded, it became less clear what a person's role in society was and so more difficult to know how to live a virtuous life.

Eventually a series of wise men, known as Sophists, appeared and argued that all morality was relative – right and wrong varied from place to place, from time to time and from person to person. Protagoras famously said: 'Man is the measure of all things.' All they saw as important was getting on in life,

Sophists

This was a name originally applied by the ancient Greeks to learned men. In the fifth century CE, the Sophists were travelling teachers. They concluded that truth and morality were matters of opinion and emphasised skills such as rhetoric.

Protagoras (c.480–c.411BCE)

Protagoras was a Greek philosopher, born in Thrace. He taught in Athens for money. He said that nothing is absolutely good or bad and that each individual is their own final authority when making decisions. Like Socrates, he was charged with impiety and fled to Sicily, but drowned on the journey.

taking part in political life and fitting in – 'truth' was a variable concept. Socrates and later Plato and Aristotle worked on proving this view to be wrong.

Socrates

It is difficult to distinguish between the views of Socrates and Plato, as Socrates left no writings and everything we know about him we know through his pupil Plato. However, Plato's dialogues have Socrates as the main protagonist who argues that all humans share a common, innate understanding of what is morally good.

Plato

Plato explained how this moral knowledge was acquired with his theory of the Forms – moral knowledge came from the highest of the forms: the Form of the Good. According to Plato, there are objective and universal moral truths – the complete opposite of the view of the Sophists.

Socrates (c.470–399 BCE)

Socrates did not leave any writings of his own but, as a Greek philosopher, he shaped Western philosophy. His pupil Plato wrote dialogues which claim to describe Socrates' views. He is also mentioned in the works of Xenophon and others. At the age of 70 he was tried for impiety and sentenced to death by poisoning (probably hemlock).

continued opposite

Aristotle

Aristotle approached ethics from a completely different angle, and although he thought universal truths could be discovered, he rejected Plato's idea of the world of the Forms as he thought that understanding of goodness and wisdom could be found in this world. According to Aristotle, we can find out how to be virtuous by looking at virtuous people and by discovering how we can better develop our character.

Socrates, Plato and Aristotle all oppose complete relativism from different angles and ask people not to just blindly follow what everyone else is thinking and doing, to consider what they believe and why they believe it, to dialogue with others and to look for truths that are not limited by their own time and culture.

It cannot be assumed that relativism means the same thing to everyone and this chapter will explore some of the different approaches.

CULTURAL RELATIVISM

You do not need to be an anthropologist to know that throughout the world there are many different ideas about how to behave and there always seem to be clashes of moral codes between one culture and another. To many people it seems obscene to chop off a person's hand as punishment for theft or to stone somebody for adultery, yet to many Muslims this is simply the required punishment, and they on their part may condemn what they see as the excessive liberalism and immorality of Western societies.

This is what is known as the *diversity thesis* – because of the diversity across and within cultures there can be no one true morality.

Many other examples of this clash of cultures may be found. Some societies practise polygamy, others monogamy; some have arranged marriages and others are free to make their own choice of spouse; we put our elderly in homes, whereas in other cultures they are valued for their wisdom and have an important place in the family home. For the relativist such differences present no problems – different tribes, different customs. Rules of conduct differ from place to place, as was noted by the ancient Greek historian Herodotus, who recounts an episode in which the King of Persia induced horror on the part of both the Greeks and the Callatians by asking them to adopt each other's funeral practices. What the Greeks took to be right and proper (e.g. burning their dead), the Callatians saw as absolutely abhorrent – Herodotus implied that since fire burned just as well in Greece as in Persia, moral practices are relative to cultural contexts. By implication there is nothing right or wrong universally. This is what is known as the *dependency thesis* – what is right or wrong depends upon the nature of the

Chief from Papua New Guinea and his four wives

society. No one can judge the morality of other cultures, as different cultures create different values, and we cannot be objective about another culture since we are all the product of our own culture.

However, for the absolutist these different forms of behaviour cause a major dilemma. Absolutism implies that forms of behaviour are universally right or wrong – an example of this is that when the nineteenth-century British missionaries went to Africa and Asia they imposed their Western **absolutes** as being more right than local customs. Thus, for example, female converts to Christianity were made to cover their breasts – surely more a sign of Victorian prudery (and the cold British climate) than any universal moral code.

Historically we can also find support for the relativist position – forms of behaviour that were condemned in the past are now considered acceptable and vice versa. We no longer allow acts of cruelty for public entertainment as in the Roman games; homosexuals can enter into same sex marriages or civil partnerships; unmarried mothers are no longer put in mental institutions; slavery is no longer legal and so on. The attitudes of society have changed on many issues.

Morality then does not exist in a vacuum, and what is considered right or wrong must be considered in context, and morality is seen as just a set of common rules and customs that over time have become socially approved and differ from culture to culture. If all morality is rooted in culture, there can be no universal moral principles valid for everyone at all times.

between Macedonia and Athens. He spent his time there investigating science and particularly biology. In 341 BCE he moved with his family back to Macedonia to become tutor to the son of King Philip II of Macedonia, Alexander (who would later become Alexander the Great). After Alexander became king, Aristotle returned to Athens and founded a school called the Lyceum. He remained in Athens teaching until 323, when Alexander the Great died. After Alexander's death it became difficult for Aristotle to stay in Athens, as he was a Macedonian. Worried that he would die like Socrates, Aristotle and his family moved to Chalcis, where he died a year later.

Aristotle was a remarkable person. He tutored students on most traditional subjects that are taught at universities today. He was fascinated with understanding the physical world around him and the universe. His biology books were not superseded by anything better until 2,000 years later. Aristotle also wrote about other areas of study, including drama, rhetoric (public speaking), meteorology, sport and physics.

Cultural relativism
What is right or wrong depends
on the culture.

Descriptive relativism
Different cultures and societies
have differing ethical systems
and so morality is relative.

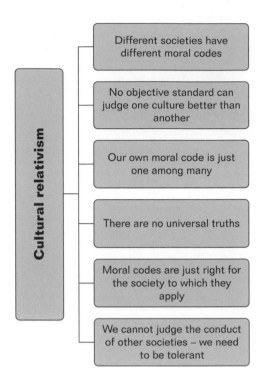

Cultural relativism

- Different societies have different moral codes
- No objective standard can judge one culture better than another
- Our own moral code is just one among many
- There are no universal truths
- Moral codes are just right for the society to which they apply
- We cannot judge the conduct of other societies – we need to be tolerant

Thought Point

1   Jesus is quoted as saying: 'The sabbath was made for humankind, and not
     humankind for the sabbath; so the Son of Man is lord even of the sabbath'
     (Mark 2: 27b–28).

     •   Does this mean that all rules are relative in human relationships? Or
          are there some rules that cannot be broken?

2   Winston Churchill's physician, Lord Moran, once remarked of the French
     President General de Gaulle: 'He's so stuffed with principles that he has
     no room for Christian Charity.'

     •   How relevant is this comment to the discussion on moral relativism?

3   There are many areas of human behaviour about which attitudes have
     changed.

- Add to this list: hire purchase; cockfighting; the role of women in society.
- Are the changes all for the better?
- What accepted practices today do you think people will look back at in horror in the future (e.g. pollution and gas-guzzling cars; the breeding and slaughter of animals for food; the use of nuclear power for energy)?

THE REASONS FOR RELATIVISM

- The decline of religious authority has meant that people look for other reasons to be ethical.
- A greater understanding of other cultures, particularly from anthropology, has led to an understanding that morality is not absolute and simply means ways of acting that are approved by a particular society.
- Relativism simply explains the differences between one time and another – for instance slavery was acceptable in the past and no longer is.
- The unacceptable effects of interfering with other cultures.
- The influence of meta-ethical analysis – asking what the terms 'ought', 'right' and 'wrong' mean. If there is no agreement about what the words mean then this implies conceptual relativism – what an intuitionist thinks is good is different from what an emotivist thinks.
- The development of competing theories – Utilitarian, intuitionist, egoist, emotivist.

THE WEAKNESSES OF RELATIVISM

Absolute
A principle that is universally binding.

- It implies that there can be no real evaluation or criticism of practices such as the burning of witches, human sacrifice, slavery, the Holocaust or the torture of the innocent.
- Relativism does not allow societies to progress (e.g. the realisation that slavery was unacceptable was slow to develop – but no one would doubt that we have made progress).
- Relativism seems to give little reason for behaving morally except to be socially acceptable.
- Although relativism is not subjectivism, it is only a step away and may come to this problematic position.
- Some statements are true absolutely (e.g. 'It is wrong to torture innocent people', 'It is right for parents to be responsible for their children').

Moral objectivism
Truth is objectively real regardless of culture.

Just because cultures vary, it does not mean that there is no objective 'good'.
*   Ethical beliefs can change when challenged – primitive practices do stop.

Note: Relativists do not reject moral principles. They say that all the different moral principles in the world are valid relative to the culture. Believing that moral values are relative does not mean that a person does not have any moral values.

Consequentialism
The rightness or wrongness of an act is determined by its consequences.

NORMATIVE RELATIVISM

Normative ethics is where actions are assessed according to ethical theories – it is about what is actually right or good and not simply about cultural diversity and cultural dependency. A relativist will normally hold at least one absolute principle: that it is wrong to impose absolute moral rules.

Both Utilitarianism and Situation Ethics are thought of as examples of normative theories, but they are different in the way they understand this. However, it is important to note that neither theory is completely relativist as they have one absolute each – love for Situation Ethics and the greatest happiness principle for Utilitarianism. Utilitarians recognise 'happiness', 'pleasure' or 'well-being' as the result of good actions, but accept that this may differ from culture to culture. Situationists, like Fletcher, reject the use of words like 'never', 'always' and 'absolute' and adopt a pragmatic approach to decision-making. The only exception is that love should be seen as the absolute. 'Love relativises the absolute.' Fletcher described his theory as relativistic.

Normative relativists reject the principle of objectivity or absolutism and see morality as something that evolves and changes.

Utilitarianism is looked at in more detail in another chapter, so this chapter will focus on Situation Ethics.

SITUATION ETHICS

Joseph Fletcher developed Situation Ethics in the 1960s in reaction to Christian legalism and antinomianism (which is the belief that there are no fixed moral principles, but that morality is the result of individual spontaneous acts).

Fletcher argues that each individual situation is different and absolute rules are too demanding and restrictive. The Bible shows what good moral decisions look like in particular situations, but it is not possible to know what God's will is in every situation. Fletcher says: 'I simply do not know and cannot know what God is doing.' As it is not possible to know God's will in every situation, *love* or *agape* is Situation Ethics' only moral 'rule'.

So it is not just the situation that guides what you should do, but the principle of agape and the guiding maxims of the Christian community: 'Do not commit murder', 'Do not commit adultery', 'Do not steal', 'Do not lie'. Situation Ethics is midway between legalism and antinomianism, and Fletcher's book, which was published in 1966, reflected the mood of the times – Christians should make the right choices without just following rules and by thinking for themselves.

Christians should base their decisions on one single rule – the rule of agape. This love is not merely an emotion but involves doing what is best for the other person, unconditionally. This means that other guiding maxims could be ignored in certain situations if they do not serve agape; for example, Fletcher says it would be right for a mother with a 13-year-old daughter who is having sex to break the rules about under-age sex and insist her daughter uses contraception – the right choice is the most loving thing and it will depend on the situation. However, the situation can never change the rule of agape which is always good and right regardless of the circumstances.

According to Fletcher's **Situation Ethics**, this ethical theory depends on four working principles and six fundamental principles.

> **Joseph Fletcher (1905–1991)**
>
> Fletcher was an American professor who founded the theory of Situation Ethics in the 1960s. He was a pioneer in bioethics and was involved in the areas of abortion, infanticide, euthanasia, eugenics and cloning. Fletcher was an Episcopalian priest, but later renounced his belief in God and became an atheist.

The four working principles

1 *Pragmatism* – what you propose must work in practice.
2 *Relativism* – words like 'always', 'never', 'absolute' are rejected. There are no fixed rules, but all decisions must be relative to agape.
3 *Positivism* – a value judgement needs to be made, giving the first place to love.
4 *Personalism* – people are put in first place, morality is personal and not centred on laws.

The six fundamental principles

1 Love (agape) is the only absolute. It is the only thing that is intrinsically 'good' and 'right', regardless of the situation.
2 This love is self-giving love, which seeks the best interests of others but allows people the freedom and responsibility to choose the right thing for themselves.
3 Justice will follow from love, because 'justice is love distributed'. If love is put into practice, it can only result in justice. Justice is concerned with

giving everyone their due – its concern is with neighbours, not just our neighbour.

4   Love has no favourites and does not give those whom we like preferential treatment – it is good will which reaches out to strangers, acquaintances, friends and even enemies.

5   Love must be the final end, not a means to an end – people must choose what to do because the action will result in love, not be loving in order to achieve some other result.

6   The loving thing to do will depend on the situation – and as situations differ, an action that might be right in one situation could be wrong in another. This is quite different from traditional Christian ethics and is far more relativistic, having just one moral rule – agape.

Strengths of Situation Ethics

* Situation Ethics is easy to understand and can be constantly updated for new problems and issues as they arise, such as genetic engineering and foetal research.
* It is flexible and can take different situations into account, but it is based on the Christian concept of love.
* It focuses on humans and concern for others – agape.
* Situation Ethics allows people to take responsibility for their own decisions and make up their own minds about what is right or wrong. Bishop John Robinson called it 'an ethic for humanity come of age'.

Weaknesses of Situation Ethics

* This method of decision-making was condemned in 1952 by Pope Pius XII, who said it was wrong to make decisions based on individual circumstances if these went against the teaching of the Church and the Bible.
* It is not possible to determine the consequences of actions – how do we know that the result will be the most loving for all concerned?

Situation Ethics has just one moral rule – agape or unconditional love – and it is relative in that it accepts that different decisions will be right or wrong according to the circumstance.

Thought Point

These examples are taken from **William Barclay**'s *Ethics in a Permissive Society* (1971). Barclay wants you to agree with the actions; can you see other ways of acting?

1   Suppose in a burning house there is your aged father, an old man, with the days of his usefulness at an end, and a doctor who has discovered a cure for one of the world's great killer diseases and who still carries the formulae in his head, and you can save only one – whom do you save? Your father who is dear to you, or the doctor in whose hands there are thousands of lives? Which is love?

2   On the Wilderness trail, Daniel Boone's trail, westward through Cumberland Gap to Kentucky, many families in the trail caravans lost their lives to the Indians. A Scottish woman had a baby at the breast. The baby was ill and crying, and the baby's crying was betraying her other three children and the rest of the party; the party clearly could not remain hidden if the baby continued crying; their position would be given away. Well, the mother clung to the baby; the baby's cries led the Indians to the position, the party was discovered, and all were massacred. There was another such occasion. On this occasion there was a Negro woman in the party. Her baby too was crying and threatening to betray the party. She strangled the baby with her own two hands to stop its crying – and the whole party escaped. Which action is love?

3   What about the commandment that you must not kill? When T.E. Lawrence was leading his Arabs, two of his men had a quarrel and in the quarrel Hamed killed Salem. Lawrence knew that a blood feud would arise in which both families would be involved, and that one whole family would be out to murder the other whole family. What did Lawrence do? He thought it out and then with his own hands he killed Hamed and thus stopped the blood feud. Was this right? Was this action that stopped a blood feud and prevented scores of people from being murdered an act of murder or of love?

4   Ethically, has humanity come of age, as Bishop John Robinson suggested in 1966?

5   To what extent is love compatible with human nature?

6   Why might critics of Situation Ethics argue that it is really Utilitarianism under a different name?

7   Explain why some critics have questioned whether Situation Ethics is really Christian.

WHAT IS ETHICAL ABSOLUTISM?

An ethical absolute is a command that is true for all time, in all places and in all situations. Certain things are right or wrong from an *objective* point of view and cannot change according to culture. Certain actions are *intrinsically* right or wrong, which means they are right or wrong in themselves.

According to moral absolutism, there are eternal moral values applicable everywhere. Absolutism gives people clear guidelines for behaviour and accepts a universal set of absolutes. This is a popular position for those who believe in a God who establishes moral order in the universe. This approach

is deontological. The consequences of an action are not taken into consideration.

This ethical system is easy and simple to apply – a crime is a crime, regardless of circumstances. If we take murder as an example – is it all right to kill someone for no reason? Both the ethical relativist and the ethical absolutist would say no. Now if we assume the murderer is a doctor who could kill one patient to save another – again both the ethical relativist and the ethical absolutist would still say this was not right. However, if we consider killing one person to save many lives, the ethical relativist will feel it is all right to kill, but for the ethical absolutist it is still wrong.

Absolute ethics allows judgements to be made about the actions of others – we can say the Holocaust was absolutely wrong. Absolute ethics allows courts of law to exist and order to be maintained.

Where do these absolute laws come from? For a theist the answer is simple – they come from God. For the agnostic or atheist the answer is more complicated – they just seem a priori in nature. They fit into Plato's world of the Forms, as there are some things we just seem to know are wrong without being taught: do you remember your parents ever telling you not to sleep with your sister? So to some extent moral absolutes can be seen as inherent in the nature of man.

Moral absolutism
There is only one correct
answer to every moral problem.

MORAL ABSOLUTISM AND RELIGION

Many religions have moral absolutist positions as they see laws as having been set by the deity or deities. Such a position is seen as unchanging and perfect; for example, the Ten Commandments.

For one person, therefore, violence may be considered wrong, even in self-defence; for another, homosexuality is considered fundamentally wrong, even when the couple are in a monogamous relationship. Many who make such claims even ignore evolving norms within their own communities, such as the rows about homosexual priests within the Anglican Church. In the past slavery was supported by religious believers, whereas today no religious group would endorse it.

Today many Christians believe there is a hierarchy of absolutes – a view called 'graded absolutism'. If there is a conflict between two absolutes, it is our duty to obey the higher one: duty to God comes first, then duty to others, followed by duty to property. Under this view, Corrie ten Boom (1892–1983) was morally right to lie to the Nazis about the Jews her family was hiding, because protecting lives is a higher moral value than telling the truth to murderers.

NORMATIVE ABSOLUTISM

The two absolutist theories that are dealt with elsewhere in this book are Natural Law, which is a religious theory, and Kantian Ethics, which is based on reason. However, even theories that are relativist in practice contain an absolute core – the greatest good for the greatest number in Utilitarianism and agape in Situation Ethics.

Strengths of absolutism

- Absolutism gives a fixed ethical code by which to measure actions.
- One culture can judge that the actions of another are wrong (e.g. genocide) and then act on that judgement.
- Absolutism can support universal laws such as the United Nations Declaration of Human Rights.

Weaknesses of absolutism

* Absolutism does not take into account the circumstances of each situation.
* Absolutists can seem intolerant of cultural diversity.
* How do we actually know what absolute morals are, as all sources of morality are open to human interpretation?
* Absolutism may often be seen as an impossible ideal.

THE DIFFERENCES BETWEEN ABSOLUTISM AND RELATIVISM

Absolutism

* There is an objective moral truth
* Absolute ethics are deontological, concerned with the action not the results
* Moral actions are intrinsically right or wrong – right or wrong in themselves regardless of culture, time, place, opinion or situation
* Moral truth is universal and unchanging
* Absolutism gives clear guidelines for behaviour and so it is easy to make ethical decisions
* Absolutism cannot take into account the circumstances
* Absolutism can seem intolerant of cultural diversity

Relativism

* There is no objective moral truth
* Moral values vary according to culture, time, place and religion
* Morals are subject to culture, time, place and religion – morals are subjective
* The existence of different views does not mean they are all equal
* Relativism explains why people hold different values and it is a flexible system that can fit a variety of lifestyles
* Relativism cannot condemn different cultural practices
* If the ideas of relativism were accepted universally, relativism would become an absolute moral code

REVIEW QUESTIONS

Look back over the chapter and check that you can answer the following questions:

1   In ten bullet points explain what is meant by Cultural relativism, including the difference between the diversity thesis and the dependency thesis.
2   List the main weaknesses of relativism.
3   What is the historical background to Situation Ethics?
4   List the principles on which Situation Ethics is based.
5   List the strengths of absolutism.

Terminology

Do you know your terminology?

Try to explain the following ideas without looking at your books and notes:

*   Consequentialism
*   Moral absolutism
*   Moral relativism
*   Moral objectivism

 Examination Questions Practice

When writing answers about absolute and relative ethics, do not just make vague assertions about Cultural relativism, but explain what the terms mean using ethical theories and even relative approaches to meta-ethics.

Remember: (a) assesses AO1 and (b) AO2. To help you improve your answers look at the AS Levels of Response. See: http://www.ocr.org.uk/qualifications/as-a-level-gce-religious-studies-h172-h572/.

SAMPLE EXAM STYLE QUESTIONS

(a) Explain what is meant by moral absolutism. (25 marks)

- You need to explain that moral absolutism considers actions are right or wrong intrinsically – consequences or circumstances have no bearing – and that a moral command is considered objectively and universally true.
- Key elements in your answer could include reference to Divine Command theory, Natural Law or Kant's theory so that you can define different kinds of absolutism.
- To make your answer clearer you could contrast moral absolutism with moral relativism, and use examples to illustrate your answer.

(b) 'Moral absolutism cannot be justified.' Discuss. (10 marks)

In your answer you need to compare different approaches to this question.

- You may point to the need to have a universal truth that transcends cultures and history.
- You may also refer to certain unchanging principles (e.g. 'do not murder', 'do not lie') and the need for a set of absolutes that apply to all people, regardless of where they live.
- However, on the other hand, you could consider that moral absolutism cannot take into account the circumstances or consequences of an action and that absolutism may seem intolerant of cultural diversity and the need to accommodate different lifestyles.

SAMPLE AS EXAM STYLE QUESTIONS

(a) Explain the main features of moral absolutism.
(b) Discuss the claim that an absolutist morality is the best way of preserving the sanctity of life.

(a) Explain moral relativism.
(b) 'Moral relativism threatens Religious Ethics.' Discuss.

FURTHER READING

Ahluwalia, L. *Foundation for the Study of Religion*, London, Hodder & Stoughton Educational, 2001.

Barclay, W. *Ethics in a Permissive Society,* London, Collins, 1971.

Kirkwood, R. 'Ethical Theory', in *Dialogue* (Special Issue), 2002.

Thompson, M. *Ethical Theory*, London, Hodder Murray, 2005.

Vardy, P. and Grosch, P. *The Puzzle of Ethics,* London, Fount, 1999.

3 Natural Moral Law

WHAT YOU WILL LEARN ABOUT IN THIS CHAPTER

- The origins of Natural Moral Law.
- Aquinas' theory of Natural Moral Law.
- The Doctrine of Double Effect.
- The strengths and weaknesses of Natural Moral Law.
- How to apply Natural Moral Law to ethical dilemmas.

KEY SCHOLARS

- Thomas Aquinas (1225–1274)
- Aristotle (384–322 BCE)

THE OCR CHECKLIST

Candidates should be able to demonstrate knowledge and understanding of:

- the origins of Aquinas' Natural Moral Law in Aristotle's idea of purpose;
- Aquinas' ideas of purpose and perfection;
- the use of reason to discover Natural Moral Law;
- the primary and secondary precepts.

Candidates should be able to discuss critically these views and their strengths and weaknesses.

From OCR A Level Religious Studies Specification H172 and H572.

WHAT IS NATURAL MORAL LAW?

Natural Moral Law includes those ethical theories which state that there is a natural order to our world that should be followed. This natural order is determined by some supernatural power. Natural Law as we understand it originated in the philosophy of the ancient Greeks, especially that of Aristotle, and was developed by Thomas Aquinas. It is an absolute theory of ethics but it is not rooted in duty, or in an externally imposed law, but in our *human nature* and our search for genuine *happiness* and *fulfilment*. Aquinas considered that by using our reason to reflect on our human nature, we could discover our specific end *telos* or purpose and, having discovered this, we could then work out how to achieve it. This understanding of God's plan for us, built into our nature at creation, Aquinas called Natural Law.

- Natural Law is *not* just about 'doing what comes naturally' – it is not about what nature does in the sense of being observed in nature. Natural Law is based on nature interpreted by human *reason*.
- Natural Law is not exactly a law in that it does not give you a fixed law – it is not always straightforward and there is some flexibility in its application.

THE ORIGINS OF NATURAL LAW

The earliest theory of Natural Law first appeared among the Stoics, who believed that God is everywhere and in everyone. Humans have within them a divine spark which helps them find out how to live according to the will of God, or in other words to live according to nature. Humans have a choice whether to obey the laws that govern the universe but they need to use their reason to understand and decide whether to obey these cosmic laws.

Thomas Aquinas linked this idea of a cosmic Natural Law with Aristotle's view that people, like every other natural object, have a specific nature, purpose and function. Aristotle considered that not only does everything have a **purpose** (e.g. the purpose of a knife is to cut), but that its *supreme good* is found when it fulfils that purpose (e.g. the knife cuts sharply).

The supreme good for humans is *eudaimonia*, which is usually translated as happiness but includes the idea of living well, thriving and flourishing with others in society. Aristotle saw this as the final goal for humans but this is to be achieved by living a life of reason. Aristotle saw reason as the highest of all human activities:

> Reason is the true self of every man, since it is the supreme and better part. . . . Reason is, in the highest sense, a man's self. (*Nichomachean Ethics*)

Reason is not just seen as the ability to think and understand, but also how to act: ethics is reason put into practice.

Deontological ethics
Ethical systems which consider that the moral act itself has moral value (e.g. telling the truth is always right, even when it may cause pain or harm).

Purpose
The idea that the rightness or wrongness of an action can be discovered by looking at whether or not the action agrees with human purpose.

Purpose

Reason

THE NATURAL LAW OF THOMAS AQUINAS

Thomas Aquinas was very influenced by Aristotle's writings, which had been lost as far as European philosophy was concerned, but preserved by Islamic scholars. Aristotle's philosophy had been 'rediscovered' just before Aquinas took up his position at the University of Paris.

Aquinas used the ideas of Aristotle and the Stoics as an underpinning for Natural Law:

1   Human beings have an essential rational nature given by God in order for us to live and flourish – from Aristotle and the Stoics.
2   Even without knowledge of God, reason can discover the laws that lead to human flourishing – from Aristotle.
3   The Natural Laws are universal and unchangeable and should be used to judge the laws of particular societies – from the Stoics.

THE PURPOSE OF HUMAN BEINGS

Like Aristotle, Aquinas concludes that humans aim for some goal or purpose – but he does not see this as *eudaimonia*. Humans, for Aquinas, are above all made '*in the image of God*' and so the supreme good must be the development of this image – *perfection*. However, unlike Aristotle, Aquinas did not think that this perfection, or perfect happiness, was possible in this life. Aquinas sees happiness as beginning now and continuing in the next life. The purpose of morality is to enable us to arrive at the fulfilment of our natures and the completion of all our desires.

In his book *Summa Theologiae*, Aquinas attempts to work out what this perfection actually is by examining the 'reflections' of Natural Moral Law as revealed by:

* Eternal Law – the principles by which God made and controls the universe and which only God knows completely. We only know these as 'reflections'; in other words, we only have a partial and approximate understanding of the laws which govern the universe.
* Divine Law – this is the Bible, which Aquinas believed 'reflects' the Eternal Law of God. However, this 'reflection' can only be seen by those who believe in God and only if God chooses to reveal it.
* Natural Law – this refers to the moral law of God which has been built into human nature; it is also a 'reflection' of the Eternal Law of God. However, it can be seen by everyone as it does not depend on belief in God or God choosing to reveal it – we simply need to use our reason to understand human nature.

Thomas Aquinas (1225–1274)

Aquinas was born in Roccasecca, in Sicily. He died in Fossanova in the Papal States. His feast day is 28 January (originally 7 March).

He studied under the German philosopher Albertus Magnus. He was an Italian Dominican theologian and the foremost medieval scholar. He worked on his own ideas from the basis of Aristotle, particularly in the metaphysics of personality, creation and Providence.

Aquinas wished to reconcile faith and intellect. His philosophical works were aimed at a synthesis of the works of Aristotle and Augustine; of the Islamic scholars Averroës and Avicenna; and of Jewish scholars such as Maimonides and Solomon ben Yehuda ibn Gabirol. His most important theological works are the *Summa Theologiae* and the *Summa Contra Gentiles*. His own system of doctrine, developed by his followers, is known as Thomism.

Eternal Law

Divine Law

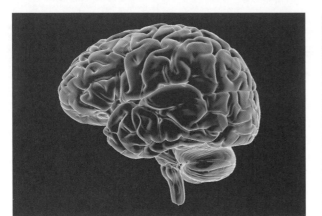

Natural Law

Human Law

Eternal Law
The principles by which God made and controls the universe which are only fully known by God.

Divine Law
The Bible – this reflects the Eternal Law.

Natural Moral Law
The theory that an eternal, absolute moral law can be discovered by reason.

Good actions should conform to all of these forms of law, but ultimately it is our own powers of reason that confirm whether the law is right. Every action which goes against reason is wrong, even if that reason is mistaken. Aquinas argues that it is the end or purpose of an act that confirms whether it is right or wrong, and this purpose is in fact revealed by Divine Law and confirmed by Natural Law.

NATURAL INCLINATIONS

Aquinas thought that God had instilled in all humans inclinations to behave in certain ways which lead us to the highest good and, by using our reason, we can discover the **precepts** (laws) which express God's Natural Law built into us.

The most fundamental inclination, according to Aquinas, is to act in such a way as to achieve good and avoid evil. He thought this because we are designed for one purpose – perfection, and so we would not knowingly pursue evil. Aquinas saw that in fact humans do not always behave like this and explained this by saying that we get things wrong and follow **apparent good** – something we think is good but in reality does not fit the perfect human ideal. For example, if someone has an affair they do not do so with the express purpose of hurting their partner but because they think they are 'in love' and it is a good thing to do. In order to work out what is a **real good** and what is an **apparent good** we need to use our reason correctly and choose the right thing to do. There is an 'ideal' human nature that we can all live up to or fall away from, and our moral actions determine whether we achieve this or not.

When humans act in accordance with their true nature, they act in accordance with their final purpose, so both the intention (interior act) and the act (exterior act) are important and need to be correct. However, Aquinas did believe that acts were good or bad in themselves and we need to use our reason correctly ('right use of reason' as Aquinas called it) to work out what to do. We can get actions wrong: if the object is evil – for example murder; if the purpose of the action is ignored – for example masturbation ignores the purpose of reproduction; if a voluntary choice is made to break Natural Law – for example choosing to sleep with someone else's wife. Aquinas recognised that we can also be influenced by our emotions, bad opinions or habits to do wrong actions.

According to Aquinas good is the very first thing understood by practical reason and all rational people will pursue good as it is the way we have been designed by God. The starting point for Natural Law is, therefore, the *synderesis* rule: do good and avoid evil. **Synderesis** is the innate, God-given tendency that, according to Aquinas, all people have to pursue good ends and avoid evil ones. *Synderesis* can also be seen as another word for conscience, then **phronesis**, or practical wisdom, enables us to make moral choices. However, our inclinations to do good are only good in so far as they are subject to reason. We need to deliberate and make responsible decisions and also make sure that these decisions agree with the Eternal Law that is also revealed in the natural world. This means that Natural Law is not unchanging: as our reason is constantly discovering new things in the world our findings may lead to a development of Natural Law.

So, looked at in this way, Natural Law is not so much a theory or a way of making moral decisions, but rather a way of stressing that our nature is knowable and that we need to use our reason to know and understand it. This becomes clearer as Aquinas explains the fundamental primary principles of Natural Law, which he believes are fixed.

Apparent good

Something which seems to be good or the right thing to do but which does not fit the perfect human ideal.

Real good

The right thing to do – it fits the human ideal.

Study hint

Aquinas thought that all humans share a single nature and so there should be a single aim or purpose for all humans. If we do not believe that there is a final purpose for all humans, then Natural Law makes no sense.

Thought Point

1   How does Aquinas use and change Aristotle's ideas?
2   Explain how Natural Law, according to Aquinas, can lead us to the supreme good.
3   Explain where Natural Law may be found and how it can show us how we ought to behave.

Primary and secondary precepts

Primary precepts
The fundamental principles of Natural Moral Law.

Aquinas saw the **primary precepts** of Natural Law as always true and applying to everybody without exception, as they are a direct 'reflection' of God's Eternal Law. These primary precepts or primary goods can be worked out by observing natural human tendencies and then using our reason. The primary precepts are as follows:

*   the preservation of life
*   reproduction
*   the nurture and education of the young (to learn)
*   living peacefully in society
*   to worship God.

These primary precepts are always true in that they point us in the right direction and are necessary for human flourishing.

Secondary precepts
These are worked out from the primary precepts.

The **secondary precepts**, on the other hand, are dependent on our own judgements of what actually to do in a given situation and are open to faulty reasoning and may lead to completely wrong choices. The secondary precepts require experience, the use of reason and the exercise of practical wisdom; they may change as we reflect on how to achieve our true purpose. The following diagram shows some applications, but be wary of taking this as some sort of absolute list.

Using excellent reason is vital and its role is to guide us towards those 'goods' that will enable us to thrive and flourish as people. You cannot simply read the secondary precepts from the primary precepts like a list of instructions; so, for example, the primary precept of reproduction might need secondary precepts that explain what is acceptable sex and what is an acceptable way to have children (e.g. IVF). You need to apply practical wisdom, which is an ability to work out what is good and what will lead humans to perfection – this needs imagination and creativity, not blanket rules.

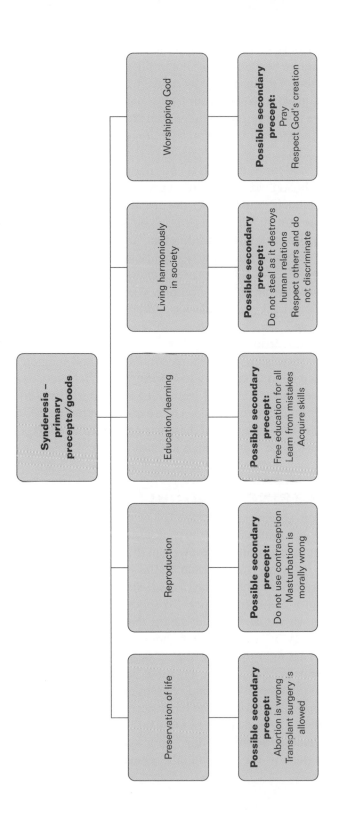

The secondary precepts make Aquinas' understanding of Natural Law realistic and quite flexible. It does not imply a body of principles from which we simply work out our moral decisions, but takes account of our human limitations and weaknesses. Natural Law may seem rigid, but the secondary precepts have to be interpreted in the context of the situation and, according to Aquinas, the more detailed you try to make it, the more the general rule allows exceptions.

What is good for us depends on our natures, not on our decisions – this allows for right and wrong decisions as we have to decide what really leads to human fulfilment, and here lies the problem. **George Hughes** says that we tend to see human fulfilment through our own life experiences and from what we have learned is human fulfilment, and forget to apply reason – both reason and practical wisdom are necessary.

There are modern Natural Law thinkers whose lists of primary goods differ somewhat from that of Aquinas. **Germain Grisez** includes self-integration, practical reasonableness, authenticity, justice and friendship, religion, life and health, knowledge of truth, appreciation of beauty and playful activities. **John Finnis** includes life, knowledge, aesthetic appreciation, play, friendship, practical reasonableness and religion. Finnis also changes procreation to marital good. **Joseph Boyle** refers to actions that 'contribute towards communal well-being and flourishing' and his list of goods is very similar to the previous two except that he stresses that nobody has the right to take away one of these basic goods from another person – so as life is a basic good, euthanasia is an immoral act.

THE DOCTRINE OF DOUBLE EFFECT

Aquinas saw the primary precepts as objectively true for everyone and he believed that by using our reason we can discover the right action in every situation by following this principle. In this he is **absolutist**.

There are times when we have moral dilemmas in which we cannot do good without a bad consequence. To solve this dilemma the doctrine of double effect was devised, roughly saying that it is always wrong to do a bad act intentionally in order to bring about good consequences, but that it is sometimes all right to do a good act despite knowing that it will bring about bad consequences. However, these bad consequences must only be unintended side-effects – the bad consequences may be foreseen but not intended. So, if a pregnant woman has cancer she could have a hysterectomy, even though this would result in the death of the foetus – but any other pregnancy-related life-threatening condition whereby deliberately killing the foetus is the only way of saving the woman would not be allowed.

Absolutism

An objective moral rule or value that is always true in all situations and for everyone, without exception.

THE CATHOLIC CHURCH AND NATURAL LAW

Aquinas' Natural Law is the basis for the morality of the Catholic Church, and it is also considered to be the morality of reason, based on the Bible and our understanding of the natural world, which can be understood by all whether they are believers or not.

The Magisterium of the Catholic Church (the teaching authority, usually the Pope and Cardinals meeting together) claims to be following in the footsteps of Peter and sees itself as an interpreter of both Divine Law (the Bible) and Natural Moral Law. The Catechism of the Catholic Church states: 'The natural law, present in the heart of each man and established by reason, is universal in its precepts and its authority extends to all men. It expresses the dignity of the person and determines the basis for his fundamental rights.' (§1956) This view of Natural Law stresses that we need to exercise responsible moral choices in order to follow the objective moral order established by God. This view was made most clear in two papal encyclicals: *Humanae Vitae* (1968) and *Veritas Splendor* (1993). *Veritas Splendor* moves away from the personal dimension of conscience and the dignity of the person, which were the focus of Vatican II (*Gaudium et Spes* §16), and stresses the act and the objective law which makes actions good or bad according to their object. The encyclical states that God is the true author of moral law, and human reason can never supersede the elements of the moral law that are of divine origin. The motives and the circumstances do not count if acts are intrinsically evil; as an example, *Veritas Splendor* reiterates the teaching against the use of contraception found in *Humanae Vitae*.

Thought Point

1   The Catholic Church has a number of secondary precepts on issues such as abortion. Would the prohibition of the abortion of a foetus growing in the fallopian tubes represent incorrect reasoning?

2   The biological purpose of sex is procreation, but it may have a secondary purpose of giving pleasure and showing love. Does sex always need to be open to the possibility of procreation? How far should the secondary purpose be considered?

3   The doctrine of double effect is often used in war. Is it possible to bomb a military command base in the centre of a civilian population and next to a hospital if the deaths of the civilians are not intended but simply foreseen?

4   'All human beings have a common human nature, and homosexuality is against human nature.' Consider arguments for and against this statement.

Intrinsically good
Something which is good in
itself, without reference to the
consequences.

SUMMARY OF NATURAL LAW

Natural Law underpins the ethics of the Catholic Church, but in reality it
attempts to establish a standard for morality which is independent of God's
will (see the Euthyphro Dilemma, Chapter 6) and does this by claiming:

The universe is controlled by laws of nature (Eternal Laws).

These laws work in harmony in a rational structure.

The laws of nature also express purpose (e.g. eyes fulfil the purpose
of seeing).

The laws of nature also express values (e.g. eyes which can see are
'good ' and those which cannot are 'bad'). To be good is to follow
our in-built purpose – do what is natural (of nature) as it is good and
avoid what is unnatural (not of nature) as it is bad.

The laws of nature are rational so we can understand them by using
our reason.

Morality then is independent of religion and both the believer and
the non-believer have to find out how to live a moral life by
listening to reason.

STRENGTHS OF NATURAL LAW

- It allows for a clear-cut approach to morality and establishes common
  rules.
- It is an autonomous, rational theory which makes as much sense to
  believers as to non-believers – the primary precept of the preservation
  of life fits in with the Darwinian idea of survival.
- The basic principles of preserving human life, reproduction, learning
  and living in society are common in all cultures and so Natural Law is
  reasonable.
- Natural Law does not simply dictate what should be done in individual
  cases from general moral principles.

- Natural Law concentrates on human character and its potential for goodness and flourishing rather than on the rightness or wrongness of particular acts, and so it allows for some measure of flexibility. The Doctrine of Double Effect is also a way through moral dilemmas when two rules conflict.
- Moral decision-making is not done by reason alone. Aquinas also involves the imagination – the body, the emotions and passions – and practical wisdom. However, we are not restricted by our emotions or our genes, and it enables us to fulfil our purpose which is inherent in our make-up and leads to both personal and societal growth.
- All those things that we require for happiness – health, friends – are morally good. The purpose of morality is the fulfilment of our natures.

WEAKNESSES OF NATURAL LAW

- Natural Law finds it difficult to relate complex decisions to basic principles in practice (e.g. should more money be spent on schools than on hospitals?).
- Natural Law depends on defining what is good, but according to **G.E. Moore**, this commits the *naturalistic fallacy*. Moore argues that goodness is unanalysable and unnatural, and so cannot be defined by any reference to nature. Aquinas argues that humans are social animals and it is part of our nature to want to live peacefully in the company of others and to care for them. He then goes on to argue that as this 'property' of caring for others is part of our human nature, it must be *good*. Moore criticises this by saying, *'You cannot derive an ought (value) from an is (fact)'* – so it may be a fact that I have within me the natural inclination to care for others, but that does not mean that I *ought* to care for them. In reality we do not make divisions between facts and values in the way we experience the world – because we are moral beings we unite these together.
- Others argue that Natural Law is based on assumptions about the world and the in-built purpose of things that are questioned by modern science. Darwin shows that nature has particular characteristics due to natural selection. The world has no rational system of laws governing it but the laws of nature are impersonal and blind with no intention of moving towards particular purposes. There is no divine purpose – it is simply the way things are.
- **Kai Neilsen** argues against Aquinas' belief in a single human nature common to all societies. Differing moral standards and Cultural relativism challenge the idea of a common Natural Law. Maybe people have

changeable natures (e.g. some are heterosexual and some are homo-sexual), and Natural Law is more complex than Aquinas thought.

- **Karl Barth** thought that Natural Law relies too much on reason, as human nature is too corrupt to be trusted, and not enough on the grace of God and revelation in the Bible.
- Some Catholic scholars also distrust philosophical theories such as Natural Law, and insist it must be supplemented by revelation or by Church teaching – this has led to some rigid interpretations of Natural Law.
- **Vardy** and **Grosch** criticise the way Aquinas works from general principles to lesser purposes and see his view of human nature as unholistic and too simplistic.

APPLICATION OF NATURAL MORAL LAW TO AN ETHICAL DILEMMA – VOLUNTARY EUTHANASIA

Natural Law is nature interpreted by human reason – by observing nature it deduces the final purpose of everything. Acting in keeping with essential nature is right, and going against it is wrong. To achieve the final purpose Natural Law sets out primary precepts as always true and applying to everybody – the first of these is the preservation of innocent life. Natural Law recognises human life as having unique value, and sees that each person has a duty to live their life in accordance with God's plan that human life should be fruitful and find its full perfection in eternal life. As a secondary precept, therefore, Natural Law prohibits suicide (and voluntary euthanasia) as this rejects God's final purpose and denies the natural instinct to live. The preservation of life could mean that more resources are put into palliative care, effective pain relief and hospice treatment, so that terminally ill people's dignity is affirmed and they can die in peace.

Another angle would be to consider the effect on the primary principle of living harmoniously in society. There could be pressure put upon the elderly and terminally ill and their contribution to society could be devalued as today's right to die becomes tomorrow's duty to die. However, **Daniel Maguire** argues that though the principle of 'no direct killing of innocent life' is true most of the time, in certain circumstances the principle would have to give way to the principle of achieving a good death. He does agree, however, that making a judgement between conflicting values is not easy and may be mistaken, but he maintains that the whole purpose of ethical reflection and using reason to reach moral decisions is to achieve a finer sensitivity to the conflicting values and make the possible options less

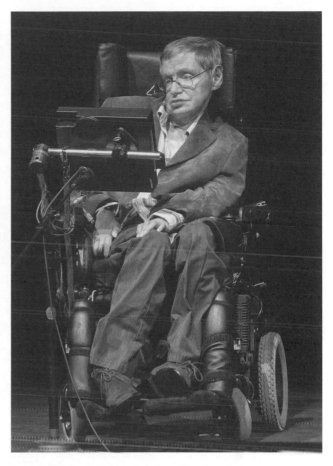

Diane Pretty died from motor neurone disease in 2002 shortly after she lost a legal battle to claim her right to die.

World-famous scientist Stephen Hawking has motor neurone disease.

arbitrary – thus voluntary euthanasia may sometimes be a good moral choice.

It is also worth looking at the doctrine of double effect and how, though Natural Law forbids any act whose direct effect is death, it is possible to allow actions (such as relief from pain) whose indirect effect may be death. There is no moral problem for Natural Law when death is merely a side-effect.

The main case for voluntary euthanasia rests on the claim that the quality of life does not justify life being allowed to continue and that it is merciful, in the patient's best interests and according to the patient's own wishes that death be assisted. Natural Law, on the other hand, maintains life as an absolute value which no other 'good' can outweigh.

REVIEW QUESTIONS

Look back over the chapter and check that you can answer the following questions:

1   Where did Natural Law come from?
2   What did Aquinas see as the purpose of human beings?
3   How do we discover the primary and secondary precepts and what are they?
4   Make a chart of the strengths and weaknesses of Natural Law.

Terminology

Do you know your terminology?

Try to explain the meaning of the following ideas without looking at your books and notes:

•   Apparent good
•   Deontological ethics
•   Intrinsically good/bad
•   Primary precepts
•   Secondary precepts

Examination Questions Practice

Read the question carefully – many candidates know all about the weaknesses of Natural Law, but not so much about its strengths. Answer the question set, not the one you would like to have been set.

Remember: (a) assesses AO1 and (b) AO2. To help you improve your answers look at the AS Levels of Response. See: http://www.ocr.org.uk/qualifications/as-a-level-gce-religious-studies-h172-h572/.

SAMPLE EXAM STYLE QUESTIONS

(a) Explain the strengths of the Natural Law theory. (25 marks)

At the beginning you should explain how the theory of Natural Law according to Thomas Aquinas is absolutist and depends on the idea that God created everything for a purpose. You also need to say that human reason is to be used to judge how to act morally and so to follow God's will; ignoring reason is ignoring God's command. You could consider some of the following strengths:

- It is clear-cut and straightforward to apply.
- All those things that we require for happiness – health, friends – are morally good. The purpose of morality is the fulfilment of our natures.
- You could also consider that Natural Law allows societies to have clear common rules and to organise moral life.
- You could also explain that Natural Law considers the importance of both the intention and the act.
- A more difficult approach is to consider that Natural Law concentrates on human character and its potential for goodness and flourishing, rather than on the rightness or wrongness of particular acts, and so it allows some measure of flexibility in the secondary precepts.

(b) To what extent could a believer in Natural Law accept embryo research? (10 marks)

- You might consider the nature of the embryo – whether it is a person or not – and God's plan for human life.
- You could point to the link between sex and childbirth.
- You may point out that human beings are led by apparent 'goods' that tempt them away from Natural Law and consider that both intention and act are important.

SAMPLE AS EXAM STYLE QUESTIONS

(a) Explain how the principles of Natural Law might be applied to the argument that every woman has the right to a child.

(b) To what extent could a believer in the Natural Law theory accept foetal research?

(a) Explain how a follower of Natural Law might respond to issues raised by abortion.

(b) 'A Natural Law approach is the best approach to abortion.' Discuss.

(a) Explain the Natural Law theory.

(b) 'The Natural Law theory has no serious weaknesses.' Discuss.

FURTHER READING

Aquinas, T. 'Summa Theologiae', in *Basic Writings of Thomas Aquinas*, Pegis, A.C. (ed.), Hackett, Indianapolis, Random House, 1997.

Hughes, G. 'Natural Law', in *Christian Ethics: An Introduction*, Hoose, B. (ed.), London, Cassell, 1998.

Macquarrie, J. and Childress, J. *A New Dictionary of Christian Ethics*, London, SCM, 1986.

Maguire, D. *Death by Choice*, New York, Image Books, 1984.

Pojman, L.P. *Ethics: Discovering Right and Wrong*, Toronto, Wadsworth, 2002.

4 Kant

Essential terminology

A posteriori
A priori
Absolute
Absolutism
Autonomy
Categorical Imperative
Copernican Revolution
Duty
Good will
Hypothetical
    Imperative
Kingdom of Ends
Law
Maxim
Summmum bonum
Universalisability

WHAT YOU WILL LEARN ABOUT IN THIS CHAPTER

- Kant's understanding of pure reason, a priori knowledge and objectivity.
- Kant's Copernican Revolution.
- Practical moral reason – the hypothetical and categorical imperatives.
- Kant's ideas of the moral law, good will, duty and the *summum bonum*.
- The strengths and weaknesses of Kant's theory of ethics.
- The theory of W.D. Ross.
- How to apply Kantian Ethics to ethical dilemmas.

KEY SCHOLARS

- René Descartes (1596–1650)
- Gottfried Wilhelm Leibniz (1646–1716)
- David Hume (1711–1776)
- Immanuel Kant (1724–1804)
- W.D. Ross (1877–1971)
- R.M. Hare (1919–2002)

THE OCR CHECKLIST

Candidates should be able to demonstrate knowledge and understanding of:

- the difference between the Categorical and the Hypothetical Imperatives;
- the various formulations of the Categorical Imperative;

continued

- Kant's understanding of the universalisation of maxims;
- Kant's theory of duty;
- Kant's ideas of the moral law, good will and the *summum bonum*.

Candidates should be able to discuss critically these theories and their strengths and weaknesses.

From OCR A Level Religious Studies Specification H172 and H572.

Immanuel Kant (1724–1804)

Immanuel Kant was born in Königsberg, Prussia, on 22 April 1724. He was educated at the Collegium Fredericianum and the University of Königsberg. He studied Classics and, at university, physics and mathematics. He had to leave university to earn a living as a teacher when his father died. Later, he returned to university and studied for his doctorate. He taught at the university for 15 years, moving from science and mathematics to philosophy. He became Professor of Logic and Metaphysics in 1770. He held unorthodox religious beliefs based on rationalism rather than revelation, and in 1792 he was forbidden by the king from teaching or writing on religious subjects. When the king died in 1797, Kant resumed this teaching and in 1798, the year after he retired, he published a summary of his religious views. He died on 12 February 1804.

WHAT IS KANT'S THEORY OF ETHICS?

Immanuel Kant believed in an objective right and wrong based on reason. We should do the right thing just because it is right and not because it fulfils our desires or is based on our feelings. We know what is right not by relying on our intuitions or facts about the world, but by using our reason. To test a moral maxim, we need to ask whether we can always say that everyone should follow it and we must reject it if we cannot.

Kant opposed the view that all moral judgements are culturally relative or subjective so that there are no such things as moral absolutes. Kant's approach to ethics was deontological, where the right takes precedence over the good, and basic rights and principles guide us to know which goods to follow.

Kant

Modern deontology avoids too close a link with Kant and rejects his absolutism and complete disregard for consequences; however, his moral theory has been and continues to be influential.

KANT'S COPERNICAN REVOLUTION

Kant's main area of study was to investigate the formal structures of pure reasoning, causality, a priori knowledge (knowledge not based on experience) and the question of objectivity. He wrote these ideas in the *Critique of Pure Reason* (1781; 2nd edn 1787). He then went on to demonstrate the formal structure of practical-moral reasoning in the *Critique of Practical Reason* (1788) and to study the conditions of the possibility of aesthetics and religion in the *Critique of Judgement* (1790).

Kant's work was a reaction against the rationalists and empiricists, and he was concerned with the problem of objective knowledge: can I have any knowledge of the world that is not just 'knowledge of the world as it seems to me'? He is asking: 'How do we know what we know and what does it mean to know?'

The views of other philosophers about knowledge

- **Descartes** (1596–1650) – the foundation of knowledge is the knowledge of one's own existence: 'I think therefore I am.' Kant criticised this, as he said it did not tell us what 'I' is, or even that it is.
- **Leibniz** (1646 1716) – thought that we can have knowledge untouched by the point of view of any observer.
- **Hume** (1711–1776) – argued that we cannot have any objective knowledge at all.

Kant is closer to the rationalist views of Descartes and Leibniz and opposed to the empiricist views of Hume, which spurred him to explain his own view. Kant considers that our knowledge is not of the world as it is in itself, but of the world as it *appears* to us. If our sense organs were different, our languages and thought patterns different, then our view of the world would be different. Kant is saying that humans can never know the world as it really is (the thing in itself) because as it is experienced it is changed by our minds – the world we now see is a *phenomenon* (like a reflection in a mirror). Kant argued that various structures or categories of thought (space, time and causality) were built into the structure of our minds – we have been pre-programmed. This means that all we can really know about scientifically are our own experiences and perceptions, which may or may not correspond to ultimate reality.

> ## René Descartes (1596–1650)
>
> René Descartes is often called the founder of modern philosophy. He was born in Touraine and was educated at a Jesuit school – La Flèche in Anjou. Here he studied mathematics and scholasticism. He then studied law at Poitiers and later took up a military career. He went to Italy on pilgrimage in 1623–4 and then, until 1628, he studied philosophy in France. He moved to the Netherlands in 1628 and, in 1637, published his first major work: *Essais Philosophiques* (Philosophical Essays). This book covered geometry, optics, meteors and philosophical method. He died from pneumonia in 1650.

Gottfried Wilhelm Leibniz (1646–1716)

Gottfried Wilhelm Leibniz was a German philosopher, mathematician and statesman. He was born in Leipzig and studied at the universities of Leipzig, Jena and Altdorf. In 1666 he began work for Johann Philipp von Schönborn, who was archbishop elector of Mainz. In 1673 Leibniz went to Paris. From 1676 until 1716 he was librarian and privy counsellor at the court of Hanover. His work comprised diplomacy, history, law, mathematics, philology, philosophy, physics, politics and theology.

Copernican Revolution
Belief that the solar system revolves around the sun.

Copernicus

Kant called this analysis the **Copernican Revolution**, as its implications for us are just as vital as the implications of believing that the solar system revolves around the sun. Science then can never give us any knowledge of objective reality, as it can never move beyond the view of the world given to us by the categories of our mind. But Kant did think that these categories could be described as objective, as they are the objective laws of our mind – this is *pure reason* and tells you what is the case.

KANT'S MORAL THEORY

Practical reason looks at evidence and argument and tells you what ought to be done. This sense of the moral 'ought' is something which cannot simply depend on external facts of what the world is like, or the expected consequences of our actions. Kant saw that people are aware of the moral law at work within them – not as a vague feeling but a direct and powerful experience.

> Two things fill the mind with ever new and increasing admiration and awe the oftener and more steadily we reflect on them: the starry heavens above me and the moral law within me.
>
> (*Critique of Practical Reason*)

Kant's moral theory is explained in the 'Groundwork of a Metaphysics of Morals' (1785) and tries to show the objectivity of moral judgement and the universal character of moral laws and attempts to base morality on reason as opposed to feelings, inclinations, consequences or religion. He roots his view of morality in reason to the exclusion of everything else, and rejects especially Hume's idea that morality is rooted in desires or feelings. He does not reject desires and feelings, but says that they have nothing to do with morality. Only reason is universal. Kant approached morality in the same way as he approached knowledge (looking at the **a priori** categories through which we make sense of the world) – he looked for the categories we use: what makes a moral precept moral? Kant declared that these were rooted in rationality, were unconditional or categorical, completely unchanging and presupposed freedom.

Freedom

For Kant, if I am to act morally then I must be capable of exercising *freedom* or **autonomy of the will**. The opposite of this is *heteronomy* – that something is right because it satisfies some desire, emotion, goal or obligation. Our reason must not be subservient to something else even if this is the happiness of the majority.

Good will

The idea of a '**good will**' is Kant's starting point for his morality.

> It is impossible to conceive of anything at all in the world, or even out of it, which can be taken as good without qualification, except a good will. Intelligence, wit, judgement and any other talents of the mind we care to name, or courage, resolution, and constancy of purpose, as qualities of temperament, are without doubt good and desirable in many respects; but they can also be extremely bad and hurtful when the will is not good which has to make use of these gifts. . . . Good will, then, like a jewel, it would still shine by its own light, as a thing which has its whole value in itself. Its usefulness or fruitfulness can neither add to nor take away anything from this value.
>
> ('Groundwork of a Metaphysics of Morals')

It is only the 'good will' which counts and which is the starting point for ethics. Abilities, talents and even virtues count for nothing, as do consequences. Only the will is within our control and so only the will can be unconditionally good and can exercise pure practical reason. This will means the total effort involved in making a conscious moral choice.

This is the opposite of Hume's argument that morality is only based on making people happy and fulfilling their desires – it is just a servant of the passions, and morality is founded on our feelings of sympathy for others and depends on our human nature.

A posteriori
A statement which is knowable after experience.

A priori
A statement which is knowable without reference to any experience.

Autonomy
Self-directed freedom, arriving at moral judgement through reason.

Absolute
A principle that is universally binding.

Absolutism
There is only one correct answer to every moral problem.

Good will
Making a moral choice expresses good will.

David Hume (1711–1776)

David Hume was born in Edinburgh on 7 May 1711. He was an historian and philosopher. He influenced the development of scepticism and empiricism. He worked in an office in Bristol for a short time and then moved to France. A *Treatise of Human Nature* was published in three volumes between 1739 and 1740. Hume went back to his family home in Berwickshire and worked on *Essays Moral and Political*, published in 1741 to 1742. Hume moved to Edinburgh in 1751 and became librarian of the Advocates' Library. Hume was a friend of Jean-Jacques Rousseau and brought him to Britain, but the friendship collapsed due to Rousseau's mental condition. Hume died on 25 August 1776.

Duty

A motive for acting in a certain way which shows moral quality.

Hume

Human nature
— Feelings and desires
— Moral principles

Duty

Duty is what makes the good will good. It is important that duty be done for its own sake and it does not matter whether you or others benefit from your action – our motives need to be pure. Doing duty for any other reason – inclination, self-interest, affection – does not count. The good will chooses duty for duty's sake.

Kant does not rule out pleasure in doing one's duty, but pleasure will not help us to know what duty is or the morality of our actions. According to Kant, there is no moral worth in the feeling of satisfaction we get from doing our duty – if giving to charity out of love for others gives you that warm glow of having helped others, it is not necessarily moral. If I give to charity because duty commands it, then I am moral. So, even though the act of giving to charity has the same result, according to Kant one way is moral and the other is not. *We are not moral for the sake of love but for duty's sake only*. He is arguing against Hume that duty and reason can help us guide our emotions so that we are not dominated and ruled by them.

Duty

Kant

Kant was looking for some sort of objective basis for morality – a way of knowing our duty. Practical reason, therefore, must give the will commands or imperatives. He makes the distinction between two kinds of imperatives – non-moral (hypothetical) and moral (categorical).

THE HYPOTHETICAL IMPERATIVE

Hypothetical imperatives are not moral commands to the will, as they do not apply to everyone. You only need to obey them if you want to achieve a certain '*goal*' – that is why a hypothetical imperative always begins with the word '*if*'.

For example: *if* I want to lose weight I ought to go on a diet and exercise more. A hypothetical imperative depends on the results and aims at personal well-being.

Hypothetical imperative
An action that achieves some goal or end.

THE CATEGORICAL IMPERATIVE

Categorical imperatives, on the other hand, are *moral commands* and do not begin with an 'if', as they tell everyone what to do and do not depend on anything, especially desires or goals. According to Kant these categorical imperatives apply to everyone (like the categories of pure reason which apply to everyone) because they are based on an *objective a priori law of reason* which Kant calls the categorical imperative. This is a test to judge whether an action is in accordance with pure practical reason.

There are a number of different forms of this, but they are variations on three basic ones:

Categorical imperative
A command to perform actions that are absolute moral obligations without reference to other ends.

1   The Universal Law
2   Treat humans as ends in themselves
3   Act as if you live in a Kingdom of Ends.

1   Act only according to that maxim whereby you can at the same time will that it should become a universal law

Law
Objective principle, a maxim that can be universalised.

Maxim
A general rule in accordance with which we intend to act.

Kant calls this the **Formula of the Law of Nature**. This first formulation of the categorical imperative asks everyone to universalise their principles or **maxims** without contradiction. In other words, before you act ask yourself whether you would like everyone in the same situation to act in the same way. If not, then you are involved in a *contradiction* and what you are thinking of doing is wrong because it is against reason.

Kant always wants to universalise rules, as he wants everyone to be free and rational, and if rules are not universalisable then others will not have the same freedom to act on the same moral principles as I use. However, Kant does not claim that everyone should be able to do the same thing as I choose to do in order for it to be moral – but rather everyone should be prepared to act on the same maxim.

Kant uses promise-keeping as an example. I cannot consistently will that promise-breaking for my own self-interest should be a universal law. If I try to make a universal law of the maxim 'I may always break my promises when it is for my benefit', the result will be that there is no point in anyone making promises – this is inconsistent and so cannot be a moral imperative.

To make his argument as clear as possible Kant uses four examples, including the one of promise-keeping:

*   A man feels sick of life as a result of a series of misfortunes that have mounted to the point of despair, but he is still so far in possession of his reason as to ask himself whether taking his own life may be contrary to his duty to himself. He now applies the test 'Can the maxim of my action really become a universal law of nature?' His maxim is 'From self-love I make it my principle to shorten my life if its continuance threatens more evil than it promises pleasure.' The only further question to ask is whether this principle of self-love can become a universal law of nature. It is then seen at once that a system of nature by whose law the very same feeling whose function is to stimulate the furtherance of life should actually destroy life would contradict itself, and consequently could not subsist as a system of nature and is therefore entirely opposed to the supreme principle of all duty.
*   Another finds himself driven to borrowing money due to need. He well knows that he will not be able to pay it back; but he sees too that he will get no loan unless he gives a firm promise to pay it back within a fixed

time. He is inclined to make such a promise; but he still has enough conscience to ask: 'Is it not unlawful and contrary to duty to get out of difficulties in this way?' Supposing, however, he did resolve to do so; the maxim of his action would be: 'Whenever I believe myself short of money, I will borrow and promise to pay it back, though I know that this will never be done.' Now this principle of self-love or personal advantage is perhaps quite compatible with my own entire future welfare; only there remains the question 'Is it right?' I therefore transform the demand of self-love into a universal law and frame my question thus: 'How would things stand if my maxim became a universal law?' I then see straight-away that this maxim can never rank as a universal law of nature and be self-consistent, but must necessarily contradict itself. For the universality of the intention not to keep it would make promising, and the very purpose of promising, itself impossible, since no one would believe he was being promised anything, but would laugh at utterances of this kind as empty shams.

- A third finds in himself a talent whose cultivation would make him a useful man for all sorts of purposes. But he sees himself in comfortable circumstances, and he prefers to give himself up to pleasure rather than bother about increasing and improving his fortunate natural aptitudes. Yet he asks himself further: 'Does my maxim of neglecting my natural gifts, besides agreeing in itself with my tendency to indulgence, agree also with what is called duty?' He then sees that a system of nature could indeed always subsist under such a universal law, although (like the South Sea Islanders) every man should let his talents rust and should be bent on devoting his life solely to idleness, indulgence, procreation and, in a word, to enjoyment. Only he cannot possibly will that this become a universal law of nature or should be implanted in us as such a law by a natural instinct. For as a rational being he necessarily wills that all his powers should be developed, since they serve him, and are given to him, for all sorts of possible ends.

- Yet a fourth is himself flourishing, but he sees others who have to struggle with great hardships (and whom he could easily help); and he thinks: 'What does it matter to me? Let everyone be as happy as heaven wills or as he can make himself; I won't deprive him of anything; I won't envy him; only I have no wish to contribute to his well-being or to support in distress!' Now admittedly, if such an attitude were a universal law of nature, mankind could get on perfectly well – better no doubt than if everyone prates about sympathy and good will and even takes pains on occasion to practise them, but on the other hand cheats where he can, traffics in human rights, or violates them in other ways. But although it is possible that a universal law of nature could subsist in harmony with this maxim, it is impossible to will that such a principle should hold everywhere as a law of nature. For a will which decided in this way would be in conflict with itself, since many a situation might arise in which the man needed love and sympathy from others, and in which by such a law of nature sprung from his own will he would rob himself of all hope of the help he wants for himself.

('Groundwork of a Metaphysics of Morals')

Kant's followers disagree about how to apply this universal law test. **R.M. Hare** suggests an alternative approach to test a proposed moral maxim:

* Try to understand the consequences of following it on affected individuals.
* Try to imagine yourself in the place of these individuals.
* Ask yourself whether you want the maxim to be followed regardless of where you imagine yourself in the situation.

The challenge then is to distinguish right maxims from wrong ones. This is the role of reason in choosing only maxims that can be universalised.

2   So act as to treat humanity, whether in your own person or in that of any other, never solely as a means but always as an end

Kant calls this the **Formula of End in Itself**. He means that we should not exploit others or treat them as things to achieve an end, as they are as rational as we are. To treat another person as a means is to deny that person the right to be a rational and independent judge of his or her own actions. It is to make oneself in some way superior and different. To be consistent we need to value everyone equally.

Kant saw the first two formulations as two expressions of the same idea. He summed this up as follows:

Principles of action are prohibited morally if they could not be universalised without contradiction, or they could not be willed as universal laws.

('Groundwork of a Metaphysics of Morals')

The third formulation follows from the other two.

3   Act as if a legislating member in the universal Kingdom of Ends

Kingdom of Ends

A world in which people do not treat others as means but only as ends.

This he calls the **Formula of a Kingdom of Ends**. Everyone should act as if every other person was an 'end' – a free, autonomous agent. Kant believed that each person is autonomous, and moral judgements should not be based on any empirical consideration about human nature, human flourishing or human destiny. However, this idea of the autonomy of the individual does not mean that everyone can just decide their own morality, but rather that each individual has the ability to understand the principles of pure practical reason and follow them. Pure practical reason must be impartial and so its principles must apply equally to everyone.

4   Any action that ignores the individual dignity of a human being in order to achieve its ends is wrong

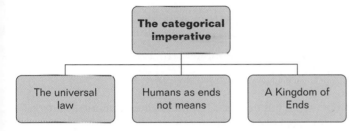

Thought Point

1   Why does Kant believe that the 'good will' is the only thing that is good without qualification? Can you think of anything else that is good without qualification? What are Kant's supporting reasons? Do you agree with him?

2   How would Kant suggest that where there is a clash of duties, we know what takes precedence by following the categorical imperative. Does this work? Discuss the following:

   (a) It is your turn to make a presentation in class and you are running late. On the way you witness a car crash and are asked to wait to make a statement to the police.

   (b) If only actual persons are ends in themselves, how would a Kantian approach a student who accidentally becomes pregnant and decides to have an abortion so as to continue her studies?

   (c) 'If I had to choose between betraying my country and betraying my friend I hope I should have the guts to betray my country.' E.M. Forster. Do you agree?

THE THREE POSTULATES OF PRACTICAL REASON

Apart from making the individual the sole authority for moral judgement, Kant's theory of ethics seems to grant freedom to do anything that can be consistently universalised. This morality sets limits but does not give direct guidance; therefore, in order for it to make sense Kant has to postulate the existence of *God, freedom* and *immortality*.

Kant's ethical theory could, in fact, be said to be a religious morality without God but he seems to take for granted God as lawgiver and he argues that there must be a God and an afterlife, as there has to be some sort of reward.

Kant has already explained that happiness is not the foundation or reason for acting morally, but he claims that it is its reward. Kant's ideas seem to be really twisted with regard to happiness. In the 'Groundwork of a Metaphysics of Morals' he writes:

> The principle of personal happiness is the most objectionable not merely because it is false and because its pretence that well-being always adjusts itself to well-doing is contradicted by experience; not merely because it contributes nothing to morality (since making a man happy is quite different from making him good) but because it bases morality on sensuous motives.

However, he also says that we have a duty to make ourselves happy, not because we want to be happy but because it is necessary for us to do our other duties. Kant seems to put duty in a sort of vacuum, totally separate from our everyday lives.

Summum bonum

The supreme good that we pursue through moral acts.

To solve this dilemma Kant looks at the postulates of *God* and *immortality*: after death, in the next world, there is no conflict between 'duty' and 'happiness', as 'duty' is part of the natural harmony of purposes created by God. Kant thought that our aim in acting morally is not to be happy but to be worthy of being happy. The **summum bonum** or highest good is a state where happiness and virtue are united – but for Kant it is the virtuous person who has a 'good will' which is vital for morality; happiness is not guaranteed. The *summum bonum*, however, cannot be achieved in this life and so there must be life after death where we can achieve it – thus for Kant, morality leads to God.

STRENGTHS OF KANT'S THEORY OF ETHICS

- Kant's morality is very straightforward and based on reason.
- There are clear criteria to assess what is moral.
- The moral value of an action comes from the action itself.
- Kant's categorical imperative gives us rules that apply to everyone and command us to respect human life.
- It makes clear that morality is about doing one's duty and not just following feelings or inclinations. This means that we cannot assume that what is good for us is morally good and so good for everyone else. This is Kant's equivalent of the Golden Rule of Christian ethics.
- It aims to treat everyone fairly and justly and so corrects the Utilitarian assumption that the minority can suffer so long as the majority are happy.
- Kant sees humans as being of intrinsic worth and dignity as they are rational creatures. Humans cannot be enslaved or exploited. This is the basis of the Declaration of Human Rights.

WEAKNESSES OF KANT'S THEORY OF ETHICS

- Kant's theory is abstract and not always easily applied to moral situations – it tells you what *types* of actions are good, but it does not tell you what is the right thing to do in particular situations. As Alasdair MacIntyre points out, you can use the universalisability principle to justify practically anything:

    > all I need to do is to characterise the proposed action in such a way that the maxim will permit me to do what I want while prohibiting others from doing what would nullify the action if universalised.
    >
    > (*A Short History of Ethics*)

Universalisability

If an act is right or wrong for one person in a situation, then it is right or wrong for anyone in that situation.

- Kant's emphasis on duty seems to imply that an action is made moral by an underlying **intention** to do one's duty. However, it is not always possible to separate 'intentions' from 'ends', as intentions are closely linked with what we do (e.g. intending to come to the help of a friend who is being beaten up is not the same as actually doing so). In addition, our motives are not always pure and people seldom act from pure practical reason; we more often help others because we like them or we feel sorry for them. Some philosophers think that putting duty above feeling is cold and inhuman. Kant's theory severs morality from everyday life and everyday feelings and emotions.
- Many people would consider that thinking about the result of an action is an important part of ethical decision-making, and if the outcome hurts another person, most people would feel guilty.

- Kant's system only seems to work if everyone has the same view of the final purpose and end of humans. It depends on some notion of God to justify this rationally ordered world. We do not all even have the same views on life and obeying the moral law could put one at a real disadvantage when dealing with people who are wicked, amoral or simply less rational.
- Kant is clear when explaining the conflict between duty and inclination but he does not help us understand the conflict between different duties, each of which could be justified.
- In addition, though Kant tells us in general terms to respect others and not treat them as ends, this does not tell us what to do in individual cases. What about the terminally ill patient who wants help to die? What about protecting the innocent victim from murderers? What about stealing a drug to help a loved one to live? What about conscription in time of war? Kant's theory here seems to lead either to a position where no decision can be made or to a situation where I may consider doing my duty as just plain wrong.

THE THEORY OF W.D. ROSS

These problems with Kant's theory of ethics led **W.D. Ross** to make certain changes.

Ross said that there were two kinds of duties:

- Prima facie duties
- Actual duties

Prima facie duties

Ross argued that exceptions should be allowed to Kant's duties – he called these *prima facie duties* (first sight duties). These duties are conditional and can be outweighed by a more compelling duty (e.g. 'Never take a life' could be outweighed by 'Never take a life except in self-defence').

> I suggest '*prima facie* duty' or 'conditional duty' as a brief way of referring to the characteristic (quite distinct from that of being a duty proper) which an act has, in virtue of being of a certain kind (e.g. the keeping of a promise), of being an act which would be a duty proper if it were not at the same time of another kind which is morally significant. Whether an act is a duty proper or actual duty depends on *all* the morally significant kinds it is an instance of.
>
> (*The Right and the Good*, pp. 19–20)

Ross lists seven prima facie duties:

1   fidelity or promise-keeping
2   reparation for harm done
3   gratitude
4   justice
5   beneficence
6   self-improvement
7   non-maleficence.

These stress the personal character of duty. The first three duties look to the past and the last four to the future, but they do not need to be considered in any particular order, but rather as to how they fit the particular situation. For example, who should I save from drowning: my father or a famous doctor? A Utilitarian would save the doctor because he could help more people. Ross says we have a special duty of gratitude to our parents which outweighs any duty to a stranger.

Ross shows that there are possible exceptions to any rule and these exceptions depend on the situation in which I do my duty, the possible consequences of doing my duty and the personal relationships involved.

However, calling these 'duties' may be a bit misleading, as they are not so much duties as 'features that give us genuine (not merely apparent) moral reason to do certain actions'. Ross later described prima facie duties as 'responsibilities to ourselves and to others' and he went on to say that our actual duty is determined by the balance of these responsibilities.

> Every act therefore, viewed in some aspects, will be *prima facie* right, and viewed in others, *prima facie* wrong, and right acts can be distinguished from wrong acts only as being those which, of all those possible for the agent in the circumstances, have the greatest balance of *prima facie* rightness, in those respects in which they are *prima facie* right, over their *prima facie* wrongness, in those respects in which they are *prima facie* wrong . . . For the estimation of the comparative stringency of these *prima facie* obligations no general rules can, so far as I can see, be laid down.
>
> (*The Right and the Good*, p. 41)

Actual duties

This is the duty people are left with after they have weighed up all the conflicting prima facie duties that apply in a particular case.

Problems with Ross's theory

- How do we know what a prima facie duty is?
- How do we know which one is right where there is a conflict between them?

Ross says that we simply **know** which acts are right by consulting our deepest moral convictions, but is this an adequate response? Can we be sure that Ross's list of duties is correct? How can we compare and rank them in order to arrive at a balance which will guide us to our actual duty?

Ross thought that people could solve problems by relying on their intuitions.

APPLICATION OF KANTIAN ETHICS TO AN ETHICAL DILEMMA – GENETIC ENGINEERING

Genetic engineering includes cloning, research on embryonic stem cells, so-called designer babies and genetically modified organisms (GMOs).

Kant says that humans should never be thought of as a means but always as an end. This second formulation of the categorical imperative is often used to protect human dignity. Creating a human life (embryo) for the purpose of obtaining cells which could be used as therapeutic material would not be protecting the dignity of that particular human life. The idea of using individuals to help others in this way is sometimes referred to as 'instrumentalisation', and if Kant is applied too rigidly his ethical theory could also prohibit blood transfusions – as the patient needing the transfusion knows nothing of the anonymous donor and is using the person's blood simply as a means to an end. It is standard practice in IVF treatment to create spare embryos – are these created instrumentally?

However, Kant's principle states: '*Act in such a way that you always treat humanity, whether in your own person or in the person of any other, never simply as a means but always at the same time as an end*'; this is rather vague and may be interpreted selectively according to one's point of view.

We also need to consider what the moral status of a human embryo is – is it the same as a born human and does Kant's principle, or indeed any other principle about persons and personhood, apply to embryos? Some people will think that an embryo is a full member of the moral community with all the rights that humans possess and cite the sanctity of life to support their position.

On the other hand, is it possible to apply Kantian Ethics to the idea of attempting to conceive a child to get a 'son and heir'? Is this any different from the idea of selecting an embryo as a genetic match for curing a sibling? Others will consider that it is too simplistic to apply Kant's categorical imperative to any form of genetic engineering and that it is better to do some good than to do no good, and from an ethical point of view it cannot be good to waste spare embryos produced from IVF when they could be used for therapeutic purposes – after all, they were not produced simply as a means.

When applying Kant's categorical imperative to difficult modern ethical dilemmas such as genetic engineering, it is important not to be too dogmatic but to look at the question from different angles.

One must also consider the question of genetically modified organisms – is it better to view this as a means to feed the hungry, or do we again treat people (small farmers) as a means to an end by putting them in thrall to the multinationals?

These are some of the questions that need to be considered and discussed when applying Kantian Ethics to genetic engineering in its many forms.

REVIEW QUESTIONS

Look back over the chapter and check that you can answer the following questions:

1   What did Kant mean by 'good will'?
2   Why is duty important to Kant?
3   Spider diagram or mind map the categorical imperative, with examples.
4   Make a chart of the strengths and weaknesses of Kantian Ethics.

Terminology

Do you know your terminology?

Try to explain the following terms without looking at your books and notes:

* The categorical imperative
* The hypothetical imperative
* Duty
* Good will
* The Kingdom of Ends
* Maxim
* The *summum bonum*
* Universalisability

Examination Questions Practice

It is a good idea always to use examples to explain the categorical imperative. Do not use phrases like 'a priori' if you cannot remember what they mean.

Remember: (a) assesses AO1 and (b) AO2. To help you improve your answers look at the AS Levels of Response. See: http://www.ocr.org.uk/qualifications/as-a-level-gce-religious-studies-h172-h572/

SAMPLE EXAM STYLE QUESTIONS

(a) Give an account of Kant's ethical theory. (25 marks)

- At the beginning you need to set the scene and explain that Kant's theory of ethics is deontological and focused on the idea of a moral law.
- You might explain that moral statements are a priori synthetic.
- You could also explain Kant's understanding of good will and duty and show that they are linked.
- Most importantly you need to explain the categorical imperative and its universalisability; that people must be considered as ends in themselves and that people work towards a Kingdom of Ends.
- A good answer would include examples, preferably Kant's own.

(b) 'Kant's ethical theory is a good approach to euthanasia.' Discuss. (10 marks)

You can argue this both ways.

- You may refer to the quality of life and compassionate love, or you could take an absolutist view and point to the importance of not treating people as means to an end and how this second formulation of the categorical imperative is often used to protect human dignity.
- However, this formulation is rather vague and may be interpreted selectively according to one's point of view.
- You may also consider the idea of universalisation and the problems involved in making euthanasia a universal maxim.
- On the other hand, you could also contrast Kant's approach with that of a more relative ethical theory, such as Situation Ethics.

SAMPLE AS EXAM STYLE QUESTIONS

(a) Give an account of Kant's theory of ethics.
(b) How helpful would this theory be when faced with the problem of dying without dignity?

(a) Describe Kant's reasons for defending the need for the categorical imperative.
(b) How useful are Kantian Ethics for drawing conclusions about the right to life?

(a) Explain Kant's concept of universalisability.
(b) Assess the view that it is always right to keep one's promises.

FURTHER READING

Kant, I. 'Groundwork of a Metaphysics of Morals', in *The Moral Law*, Paton, H.J. (trans.), London, Routledge, 2005.

MacIntyre, A. *A Short History of Ethics*, London, Routledge, 1968.

Norman, R. *The Moral Philosophers*, Oxford, Oxford University Press, 1998.

Pojman, L.P. *Ethics: Discovering Right and Wrong*, Toronto, Wadsworth, 2002.

Ross, W.D. *The Right and the Good*, Oxford, Oxford University Press, 1930, 2002.

Scruton, R. *Kant*, Oxford, Oxford University Press, 1982.

Ward, K. *The Development of Kant's View of Ethics*, Oxford, Blackwell, 1972.

5 Utilitarianism

WHAT YOU WILL LEARN ABOUT IN THIS CHAPTER

*   The principle of utility, the hedonic calculus, Act and Rule Utilitarianism.
*   Classical forms of Utilitarianism from Bentham, Mill and Sidgwick; modern versions from Hare, Singer, Brandt and Popper.
*   The strengths and weaknesses of Utilitarianism.
*   How to apply Utilitarianism to ethical dilemmas.

KEY SCHOLARS

*   Epicurus (341–270 BCE)
*   Jeremy Bentham (1748–1832)
*   John Stuart Mill (1806–1873)
*   Henry Sidgwick (1838–1900)
*   W.D. Ross (1877–1971)

*   Richard Brandt (1910–1997)
*   R.M. Hare (1919–2002)
*   John Rawls (1921–2002)
*   Bernard Williams (1929–2003)
*   Peter Singer (1946–)

THE OCR CHECKLIST

Candidates should be able to demonstrate knowledge and understanding of:

*   the classical forms of Utilitarianism from Bentham and Mill;
*   the principle of utility;
*   the differences between the Utilitarianism of Bentham and of Mill;

- the hedonic calculus, higher and lower pleasures, quantity vs. quality, and Act and Rule Utilitarianism;
- the Preference Utilitarianism of Peter Singer.

Candidates should be able to discuss critically these issues and their strengths and weaknesses.
From OCR A Level Religious Studies Specification H172 and H572.

WHAT IS UTILITARIANISM?

You have probably heard someone justify their actions as being for the greater good. Utilitarianism is the ethical theory behind such justifications.

Utilitarianism is a **teleological** theory of ethics. It is the opposite of *deontological* ethical theories that are based on moral rules, on whether the action itself is right or wrong. Teleological theories of ethics look at the consequences – the results of an action – to decide whether it is right or wrong. Utilitarianism is a **consequentialist** theory.

The theory of Utilitarianism began with **Jeremy Bentham** as a way of working out how good or bad the consequence of an action would be. Utilitarianism gets its name from Bentham's test question: 'What is the use of it?' He thought of the idea when he came across the words 'the greatest happiness of the greatest number' in **Joseph Priestley**'s *An essay on the first principles of government; and on the nature of political, civil, and religious liberty* (1768). Bentham was very concerned with social and legal reform and he wanted to develop an ethical theory which established whether something was good or bad according to its benefit for the majority of people.

Bentham called this the **principle of utility**. Utility here means the *usefulness* of the results of actions. The principle of utility is often expressed as 'the greatest good of the greatest number'. 'Good' is defined in terms of *pleasure* or *happiness* – so an act is right or wrong according to the good or bad that results from the act and the good act is the most pleasurable. Since it focuses on the greatest number, Bentham's theory is quantitative.

THE ORIGINS OF HEDONISM

The idea that 'good' is defined in terms of pleasure and happiness makes Utilitarianism a **hedonistic** theory. The Greek philosophers who thought along similar lines introduced the term *eudaimonia*, which is probably best

Teleological
Moral actions are right or wrong according to their outcome or *telos* (end).

Consequentialist
Someone who decides whether an action is good or bad by its consequences.

Principle of utility
The theory of usefulness – the greatest happiness for the greatest number.

Hedonism
The view that pleasure is the chief 'good'.

Jeremy Bentham (1748–1832)

Jeremy Bentham was born in London on 15 February 1748. He could read scholarly works at age 3, played the violin at 5, and studied Latin and French at 6. At age 12 he went to Oxford and trained as a lawyer. Bentham was the leader of the Philosophical Radicals who founded the *Westminster Review*. He died in London on 6 June 1832. His body was dissected and his clothed skeleton is in a glass case in University College, London. Bentham advanced his theory of Utilitarianism as the basis for general political and legal reform.

translated as 'well-being'. Both Plato and Aristotle agreed that 'good' equated with the greatest happiness, while the Epicureans stressed 'pleasure' as the main aim of life. The ultimate end of human desires and actions, according to Aristotle, is happiness and though pleasure sometimes accompanies this, it is not the chief aim of life. Pleasure is not the same as happiness, as happiness results from the use of reason and cultivating the virtues. It is only if we take pleasure in good activities that pleasure itself is good. This idea of Aristotle's is taken up by John Stuart Mill, as we will see later.

JEREMY BENTHAM'S APPROACH

Jeremy Bentham developed his ethical system around the idea of pleasure and it is based on ancient hedonism, which pursued physical pleasure and avoided physical pain. According to Bentham, the most moral acts are those that maximise pleasure and minimise pain. This has sometimes been called the 'Utilitarian calculus'. An act would be moral if it brings the greatest amount of pleasure and the least amount of pain.

Pain vs. pleasure

Bentham said: 'The principle of utility aims to promote happiness which is the supreme ethical value. Nature has placed us under the governance of two sovereign masters, *pain* and *pleasure*. An act is right if it delivers more pleasure than pain and wrong if it brings about more pain than pleasure.'

By adding up the amounts of pleasure and pain for each possible act we should be able to choose the good thing to do.

Happiness = pleasure minus pain

The hedonic calculus

Hedonic calculus
Bentham's method for measuring the good and bad effects of an action.

To help us choose the good thing to do and work out the possible consequences of an action, Bentham provided a way of measuring. This is the **hedonic calculus**.

It has seven elements:

1   the intensity of the pleasure (how deep)
2   the duration of the pleasure caused (how long)
3   the certainty of the pleasure (how certain or uncertain)
4   the remoteness of the pleasure (how near or far)
5   the chance of a succession of pleasures (how continuous)

The quantity of happiness

Epicurus (341–270 BCE)

Epicureans are followers of Epicurus who was born on the island of Sámos. In 322 he began teaching in Colophon. In 311 he founded a philosophical school in Mitilíni on the island of Lésvos and then became head of a school in Lampsacus. He returned to Athens in 306 and taught his group of followers there. Epicurus developed a system of ethics but later thinkers have used his philosophy as an equivalent to hedonism teaching that pleasure or happiness is the chief good, which people should aim to achieve.

6   the purity of the pleasure (how secure)
7   the extent of the pleasure (how universal).

This calculus gave Bentham a method of testing whether an action is morally right, in that if it was good it would result in the most pleasurable outcome, having weighed up all the elements. Whatever is good or bad can be measured in a **quantitative** way.

Overleaf there is an example of how the hedonic calculus might be applied to a young totally paralysed man who is deciding whether to have euthanasia or not.

It is actually quite difficult to decide which decision would bring the most pleasure and the least pain and this is one of the problems when using the hedonic calculus as it is not possible for us to see into the future; we can only make educated guesses and these are often clouded by our emotional state at the time.

Quantitative
Looking at the quantity of the happiness.

Hedonism

Bentham's Utilitarianism is a universal hedonism – the highest good is the greatest happiness for the greatest number. Actions are judged as a *means to an end*. What is right is that which is calculated to bring about the greatest balance of good over evil, where good is defined as pleasure or happiness.

Bentham's view is described as **Act Utilitarianism**.

Act Utilitarianism
A teleological theory that uses the outcome of an action to determine whether it is good or bad.

Hedonic calculus	Have euthanasia	Do not have euthanasia
Intensity	He could be at peace and his family would not have to devote their lives to caring for him. However, his death could bring intense feelings of pain to his family and friends	His continuing existence gives intense feelings of joy to his family and friends, but may also lead to resentment in those who care for him
Duration	Death is permanent but the grieving of family and friends might last a long time	The young man will need looking after for a lifetime
Certainty	The freedom from the pain of his situation is certain	It is uncertain what pleasures continuing to live totally paralysed will bring
Remoteness	The relief from his situation is immediate	Any possibility of a cure or of learning to live successfully with his situation is a long way off
Succession	There will be no more choices The relief that he is no longer suffering may help his family and friends to accept his death	Pleasure that he is still living, but pain that he is still suffering will cancel each other out
Purity	If he regrets his decision it will be too late	May live a miserable life stuck on a bed or in a wheelchair, totally dependent on others
Extent	The young man and his family and friends are the most directly affected	His continuing existence will bring both pain and pleasure for a lifetime

Bentham argued that we should be guided by the principle of utility and not by rules. However, it may be necessary to use rules of thumb based on past experience, especially if there is no time to work out the consequences.

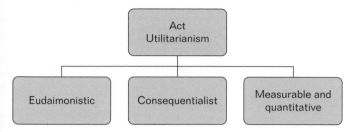

Thought Point

1 What would be the problems if everyone acted as an Act Utilitarian all the time?
2 Are all actions only good because they have good results?
3 Suppose a rape is committed that is thought to be racially motivated. Riots are brewing that may result in many deaths and long-term racial antagonism. You are the police chief and have recently taken a man into custody. Why not frame him? He will be imprisoned if found guilty and this will result in peace and safety. Only you, the innocent man and the real rapist (who will keep quiet), will know the truth. What is the morally right thing to do? Look at all the consequences of any action.
4 Suppose a surgeon could use the organs of one healthy patient to save the lives of several others. Would the surgeon be justified in killing the healthy patient for the sake of the others?
5 You are an army officer who has just captured an enemy soldier who knows where a secret time bomb is planted. If it explodes it will kill thousands. Will it be morally permissible to torture the soldier so that he reveals the bomb's location? If you knew where the soldier's children were, would it also be permissible to torture them to get him to reveal the bomb's whereabouts?

JOHN STUART MILL'S APPROACH

Mill was also a hedonist and accepted that happiness is of the greatest importance. He stressed happiness rather than pleasure.

The Greatest Happiness Principle

Mill said: 'The Greatest Happiness Principle holds that actions are right in proportion as they tend to promote happiness, wrong as they tend to produce

John Stuart Mill (1806–1873)

John Stuart Mill was born on 20 May 1806, the son of James Mill, who had a significant influence on nineteenth-century British thought in philosophy, economics, politics and ethics. From 1822 he worked for his father in India House and stayed there until 1858, when the company closed and he retired. Mill then lived in St Véran, France, until 1865, when he became a Member of Parliament. He went back to France in 1868, and lived there until his death on 8 May 1873. He is most famous for his essay *On Liberty* (1859).

the reverse of happiness. By happiness is intended pleasure, and the absence of pain; by unhappiness, pain and the privation of pleasure.' Happiness for Mill is more than just pleasure and also includes having goals and virtues. This is closer to Aristotle's idea of *eudaimonia* (see Chapter 12 on Virtue Ethics).

The quality of pleasure

Having affirmed his agreement with the principle of utility, Mill then modifies Bentham's approach, especially the quantitative emphasis. He says: 'Some kinds of pleasures are more desirable and more valuable than others, it would be absurd that while, in estimating all other things, quality is not also considered as well as quantity.'

According to Mill, quality of pleasure employs the use of the higher faculties. Here he is answering the objection to Bentham's approach that Utilitarians are just pleasure-seekers. For example, consider the case of the Christians and the Romans: many Romans get a lot of pleasure from seeing a few Christians eaten by lions – here the greatest happiness (that of the Romans) is produced by an act (Christians being eaten by lions) that is surely quite wrong. Mill says that the quality of pleasure that satisfies a human is different from that which satisfies an animal. People are capable of more than animals, so it takes more to make a human happy. Therefore, a person

Qualitative
Looking at the quality of the pleasure.

The quality of happiness

will always choose higher quality, human pleasures, and reject all the merely animal pleasures. As Mill puts it:

> Few human creatures would consent to be changed into any of the lower animals for a promise of the fullest allowance of the beast's pleasures. . . . It is better to be a human being dissatisfied than a pig satisfied; better to be Socrates dissatisfied than a fool satisfied. And if the fool or the pig are of a different opinion, it is because they only know their side of the question. (*On Virtue and Happiness*, 1863)

So since the Romans are only enjoying 'animal' pleasure, it does not matter that they are getting a lot more of it than the Christians – it is the quality not the quantity of the pleasure that really counts. For Mill, it is intellectual pleasures (e.g. reading poetry or listening to music) that really count and are more important than such pleasures as eating, drinking or having sex.

Happiness, he argues, is something that people desire for its own sake, but we need to look at human life as a whole – happiness is not just adding up the units of pleasure but rather the fulfilment of higher ideals.

Universalisability

Mill next develops the argument that in order to derive the principle of the greatest good (happiness) for the greatest number we need the principle

Universalisability

If an act is right or wrong for one person in a situation, then it is right or wrong for anyone in that situation.

of universalisability. He says: 'Each person's happiness is a good to that person, and the general happiness, therefore, is a good to the aggregate of all persons.' This means:

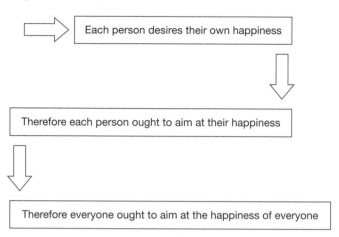

Each person desires their own happiness

Therefore each person ought to aim at their happiness

Therefore everyone ought to aim at the happiness of everyone

As you can see, the last proposition does not follow logically from the previous one. To move from each person to everyone is a fallacy. Mill makes this move because he wants to justify 'the greatest number'. This can mean that Utilitarianism demands that people put the interests of the group before their own interests, and Mill compares this to 'the Golden Rule of Jesus of Nazareth'. Mill has a positive view of human nature and thinks that people have powerful feelings of empathy for others which can be cultivated by education and so on.

Mill also separates the question of the motive and the morality of the action. There is nothing wrong with self-interest if it produces the right action.

Rule Utilitarianism

Rule Utilitarianism

Establishing a general rule that follows Utilitarian principles.

Another aspect of Mill's approach is the idea that there need to be some moral *rules* in order to establish social order and justice – but the rules should be those which, if followed *universally*, would most likely produce the greatest happiness. Mill has been seen as a **Rule Utilitarian** in contrast to Bentham's Act Utilitarianism – though Mill never discussed Act or Rule Utilitarianism in these terms. Also, like many philosophers, Mill's approach was not consistent throughout his writings – at first Mill appears to be an Act Utilitarian, saying that pleasures can be described as either higher or lower, and later he writes that rights and rules are principles of utility. He argues that some rights need to be guaranteed in order to ensure general happiness and the greater good. He seems to assert that when one is uncertain as to

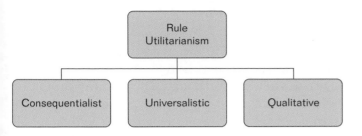

which action to take, the rules of justice and rights (life, liberty and property) must be considered as most important.

As Mill's position is unclear it is perhaps better to describe him as a **weak** Rule Utilitarian, as when a strong Utilitarian reason exists to break the rule, the rule should be disregarded.

Comparing Bentham and Mill

Bentham	Mill
'The greatest good [*pleasure*] for the greatest number'	'The greatest *happiness* for the greatest number'
Focused on the *individual* alone	We should protect the common good, *universalistic*
Quantitative – hedonic calculus	*Qualitative* – higher/lower pleasure
Act Utilitarianism	Rule Utilitarianism
In search of maximisation of happiness	
Consequentialist	Consequentialist

HENRY SIDGWICK'S APPROACH

Another important Utilitarian was **Henry Sidgwick**. In *The Methods of Ethics* he argues that the balance of pleasure over pain is the ultimate goal of ethical decisions. His argument is closer to Bentham than to Mill, as he questions how it is possible to distinguish between higher and lower order pleasures, and how we can distinguish one higher order pleasure from another. However, Sidgwick does argue that the process of deciding is *intuitive* – we make self-evident judgements about what we ought to do.

Henry Sidgwick (1838–1900)

Sidgwick was born in Skipton, Yorkshire. He became Professor of Moral Philosophy at Cambridge in 1883. The requirement for him to subscribe to Anglican Christianity before taking the post was waived because he was unable to do so on conscientious grounds. He concentrated on ethical problems and thought that many could be resolved by appeal to a god, but he could not himself subscribe to this view. He could not accept that the maximising of human pleasure could be aligned with an idea of 'universal values'. Sidgwick supported higher education for women and was a founder of Newnham College, Cambridge. He was the first President of the Society for Psychical Research. His principal works include *The Methods of Ethics* (1874), *Principles of Political Economy* (1883) and *Elements of Politics* (1891).

Justice

Sidgwick was concerned with justice in society and, like Mill, he had a positive view of human nature, hoping that the future would bring a growth in human empathy and moral motivation. He argued that justice is the similar and injustice the dissimilar treatment of similar cases: 'Whatever action any of us judges to be right for himself, he implicitly judges to be right for all similar persons in similar circumstances.' It cannot be right for Jack to treat Tom in a manner in which it would be wrong for Tom to treat Jack, simply on the grounds that they are two different individuals and without there being any difference in their circumstances or their natures. This argument that we must act according to just laws raises the issue of which laws are just, and the whole issue of justice seems to sit uncomfortably with the principle of utility and the Act Utilitarian position.

SIDGWICK AND BENTHAM

There are obvious differences between Bentham and Sidgwick, but both may be described as Act Utilitarians – moral actions are not only judged by their consequences, but also by how they benefit the welfare of people. The act that brings happiness to the greatest number is a right act. Sidgwick's approach to Utilitarianism is the starting point for modern-day approaches to this ethical theory.

ACT AND RULE UTILITARIANISM

Before looking at modern approaches to Utilitarianism, it is important that you fully understand the two variations – Act Utilitarianism and Rule Utilitarianism.

The distinction is to do with what the principle of utility is applied *to*.

- According to Act Utilitarianism the principle is applied directly to a particular action in a particular circumstance.
- According to Rule Utilitarianism the principle is applied to a selection of a set of rules which are in turn used to determine what to do in particular situations.

ACT UTILITARIANISM

You must decide what action will lead to the greatest good in the particular situation you are facing and apply the principle of utility directly. You need to look at the consequences of a particular act and what will bring about the greatest happiness.

Flexibility

Since the same act might in some situations produce the greatest good for the greatest number, but in other situations not, Utilitarianism allows moral rules to change from age to age, from situation to situation.

There are no necessary moral rules except one: that we should always seek the greatest happiness for the greatest number in all situations.

Act Utilitarianism is linked to Bentham's form of Utilitarianism.

Weaknesses of Act Utilitarianism

- It is difficult to predict the consequences.
- There is potential to justify any act.
- There is difficulty in defining pleasure.
- There is no defence for the minorities.
- It is impractical to say that we should calculate the morality of each choice.
- *Teleological* – aims for a maximisation of pleasure for the majority. It has an end aim or goal.
- *Relative* – no notion of absolute right/wrong. No external source of truth. Nothing in itself is right or wrong.
- *Consequential* – the consequences of an act alone determine its rightness/wrongness.

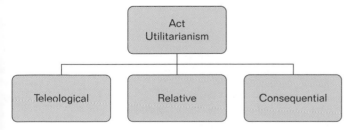

RULE UTILITARIANISM

Rule Utilitarians believe that rules should be formed using Utilitarian principles for the benefit of society. Your action is judged right or wrong by the goodness or badness of the consequences of a rule that everyone should follow in similar circumstances. Rule Utilitarianism enables us to establish rules that will promote the happiness of humanity and will generally be right in most circumstances (e.g. telling the truth, keeping your promises).

Strong Rule Utilitarians believe that these derived rules should never be disobeyed.

Weak Rule Utilitarians say that although there should be generally accepted rules or guidelines, they should not always be adhered to indefinitely. There may be situations where the better consequence might be achieved by disregarding the rule (e.g. where it might be better to tell a lie).

Weak Rule Utilitarianism is commonly linked with Mill.

Weaknesses of Rule Utilitarianism

* It is difficult to predict the consequences.
* It is difficult to define what constitutes happiness.
* There is no defence for the minorities.
* To invoke rules means that the approach becomes deontological not teleological.
* Followers of Rule Utilitarianism can either be strict rule-followers or rule-modifiers, but neither seems satisfactory. Strict rule-followers can be irrational: obeying the rule even when disobeying it will produce more happiness. Rule-modifiers can end up being no different from Act Utilitarians.
* *Deontological* – rules take priority.
* *Relative* – what is right/wrong is established as the maximisation of pleasure for the particular community/society within which it operates.
* *Consequential* – the overall consequences determine its rightness/ wrongness.

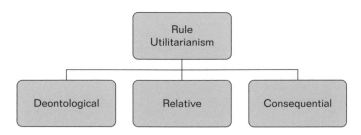

Thought Point

1   Suppose that you were God, and because you are onmibenevolent, you want your creatures to be as happy as possible across time (i.e. you believe in Utilitarianism). If you were choosing a moral code to teach your created people that would make them all happy, what code would you teach them?

2   Explain the distinction between Act and Rule Utilitarianism and why Rule Utilitarianism came about.

3   The country is threatened with drought, so people are urged to conserve water, and hose-pipe bans are in force. Joe lives in an isolated part of the country and nobody ever drives past his house. The water company has forgotten Joe exists and so he is never billed for his water. Joe knows about the hose-pipe ban, but he really wants a green lawn. His lawn is tiny, so he knows he will not be harming anyone if he waters it and the small amount he uses will not affect the drought. Joe continues to use water. What would an Act Utilitarian say about this? What would a Rule Utilitarian say? Give reasons.

PREFERENCE UTILITARIANISM

Preference Utilitarianism is a more recent form of Utilitarianism and is associated with **R.M. Hare, Peter Singer** and **Richard Brandt**.

An Act Utilitarian judges right or wrong according to the maximising of pleasure and minimising of pain, a Rule Utilitarian judges right or wrong according to the keeping of rules derived from utility, but a Preference Utilitarian judges moral actions according to whether they fit in with the preferences of the individuals involved. This approach to Utilitarianism asks: 'What is in my own interest? What would I prefer in this situation? Which outcome would I prefer?' However, because Utilitarianism aims to create the greatest good for the greatest number, it is necessary to consider the preferences of others in order to achieve this.

Preference Utilitarianism
Moral actions are right or wrong according to how they fit the preferences of those involved.

R.M. Hare's approach

Hare argues that in moral decision-making we need to consider our own preferences and those of others. He says that 'equal preferences count equally, whatever their content'. People are happy when they get what they prefer, but what we prefer may clash with the preferences of others. Hare says we need to 'stand in someone else's shoes' and try to imagine what someone

Peter Singer (1946–)

Peter Singer was born on 6 July 1946 in Melbourne. He studied at Melbourne and Oxford. In 1999 he was appointed DeCamp Professor of Bioethics at the University Center for Human Values, Princeton University. Singer's system is based on reason and not on self-interest or social conditioning. His work deals with issues such as embryo experimentation, genetic engineering, surrogacy, abortion and euthanasia. Singer's best-known work is *Animal Liberation* (1975). He is a vegetarian and donates the royalties from his books to international aid and animal liberation. He gives between 10 and 20 per cent of his income to the poor.

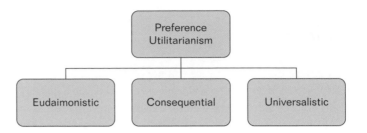

else might prefer. We should treat everyone, including ourselves, with impartiality – he also argues for universalisability.

Peter Singer's approach

Singer also defends Preference Utilitarianism and suggests that we should take the viewpoint of an *impartial spectator* combined with a broadly Utilitarian approach. He says that 'our own preferences cannot count any more than the preferences of others' and so, in acting morally, we should take account of all the people affected by our actions. Ethical judgements must be made from a universal point of view. This view accepts that our own wants, needs and desires cannot count for more than those of anyone else. Singer uses the example of sharing the abundance of nature's fruits – everyone is entitled to an equal share. These have to be weighed and balanced and then we must choose the action that gives the best possible consequences for those affected, however. Singer says society is made up of a collection of individuals, each with their own preferences; trade-offs, however, have to be made for the general welfare – in other words some preferences have to be accepted and others rejected so that the good of all may be achieved.

For Singer, the 'best possible consequences' means what is in the *best interests* of the individuals concerned – this is different from Bentham, Mill and Sidgwick, as he is not considering what increases pleasure and diminishes pain. In *Practical Ethics* (1993) Singer wrote that 'an action contrary to the preference of any being is, unless this preference is outweighed by contrary preferences wrong.' The more preferences satisfied in the world, the better – so killing someone like Hitler, which would save the lives of many others and lead to many preferences being fulfilled, would be the right thing to do.

This principle of equal consideration of preferences or interests acts like a pair of scales – everyone's preferences or interests are weighed equally. So, in Singer's view, killing a person who prefers to go on living would be wrong and not killing a person who prefers to die would also be wrong. Racism is wrong, as it goes against the principle of acknowledging other people's interests or preferences and gives greater value to the preferences of one's own race.

If Singer's principles were put into practice, they would prove radical – for example he argued that since $1,000 can keep several children alive for years, each of us is obligated not to spend it but to donate it to Oxfam or the Red Cross. Singer's principle is, 'If it is in our power to prevent something bad from happening, without thereby sacrificing anything of comparable moral importance, we ought, morally, to do it.' ('Famine, Affluence, and Morality', *Philosophy and Public Affairs*, vol. 1, no. 1 (Spring 1972), pp. 229–243 (revised edition.))

> A moment's reflection on the implications of this principle should convince you of its radicalness. If we were to follow it, we would be left just slightly better off than the worst off people in the world (who would be much better off). People would have to turn in their second cars and second homes and share the ones they already have.
> (Louis Pojman, *Ethics: Discovering Right and Wrong*, 2002)

There are always going to be issues with this as one could argue that it is not always possible to know people's true preferences, as these change over time as our knowledge and understanding change, and according to Singer's principle of equal consideration this shows that the ties of love and kinship do not count.

Some of Singer's approaches seem difficult to accept for many people – he argues that some animals have a higher moral status than some humans. He begins this argument by observing that many animals prefer to avoid pain and enjoy pleasure. Singer argues that causing animals pain by killing them for food, caging them, separating them from their mates and families, etc., is against their preferences and is therefore wrong. He does not consider humans to be above animals and states that an intelligent adult ape has more conscious preferences than a newborn infant. To think otherwise is to be guilty of speciesism. He approves of Bentham's dictum: 'the question is not, Can they *reason*? nor, Can they *talk*? but, Can they *suffer*?', and follows Mill's idea when he talks of extending 'the standard of morality so far as the nature of things permits, to the whole of sentient creation' (*Utilitarianism*). Singer accords animals rights as sentient (feeling) beings; they have valid interests. So according to Singer's Preference Utilitarianism, it is preferences rather than human life that we should value.

This view obviously brings out the problem of those people who are unable to express preferences – the newborn, the severely mentally disabled and those who have no rational self-consciousness such as people suffering from Alzheimer's. Also, according to Singer, an early foetus would have no preferences as it cannot feel pain, and even a late foetus would have its limited preferences outweighed by those of the parents: for Singer the worth of human life varies. The same philosophy applies to the dying or those with Alzheimer's – they may have no preferences left, but the family and friends who love them do.

Richard Brandt's approach

Richard Brandt was one of the leading Utilitarian philosophers of the twentieth century. He defended a version of Rule Utilitarianism, but later, in his book *A Theory of the Right and the Good* (1979), he talks about the preferences you would have if you had gone through a process of cognitive psychotherapy and explored all the reasons for your preferences and rejected any you felt were not true to your real values. He argued that the morality you would then accept would be a form of Utilitarianism – with your preferences free from any psychological blocks and you in full possession of all the facts. Such a person would not, therefore, be influenced by advertising.

NEGATIVE UTILITARIANISM

Karl Popper's approach

Negative Utilitarianism
The principle of minimising pain.

Karl Popper coined the term **Negative Utilitarianism** and this idea has clear links to Buddhism as it argues that we should aim to minimise suffering rather than maximise pleasure. He considered that the principle of utility and the search for the happiness of the majority could easily lead to benevolent dictatorship. Popper himself had lived through the early years of the Nazi regime before leaving Austria for England, and he was well aware of the effects of Communism, which promised so much and delivered so little. He thought that the increase in happiness should be left to private initiative and public policy should aim to minimise suffering.

> I believe that there is, from the ethical point of view, no symmetry between suffering and happiness, or between pain and pleasure. Both the greatest happiness principle of the Utilitarians and Kant's principle, 'Promote other people's happiness . . .', seem to me (at least in their formulations) fundamentally wrong on this point, which is, however, not one for rational argument . . . In my opinion . . . human suffering makes a direct moral appeal for help, while there is no similar call to increase the happiness of a man who is doing well anyway.
>
> (*The Open Society and Its Enemies*, 1952)

Those who support Negative Utilitarianism argue that it is more effective since there are more ways to do harm than to do good, and the greatest harms have more consequences. However, other philosophers, such as R.N. Smart, suggest that Negative Utilitarianism aims ultimately to kill off all humanity, as this would effectively minimise pain. They argue that Negative Utilitarians seem to argue for the destruction of the world to avoid the pain of a pin prick, though in response to this a Negative Utilitarian could argue that a pin prick is not quite the same as the suffering caused by genocide, torture or cancer. But this still fails to say how much mild suffering is morally allowed and how we measure it.

Newer versions of Negative Utilitarianism do not attempt to minimise all types of suffering but, by linking with Preference Utilitarianism, only those kinds that result from preferences not being met. In most supporters of moderate Negative Utilitarianism the preference to survive is greater than the desire to be free from suffering, so they reject Smart's idea of a quick and painless destruction of the entire human race. Today many followers believe that with the rise of modern biotechnology many of the worst cases of suffering will be no more, and we would then be able to better cope with cases of minor suffering such as a pin prick.

STRENGTHS OF UTILITARIANISM

- It is straightforward and based on the single principle of minimising pain and maximising pleasure and happiness. A system which aims to create a happier life for individuals and groups is attractive.
- It relates to actions that can be observed in the real world (e.g. giving to charity promotes happiness for poor people and is seen to be good, whereas an act of cruelty is condemned as bad).
- Its consequentialism is also a strength, as when we act it is only natural to weigh up the consequences.
- Utilitarianism's acceptance of the universal principle is essential for any ethical system. It is important to go beyond your own personal point of view.
- The idea of promoting the 'well-being' of the greatest number is also important – this is the basis of the healthcare system: care is provided to improve the health of the population and if more money is spent on the health service, people are healthier and therefore happier.
- Preference Utilitarianism also gives us the valuable principle of being an impartial observer or, as Hare puts it, 'standing in someone else's shoes'. It is important to think about others' interests or preferences as long as one also includes behaving justly.

WEAKNESSES OF UTILITARIANISM

Bernard Williams (1929–2003)

Bernard Williams was born in Southend-on-Sea and studied at Balliol College, Oxford. In 1967 he was made Knightsbridge Professor of Philosophy at the University of Cambridge. In 1988 he moved to the USA. He was Professor at Berkeley, California, and White's Professor of Moral Philosophy at Oxford until his retirement in 1996. He was very interested in politics and sat on several government committees, including those on gambling, drugs and pornography.

John Rawls (1921–2002)

John Rawls was known for his theory of 'justice as fairness'. He taught at Cornell University and Massachusetts Institute of Technology, then moved to Harvard. He is known for *A Theory of Justice* (1971) and *Political Liberalism* (1993).

- It is good to consider the consequences of our actions, but these are difficult to predict with any accuracy.

- Utilitarianism can also be criticised because it seems to ignore the importance of *duty*. An act may be right or wrong for reasons other than the amount of good or evil it produces. The case of the dying millionaire illustrates this. The millionaire asks his friend to swear that on his death he will give all his assets to his local football club. The millionaire dies and his friend sets about fulfilling his last wishes, but he sees an advertisement to save 1,000,000 people who are dying of starvation. Should he keep his promise or save 1,000,000 people? However, some promises may be bad and should not be kept. Duty does not stem from self-interest and is non-consequential – is motive more important than outcomes? Should promises be kept, the truth told and obligations honoured? **W.D. Ross** thought that the role of duty had some importance and advocated prima facie duties as more acceptable.

- Utilitarianism can also advocate injustice, as in the case above where the innocent man is unjustly framed for rape to prevent riots.

- Another weakness is the emphasis on pleasure or happiness. If I seek my own happiness it is impossible for me to seek general happiness and to do what I ought to do. The qualitative and quantitative approaches also pose problems, as all we can really do is guess the units of pleasure – how do we measure one pleasure against another? Should we try to maximise the average happiness or the total happiness (e.g. should the government give tax cuts for the minority with the lowest income or spread the cuts more thinly across all tax payers?). Bentham would allow an evil majority to prevail over a good minority and the exploitation of minority groups – does this not go against what we would consider ethical behaviour?

- Utilitarianism does not consider motives and intentions and so rejects the principle of treating people with intrinsic value. Utilitarianism does not take any notice of personal commitments but only considers the consequences of an action. **Bernard Williams** said that we should not ignore integrity and personal responsibility for moral actions, and he uses the story of Jim and the Indians, where Jim is asked to choose between killing one Indian and letting 19 go free, or refusing and having all 20 shot, to illustrate this and argues that people need to retain their integrity even if this leads to unwelcome consequences.

- **John Rawls** also argues that Utilitarianism is too impersonal and does not consider the rights of individuals in its attempt to look for the 'greater good'.

Utilitarianism has some major weaknesses as far as duty, justice, motives, intentions and consequences are concerned, and the principles of 'the greatest good for the greatest number' and 'treating people as a means to an end' are rather dubious moral principles. The principles of seeking to act in a benevolent way, trying to apply universality and a consideration of consequences (even if only estimated) are principles that may be used with other, more deontological principles such as duty and integrity. Perhaps we need to combine the best principles from both the teleological and deontological approaches to ethics.

APPLICATION OF UTILITARIANISM TO AN ETHICAL DILEMMA – ABORTION

Utilitarianism has little to say on this issue as arguments over whether the foetus is a 'person', whether one person has the 'right' to the use of another's body, whether someone has the 'right' to determine what happens in their own body (Judith Jarvis Thompson) and whether having sex amounts to an 'invitation', and the effects of this, are of little interest to the Utilitarian.

The hedonistic approach to Utilitarianism is concerned only with the balance of pleasure and pain. Therefore it is concerned with the amounts of pleasure and pain in situations where abortion is allowed as contrasted with the amounts of pleasure or pain where abortion is forbidden.

One approach to this issue might be to consider the parties involved. If you believe the main consideration to be the interests of the *foetus*, you need to estimate its future happiness and so the conditions of its family and so on. Any suffering involved in the abortion procedure itself can be avoided by simply aborting the pregnancy sooner, before the foetus has developed the capacity to suffer.

The next party to consider are the *parents* and *other family*. Here again the situation needs to be taken into account when determining present and future happiness – financial situation (e.g. single mother on benefits), absent or unknown father, continuation of genetic abnormalities and so on. According to some studies, having a baby appears to decrease the happiness in a relationship, even in those cases where the baby is wanted.

Utilitarianism also considers the *community* at large – here there may be no consideration of rights or of emotional or religious arguments, but a consideration of maintaining a population level which is felicifically optimal. Thus Utilitarianism is generally against abortion only when it is generally in favour of raising the population and vice versa.

In Utilitarian terms, a general prescription either for or against abortion is hard to justify as each case would be unique – you could argue that if a Utilitarian finds herself unexpectedly pregnant she should seek an abortion;

if Utilitarianism was in favour of her having a child she should have been trying for a baby and so the pregnancy would be expected. This is of course assuming that the decision is not influenced by her personal desires. (Followers of Hare might wonder if abortion is contrary to prima facie principles and whether these should be changed in the face of the happiness of the whole community.)

Utilitarians faced with the dilemma of abortion have to consider more than the questions of rights and personhood; nor can they decide the rightness or wrongness of abortion simply by considering the consequences and the effects on those involved.

REVIEW QUESTIONS

Look back over the chapter and check that you can answer the following questions:

1 Explain the main principle of Utilitarianism.
2 Explain the Utilitarianism of Bentham.
3 Explain the Utilitarianism of Mill.
4 Explain the differences between Act and Rule Utilitarianism.
5 Complete the following diagram:

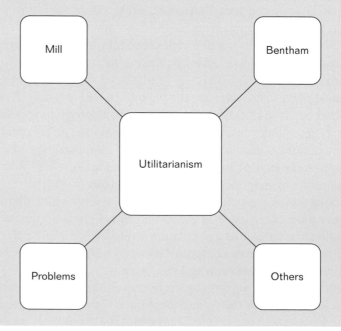

Terminology

Do you know your terminology?

Try to explain the following key ideas without looking at your books and notes:

* Consequentialist
* Teleological ethics
* Act Utilitarianism
* Rule Utilitarianism
* Preference Utilitarianism

Examination Questions Practice

When writing answers to questions on Utilitarianism, make sure you can explain clearly the different types, as Utilitarianism is more a family of theories than one simple theory.

Remember: (a) assesses AO1 and (b) AO2. To help you improve your answers look at the AS Levels of Response. See: http://www.ocr.org.uk/qualifications/as-a-level-gce-religious-studies-h172-h572/.

SAMPLE EXAM STYLE QUESTIONS

(a) Explain how Bentham's version of Utilitarianism may be used to decide on the right course of action. (25 marks)

You will need to begin by giving an explanation of Utilitarianism – the rightness or wrongness of an action is determined by its 'utility' or usefulness, which is the amount of pleasure or happiness caused by the action. An action is right if it produces the greatest good for the greatest number.

* You should explain the hedonic calculus (intensity, duration, certainty or uncertainty, closeness or remoteness, the chance it has of being followed by sensations of the same kind, the purity and extent) and how it may be used to measure pleasure and pain.
* You could give examples to illustrate this.
* You may explain that Bentham's version of Utilitarianism is often called Act Utilitarianism, where the principle of utility must be applied for each individual situation.

(b) Evaluate a Utilitarian approach to abortion. (10 marks)

Here the question is asking you to assess the different approaches of the various types of Utilitarianism or to contrast the Utilitarian approach with that of another ethical theory, perhaps one that considers the foetus as a human being.

- You may consider that most abortions are acceptable to a Utilitarian, though they need to consider the long-term consequences.
- The Utilitarian view may be contrasted with the idea of the sanctity of life, and the rights of the mother and the rights of the foetus discussed.

SAMPLE AS EXAM STYLE QUESTIONS

(a) Explain the main differences between Act and Rule Utilitarianism.
(b) To what extent is Utilitarianism a useful method of making decisions about euthanasia?

(a) Explain the main strengths of a Utilitarian ethical system.
(b) To what extent is Utilitarianism a useful method of making decisions about abortion?

(a) Explain the main strengths and weaknesses of Utilitarianism.
(b) Evaluate a Utilitarian approach to genetic engineering.

FURTHER READING

Bentham, J. *Introduction to the Principles of Morals and Legislation*, Harrison, W. (ed.), Cambridge, Cambridge University Press, 1948.

Gensler, H., Earl, W. and Swindal, J. *Ethics: Contemporary Readings*, New York/London, Routledge, 2004 (contains original writings of many classic and contemporary philosophers).

Mill, J.S. *Utilitarianism*, Indianapolis, Hackett Publishing, [1861, 1863], 2002.

Norman, R. *The Moral Philosophers*, Oxford, Oxford University Press, 1998.

Pojman, L.P. *Ethical Theory*, Toronto, Wadsworth, 1989.

Pojman, L.P. *Ethics: Discovering Right and Wrong*, Toronto, Wadsworth, 2002.

Pojman, L.P. *Ethics: Inventing Right and Wrong* (5th edn), Belmont, CA, Thomson/Wadsworth, 2006.

Singer, P. *Practical Ethics*, Cambridge, Cambridge University Press, 1993.

Smart, J.J.C. and Williams, B. *Utilitarianism: For and Against*, Cambridge, Cambridge University Press, 1973.

6 Religious Ethics
Christian Ethics

Essential terminology

Absolutism
Conscience
Deontological ethics
Divine Command
    theory
Euthyphro Dilemma
Natural Law
Relativism
Situation Ethics
Teleological Ethics
Utilitarianism

For the purpose of this book only Christian ethics will be studied. This chapter covers the requirements for both AS and A2 Religious Ethics.

Examination questions may be approached by reference to biblical texts and teachings, or by reference to an ethical theory which is essentially religious, or both.

WHAT YOU WILL LEARN ABOUT IN THIS CHAPTER

- The origins of Christian ethics in Judaism.
- Christian ethics from the New Testament.
- The role of authority, tradition and conscience in Christian ethics.
- The link between religion and morality.
- Absolutism and relativism in Christian ethics.
- Christian ethical theories: Divine Command theory, Natural Moral Law and Situation Ethics.
- Virtue Ethics.
- The relationship between Christian ethics and Utilitarianism.
- The relationship between Christian ethics and Kantian Ethics.
- The relationship between Christian ethics and contemporary moral thought.

KEY SCHOLARS

- Thomas Aquinas (1225–1274)
- Jeremy Bentham (1748–1832)
- Joseph Fletcher (1905–1991)
- Immanuel Kant (1724–1804)
- John Stuart Mill (1806–1873)
- Plato (428–347 BCE)

THE OCR CHECKLIST

Candidates should be able to demonstrate knowledge and understanding of:

- the main ethical principles of the religion studied and how the followers of the religion make ethical decisions;
- the ways in which religion and morality may seem to be linked or be seen as separate from each other;
- how far morality may be seen as dependent on God (Divine Command theory);
- how far religious ethics may be seen as absolutist or relativist;
- how ethical theories may be considered religious.

Candidates should be able to discuss critically these issues and their strengths and weaknesses.

From OCR A Level Religious Studies Specification H172 and H572.

WHAT IS CHRISTIAN ETHICS?

Natural Law
The theory that an eternal, absolute, moral law can be discovered by reason.

Situation Ethics
The morally right thing to do is the most loving in the situation.

There is no easy answer to this question, as there is so much diversity within Christianity. Some Christians will base their ethics solely on the Bible and its teachings, others will base their ethics on the biblical teachings but also on Church tradition and **Natural Law**, others will follow a **Situation Ethics** approach and others will look to their conscience as a guide. As a result of this diversity, Christians have different responses to ethical issues, whether it is euthanasia, abortion, genetic engineering, foetal research, sex and relationships, war, peace or justice. It is important to understand not only what Christians think on different ethical issues, but also why they think as they do and the basis of their ideas.

In many ways Christian ethics does not look at right and wrong actions, but at the sort of person we are called to become. The Bible teaches that humans are created by God in his image and called to live free and responsible lives, but sin and ignorance have led us to misuse this freedom. In many ways, therefore, Christian ethics has more in common with Virtue Ethics than any other ethical theory.

The Jewish roots of Christian ethics

The early Church brought into Christianity much that belonged to Judaism, and many today would still claim that we can obtain absolute moral rules from the Bible: the Ten Commandments are rules that must be followed without exception, and in the Bible we can find many acts such as homosexuality and divorce that are utterly condemned. However, it is clear that Christianity left behind the Jewish ethic of law as a Divine Command made known in a comprehensive legal code and interpreted by lawyers into many ritual requirements and practices. Christians attempted to drop the legalism and keep the law, especially the Ten Commandments, which were seen as an important part of God's revelation and good guidelines for human existence and human flourishing, in accordance with the human nature which God gave us. Jewish ethical teaching, at its core, is based on relationships: our relationship with God and all our many and varied relationships with other people.

Moses and the Ten Commandments

The basis of Christian ethics in the Bible

The use of the Bible, both the Old and New Testaments, in Christian ethics is not as straightforward as some would believe; some passages need careful exegesis which is beyond the scope of this book. The Bible is a collection of writings put together over a long period of time and reflecting many different cultural contexts. It is important that this fact is borne in mind and that its diversity is recognised. There is no biblical morality or even New Testament teaching that can be followed in every detail, as it all needs to be understood in its cultural context. Christian denominations have always chosen the Bible teachings that back up their particular take on Christianity, such as the Catholic use of Mark's teaching on divorce and total disregard for Matthew's exception clause, or the Lutheran misuse of Romans (7:1–20):

> For we know that the law is spiritual; but I am of the flesh, sold into slavery under sin. I do not understand my own actions. For I do not do what I want, but I do the very thing I hate. Now if I do what I do not want, I agree that the law is good. But in fact it is no longer I that do it, but sin that dwells within me. For I know that nothing good dwells within me, that is, in my flesh. I can will what is right, but I cannot do it. For I do not do the good I want, but the evil I do not want is what I do. Now if I do what I do not want, it is no longer I that do it, but sin that dwells within me.

The following section will necessarily take a broad-brush approach and follow general themes.

The ethics of Jesus

Although Christian ethics carries with it the Ten Commandments, it is of a totally different mindset from a law-based ethic. It was, from the beginning, attempting to reply to the philosophical questions of *happiness* and *salvation*. Therefore the most concentrated body of ethical teaching in the Gospels, the Sermon on the Mount, begins with the Beatitudes: 'Blessed are the poor . . .'.

The Sermon on the Mount may seem to be a set of impossible commands, but although its teaching is challenging, underlying it all is the commandment of love. However, it is not always easy to see what is meant by 'love': for Jesus in the Synoptics it is love of God and love of neighbour; for Paul it is mostly love of neighbour, especially Christians; John's Gospel seems to speak of love in an even narrower sense. It may be summed up as follows:

> 'You shall love the Lord your God with all your heart, and with all your soul, and with all your mind.' This is the greatest and first commandment. And a second is like it: 'You shall love your neighbour as yourself.'
>
> (Matthew 22:37b–39)

Or:

'In everything do to others as you would have them do to you.'

(Matthew 7:12a)

The ultimate Christian ethical teaching seems to centre on love:

Love is the fulfilling of the law.

(Romans 13:10b)

This New Testament ethical teaching is part of the relationship with God – what makes Christian ethics different is the 'faith' element; Christian ethics comes from a need to interpret, understand and respond to ethical issues from the point of their particular relationship with God.

Thought Point

Look up some of the following texts to see how Jesus' ethics is based on, yet seems to reinterpret, the Jewish law:

- Matthew 5–7
- Mark 2:23 to 3:6
- Mark 7:1–23

This idea of the special relationship with God is carried on in the idea of the *Kingdom of God*. What the Kingdom of God actually means has been debated endlessly, but it seems to be a state which has arrived, but not yet – a little like a visitor who has arrived at a friend's house and rung the doorbell, but the door has not yet been opened. The problem is how this paradox is to be maintained as far as ethics is concerned. Jesus' ethics can only be connected with the idea of the Kingdom of God by seeing entry into the Kingdom as a result of responding to the appeal to the desire to be children of God; a joyful acceptance of forgiveness and a desire to do God's will. This is no blind obedience, nor is it a morality of law, command, duty and obligation; nor is it motivated by the promise of reward in heaven or punishment in hell, but by a desire to follow God's will – the love commandment.

The ethics of Paul

The other source of biblical Christian ethics is found in the Epistles of Paul. He wrote at a time when the early Christians were attempting to interpret the teachings of Jesus and apply them to a variety of new situations. Paul stresses the importance of Christian freedom, but to be free from the law means to be united with Christ and with one another in love and service. It is *life lived in the Spirit*:

> Live by the Spirit, I say, and do not gratify the desires of the flesh. . . . But if you are led by the Spirit, you are not subject to the law. . . . If we live by the Spirit, let us also be guided by the Spirit.
> (Galatians 5:16, 18, 25)

For Paul, the whole law may be summed up in *love of neighbour* and this love is limitless, as is shown in the great hymn to love in the Letter to the Corinthians. Paul also calls the Christians to imitate the virtues of Jesus in their daily lives: meekness; gentleness; humility; generosity; mercy and self-giving love. However, the words and life of Jesus could not be made into a blueprint for Christian ethics in the early Church without becoming legalistic, and so it was recognised that following Christ depended on the gift and guidance of the Holy Spirit which was given to the *community* of believers. Paul's list of virtues is called 'the fruit of the Spirit' (Galatians 5:22–23) and love is the greatest sign of the presence and activity of the Holy Spirit (I Corinthians 13).

Christian ethics in this developing Church could be called a *community ethic*: the ethic of a community guided by the Holy Spirit, rather than by law or tradition.

> If then there is any encouragement in Christ, any consolation from love, any sharing in the Spirit, any compassion and sympathy, make my joy complete: be of the same mind, having the same love, being in full accord and of one mind. Do nothing from selfish ambition or conceit, but in humility regard others as better than yourselves. Let each of you look not to your own interests, but to the interests of others.
> (Philippians 2:1–4)

However, there is no explicit concern with changing society as a whole. The main attitude towards rulers was that of obedience, as their authority was given by God, but if the commands of the state and those of God conflict, then the Christian should obey God. According to Paul the barriers between slaves and free men and women have been broken, both marriage and celibacy are seen as gifts, and wealth is to be shared with those in need. However, there is no evidence of struggling for justice, as it was believed that

God would soon intervene in history and establish his kingdom, apart from which Christians were few in number with no political clout. The teaching of love for one's neighbour, however, did eventually lead Christians to exercise greater social responsibility.

Love

This distinctive moral teaching based on love continued to dominate the work of Christian thinkers:

> Love, and do what you will. If you keep silence, keep silence in love; if you speak, speak in love; if you correct, correct in love; if you forbear, forbear in love. Let love's root be within you, for from that root nothing but good can spring.
>
> (Augustine, *Epistola Joannis* 7.8)

Love, according to **Thomas Aquinas**, is the reason why we were made; it unites us with God, and to love is to share his life. Without love no virtue is possible, and love alone leads to happiness and fulfilment.

AUTHORITY AND TRADITION IN CHRISTIAN ETHICS

Although Aquinas followed the early Christian idea of morality as love and grace, not law, it is true that legalism has justifiably been associated with Christian ethics, both in theory and in practice. **Peter Singer** criticises this legalism and accuses Christianity of obscuring the true nature of morality: human fulfilment – happiness. He thinks that the end of the Christian influence on our moral standpoints will open up a 'better way of life for us' and the Judaeo-Christian ethic is 'an empty shell, founded on a set of beliefs that most people have laid aside'. Christian ethics have been seen as deontological and authoritarian, with an emphasis on certain acts as being either right or wrong.

The issue of authority and tradition is treated differently by the different Christian Churches. Some *Protestants* see the Bible as the sole authority in every matter and this is more important than the role given to tradition in Catholicism. *Catholics* would argue that scripture does not give guidance on many important matters and so tradition is important, as interpreted by the *Magisterium* (the Pope and the bishops). This teaching does not claim to be absolutely accurate or infallible, but is teaching on behalf of the community of the people of God. It can become authoritarian, especially when the issues are new or there is no consensus of views among the episcopacy or the Catholic community – for example, the teaching of *Humanae Vitae* (1968), which banned artificial contraception and has been totally ignored by many Catholics.

This idea of the 'agreement of the faithful' has been further developed by many free churches, which have built their forms of church government on congregational lines – this is going back to Paul's idea of attempting to discern the will of God by the Holy Spirit working in the Christian community. However, many Christian legalists would argue that Christians should keep rules because God has revealed them – is this why Christian ethics has become so irrelevant?

DIVINE COMMAND THEORY

If God's will is taken as arbitrary, then this does not give any satisfactory explanation for why anyone is morally bound to follow it. If God commands something for good reasons, then it is these reasons that are the source of moral obligations, regardless of God or any religious law.

Does religion give people a reason to be moral? Is there any meaning to life that would make it even possible to talk about morality? In Dostoyevsky's *The Brothers Karamazov*, Ivan says that 'without God everything is permitted' – so does God give a reason to be moral? In Albert Camus' *The Stranger*, the issue of meaning is a central theme – Mersault does not condemn any action as wrong and, when he ends up shooting a complete stranger, he is only sorry that he got caught – killing someone has no more meaning than any other action. However, we do make judgements about what is right and wrong, and many people do so without seeing any involvement from God.

The whole problem of doing something because God commands it was examined by **Plato** in what has become known as the **Euthyphro Dilemma**. Plato asks: 'Is X good because God wills it or does God will it because it is good?'

Euthyphro Dilemma

The dilemma first identified by Plato – is something good because God commands it or does God command it because it is good?

The first option says that certain actions are good because God commands them – it is the command of God that makes something good or bad. This means that if God commanded 'Make a fat profit', then it would be right – this makes God's commands arbitrary. **Leibniz** in his *Discourse on Metaphysics* sums this up:

> So in saying that things are not good by any rule of goodness, but sheerly by the will of God, it seems to me that one destroys, without realising it, all the love of God and all his glory. For why praise him for what he has done if he would be equally praiseworthy in doing the contrary?

The idea that moral rules are true because God commands them is called the **Divine Command theory**. In many ways the laws of the Old

Testament may be seen as a good example of this theory (e.g. 'Thou shalt not commit murder'). This view of Christian ethics goes completely against the morality of love and grace, but it was held by many Christian thinkers such as **Duns Scotus**, **William of Ockham** and **Descartes** as well as many conservative Protestants today. If we do good acts simply out of obedience to God, are we being good for the right reasons?

The second option says that God commands things because they are right or wrong in themselves. Murder is wrong in itself and that is why God forbids it. God can see that it destroys life and makes people unhappy, and so it is unlikely that he would ever command it. However, this option seems to be arguing that there is a standard of right and wrong which is independent of God and which influences his commands. **James Rachels** argued that it is unacceptable for religious belief to involve unqualified obedience to God's commands as it means abandoning personal autonomy – the rightness of an action must come from the fact that the action is right in itself.

> **Divine Command theory**
> Actions are right or wrong depending on whether they follow God's commands or not.

Thought Point

1   Do we need God to give meaning to life?
2   Do you agree that 'without God everything is permitted'?
3   Explain the difference between 'X is good because God wills it' and 'God wills X because it is good'.
4   Read the Euthyphro Dilemma and work out the key criticisms of the argument.
5   Can morality ever be founded on authority?
6   How do you decide what is good or bad? Justify your view.

SITUATION ETHICS

Situation Ethics presumes that it is not necessary to abandon moral autonomy, nor is it necessary to allow everything (antinomianism) or to be totally legalistic. In any situation people need to avoid subjectivism and individualism, and to use in each situation the moral rules of the community, but they should also be prepared to set these aside if love is better served by doing so. Reason, then, is to be used, but based on the Christian principle of *agape*. This centralisation of love is explained most clearly by **Joseph Fletcher** in his book *Situation Ethics* (1966) – nothing is intrinsically good except love. Rules can help us, but they cannot tell us what to do – they are subservient to love. Love wills the good of neighbour, whether we like him

Relativism
Nothing may be said to be
objectively right or wrong; it
depends on the situation,
culture and so on.

Teleological ethics
The morally right or wrong thing
to do is determined by the
consequences.

or not; love is to be the only motive for action, and consequences need to be taken into account and only the end justifies the means.

Situation Ethics has been criticised for being Utilitarian and simply substituting love for pleasure, and Fletcher is thought to be rather vague; values and situations are so variable that we cannot easily see all the ramifications, past, present and future. Can Situation Ethics be considered Christian? It certainly puts love at the centre, but there are many differences among Christians about what exactly love is and how it is shown. Fletcher's examples are all exceptional cases: Mrs Bergmeier; dropping the atomic bomb on Hiroshima; a man considering stopping his medication so that he would die and his family would receive his life insurance; and a woman who has to seduce and sleep with an enemy spy to end a war. Fletcher's idea of love is not exactly the same as that of Jesus, who individualised love; take, for example, the woman with the haemorrhage, or the healing of the centurion's servant – not a very popular act of love. Fletcher either reinterprets Jesus' actions or dismisses them, so it is hardly surprising that in later life religion played no part in his life and he ceased to describe himself as a Christian Situationist.

Thought Point

1   Do you think Fletcher's ethics are Christian?
2   Analyse Fletcher's view that 'the end of love justifies the means'.
3   Is Situation Ethics a useful guide for everyday ethical decisions?
4   Are moral rules totally useless in moral decision-making or can you see a role for them?
5   Is the choice for Christian ethics just between legalism and situationism?

NATURAL LAW

A full treatment of Natural Law may be found in Chapter 3.

Natural Law is often seen as centred on law, and so on obligation, and Aquinas himself speaks of the Natural Law. However, by this he meant that our nature is objectively knowable and our reason will help us to understand what is meant by it. Ethics is a matter of our common humanity, not a set of principles from which we make moral decisions, and its purpose is to enable us to become complete and whole humans, and to achieve our desires. Morality is rooted in the desire for happiness, but, for Aquinas, Natural Law is not enough if we are to attain final happiness – for this God's grace is needed.

Natural Law has come to be seen as **deontological** and authoritarian with its application of the primary precepts, but Aquinas said that the primary precepts were always true, as they point us in the right direction; however, different situations require secondary precepts and if our reasoning is faulty these may be wrong – we need to discern what is good and what will help us to become complete and whole human beings. Intention is important, but in Natural Law it is not possible to say that the end justifies the means, although there is certainly flexibility in the Natural Law approach. Aquinas wrote: 'The more you descend into the details the more it appears how the general rule admits of exceptions, so that you have to hedge it with cautions and qualifications.'

However, Aquinas is certain that there is an absolute Natural Law and this has led the Catholic Church, following Aquinas, to emphasise reason as a tool for showing that certain acts are intrinsically right or wrong, as they go against our true purpose; certain **absolutes**, such as the sanctity of life, cannot be changed by the circumstances.

CONSCIENCE

Catholics consider that **conscience** plays an important part in Christian ethical decision-making. Here conscience is not seen as some inner voice or oracle that will point us in the right direction – conscience is not about feelings but about reason and judgement. Aquinas saw conscience as reason making moral decisions. But conscience as the 'voice of God' can easily become what we mean by 'right' and 'wrong' – so men persecute 'heretics', slaughter enemies and become suicide bombers in the name of God.

However, conscience does not make the law; it recognises law and uses it to assess conduct. So, for Religious Ethics, conscience is not so much the voice of God as a response to God's voice. Conscience can be mistaken; doing a bad action when following the guidance of conscience does not make that action good. Conscience is just a way of using reason to come to a decision, but it needs to be informed, and in following conscience we need to be prepared to accept the costs, not just do what we want.

VIRTUE ETHICS

Virtue Ethics is also an important source for Christian ethics. Virtue Ethics refers to the character of being a good person. This again links back to love as being the highest of all virtues and also the rationale for all the virtues, which simply spell out the form love takes in different circumstances. The virtues, for Christian ethics, point to the goal for which we aim, even if we do not achieve

Deontological ethics
Ethical systems which consider that the moral act itself has moral value (e.g. telling the truth is always right, even when it may cause pain or harm).

Absolutism
An objective moral rule or value that is always true in all situations and for everyone without exception.

Conscience
Our sense of right and wrong.

it in this life. This approach to ethics cultivates the inner person and so leads to good actions. For a full treatment of Virtue Ethics see Chapter 12.

CHRISTIAN ETHICS AND UTILITARIANISM

Is there any link between the deontological commands of the Ten Commandments and the teleological approach of **Utilitarianism**? Natural Law is very different from Utilitarianism, as it maintains that by using our reason we can arrive at moral knowledge and does not believe that the ends justify the means.

Utilitarianism
Only pleasure and the absence of pain have utility or intrinsic value.

Jeremy Bentham reacted against the rule-based morality of his time, with certain actions being intrinsically right or wrong. He was therefore dismissive of any reference to the Bible, conscience or Natural Law as a means of knowing right and wrong. As an empiricist he believed that knowledge had to come from the senses and he tried to make a scientific basis for morality. People should measure the rightness or wrongness of any action in terms of how many units of pain or pleasure it produced – these could be measured quantitatively using the hedonic calculus.

John Stuart Mill calculated pleasures in a qualitative way, regarding intellectual pleasures as superior to merely physical ones. He also thought that most ordinary people should normally stick to some traditional rules, based on Utilitarian principles, rather than calculate what they should do in each situation. He likened the principle of utility to Jesus' Golden Rule:

'Love your neighbour as yourself.'
'Do unto others as you would have them do unto you.'

He saw Utilitarianism as universal benevolence, doing good to others and denying self-love. Bentham, in fact, thought that Christianity would support Utilitarianism, as God is supposed to be benevolent.

Situation Ethics is accused of being Utilitarian, and Fletcher recognised the similarity between the two theories. Both are relativist in approach and Fletcher saw love as 'justice distributed' – justice means working out the most loving thing to do for all – which simply replaces the 'good' of Utilitarianism with 'agape'.

Natural Law is very different from Utilitarianism, as it sees certain actions as intrinsically wrong, regardless of the consequences. Both Utilitarianism and Situation Ethics fail to see that love is not always about the collective good, but also about the individual. Love that cares about the individual will not sacrifice the few for the sake of the majority without any attention being given to their particular needs and welfare. Utilitarianism ignores the idea that some actions are intrinsically wrong (e.g. murder).

The empiricism of Utilitarianism results in a very particular under-standing of human nature as only motivated by pleasure/pain. The value of a person, and humanity as a whole, is measured only in terms of experiences with no room for the idea of a human made in the 'image of God' with intrinsic value and rights. The teachings and life of Jesus do not fit with Utilitarianism, except for the manner of his death: 'it is expedient for you that one man should die' (John 11:50a). According to the New Testament Christian ethics, others should always be placed first; we should turn the other cheek, forgive unto seventy times seven and real happiness comes in serving others – how can this be measured using the hedonic calculus?

In Utilitarian ethics motives and character are unimportant compared with the consequences. Unlike Virtue Ethics, the act is more important than the agent. In Christian ethics, moral decision-making is about habitual actions, not one-off acts – the virtuous person becomes virtuous by practice. In Galatians 5:22–23 the fruits of the Spirit are shown by the characteristics of Christian living: love, joy, peace, patience, kindness, goodness, faith-fulness, gentleness, self-control. Living a Christian ethical life involves modelling one's character on that of Christ.

CHRISTIAN ETHICS AND KANTIAN ETHICS

Kantian Ethics would seem, at first glance, to fit in nicely with Christian ethics, especially the second formulation of the categorical imperative which gives humans intrinsic value and says that they should not be treated as 'means to an end but as ends in themselves'. This intrinsic value is clearly seen in biblical ethics: 'So God created man in his own image' (Genesis 1:27a).

For Kant, as for Christian ethics, the end can never justify the means. Kant's idea of universalisability is if you can will your action to be uni-versalised, then it would be an action that would be considered good in all situations, including your own. Again this is the same as Jesus' Golden Rule.

However, Jesus teaches that rules are not paramount and that law is given to humans to help them live a good life. Jesus cured people on the Sabbath and, when questioned about this, replied that the Sabbath was made for man, not man for the Sabbath (i.e. man is not subordinate to the law), but Kant enforces rigid rules with no exceptions under his principle of universalisability.

Kant also argues that right moral action can be deduced using reason alone, leaving no room for authority, tradition or even biblical revelation. Kantian Ethics are a priori (morality is innate and knowable through reason), unlike Natural Law which is a posteriori and discovers what is right through experience.

APPLICATION OF CHRISTIAN ETHICS TO PRACTICAL ETHICS – THE ENVIRONMENT

The media are full of stories concerning environmental disasters of one kind or another, from global warming to endangered species to destruction of the rain forest. However, there is not a lot of emphasis on this among Christians: some see it as just a liberal or New Age issue; some see it as just plain unimportant, as God will soon destroy everything. However, others do look to Christian ethics to find an answer to the question of our responsibility to the Earth and the creatures on it.

Some people blame Judaeo-Christian teaching for the environmental crisis we now face – they point to Genesis (1:26–28) where humans are given dominion over the Earth. This, they say, has given humanity a licence to exploit the Earth.

Christian ethics, however, points to the creation story – God as creator and man as his steward. All of nature, including man, is equal in its origin, and nature has intrinsic value because God created it and he alone is the owner. In the second creation story God told Adam and Eve to cultivate the garden (Genesis 2:15), and we may certainly use nature for our benefit, but only as God intends. Having dominion means holding in trust.

However, all too often, people evaluate projects in a Utilitarian way, by looking at their impact upon humans. The Bible contains many examples of how we are to care for the land and animals (e.g. Leviticus 25:1–12; Deuteronomy 15:4; Isaiah 5:8–10).

Ultimately, Christian ethics is rooted in the relationship with God, and a Christian's relationship with God depends on how he uses creation and contributes to bringing about the Kingdom of God (I Corinthians 15:21–22; Romans 5:12–21). Christians must also observe environmental justice, which means considering how their lifestyles impact on the world. Love of God and love of one's neighbour are fundamental in Christian ethics and apply to the environment also.

REVIEW QUESTIONS

Look back over the chapter and check that you can answer the following questions (Q.5 is more suitable for A2 candidates):

1   Explain the Euthyphro dilemma and how it can be used to criticise Divine Command theory.

2   Is Christian ethics absolute, relative or both? Give your reasons.

3   Is Christian ethics communitarian or individualistic? Give clear explanations.

4   Explain the different approaches of Natural Law and Situation Ethics.

5   Can Christian ethics be considered Utilitarian?

Examination Questions Practice

As you can see from this chapter, the subject of religious (Christian) ethics is vast and varied. Make sure you know the biblical background and the different approaches.

Remember: (a) assesses AO1 and (b) AO2. To help you improve your answers look at the AS Levels of Response. See: http://www.ocr.org.uk/qualifications/as-a-level-gce-religious-studies-h172-h572/.

SAMPLE EXAM STYLE QUESTIONS

(a) Explain the ethical teachings of the religion you have studied. (25 marks)

- You may start with biblical ethics and explain ethics as a result of religious belief, and describe the rules, duties and commands from revelation.
- You could also explain that religious ethical behaviour comes from a sense of obedience to God and a desire to live life in the way God wishes it to be lived.
- When explaining Christian ethics you can refer to and explain Natural Law, Situation Ethics and Virtue Ethics.
- If you have studied a different world religion for your AS examination, such as Islam, Judaism, Buddhism or Hinduism, you can explain the main principles of that religion.

(b) 'Religious Ethics are too rigid for moral decision-making.' Discuss. (10 marks)

Here you need to evaluate the deontological and teleological approaches to ethics in the context of Religious Ethics.

- Some may argue that an absolute approach is right and others may reject this.
- If you are answering from the viewpoint of Christian ethics, you may consider that Christian ethics is mainly deontological and contrast this with a situationist approach or that of Virtue Ethics.

SAMPLE AS EXAM STYLE QUESTIONS

(a) Explain any one religious method of ethical decision-making.

(b) How far can a religious theory of ethics be justified?

(a) Explain the main ethical principles of the religion you have studied.

(b) '"Treat others the way you would like to be treated yourself" is the most important ethical principle.' How fair is this claim in relation to the religion you have studied?

(a) Explain the main ethical principles of the religion you have studied.

(b) 'A right ethical act is one approved by God.' Discuss.

(a) Explain one ethical theory that has its basis in religion.

(b) 'It is indefensible to base ethics on religion.' Discuss.

SAMPLE A2 EXAM STYLE QUESTIONS

• Discuss the view that only a religious ethic can provide an acceptable basis for environmental ethics.

• 'Only Religious Ethics can provide answers to the issues surrounding sexual ethics.' Discuss.

FURTHER READING

Cook, D. *The Moral Maze*, London, SPCK, 1983.

Hoose, B. (ed.) *Christian Ethics: An Introduction*, London, Cassell, 1998 – contains an excellent chapter on the Bible and Christian ethics by Tom Deidum.

Macquarrie, J. and Childress, J. *A New Dictionary of Christian Ethics*, London, SCM, 1986.

Plato, 'Euthyphro', in *The Last Days of Socrates*, Tredennick, H. (trans.), London, Penguin, 1969.

Rachels, J. and Rachels, S. *The Elements of Moral Philosophy*, New York, McGraw-Hill, 2007.

7 Medical Ethics 1
Abortion and the Right to a Child

WHAT YOU WILL LEARN ABOUT IN THIS CHAPTER

- The idea of the sanctity of life and how it applies to abortion.
- Ideas of personhood and the status of the foetus.
- The rights of all those involved.
- The approaches of different ethical theories to abortion.
- The question of infertility and the right to a child.
- What IVF involves.
- The approaches of different ethical theories to the question of the right to a child.

KEY SCHOLARS

- Thomas Aquinas (1225–1274)
- Immanuel Kant (1724–1804)
- Jeremy Bentham (1748–1832)
- John Stuart Mill (1806–1873)
- Pope Pius XI (1857–1939)
- Pope Paul VI (1897–1978)
- Judith Jarvis Thomson (1929–)
- Jonathan Glover (1941–)
- Rosalind Hursthouse (1943–)
- Peter Singer (1946–)
- Helga Kuhse (1940–)
- Mary Anne Warren (1946–2010)

THE OCR CHECKLIST

Candidates should be able to demonstrate knowledge and understanding of:

- the concept of the 'Sanctity of Life' and how it applies to abortion;
- the concept of personhood as applied to abortion;
- the right to life as applied to abortion and the rights of all those involved;
- the issues of infertility and the right to a child;
- the status of the embryo;
- whether a child is a gift or a right;
- the application and the different approaches of the ethical theories listed below to abortion and the right to a child.

The ethical theories:

- Natural Law;
- Kantian Ethics;
- Utilitarianism;
- Religious Ethics.

Candidates should be able to discuss critically these issues and their strengths and weaknesses.

From OCR A Level Religious Studies Specification H172.

Abortion

The termination of a pregnancy by artificial means.

Foetus

An organism in the womb from nine weeks until birth.

Hippocratic Oath

Written in the fifth century BCE, it became the basis for doctors' ethics. Other promises now replace it, but it is specifically against abortion.

WHAT IS ABORTION?

Abortion is the induced termination of a pregnancy to destroy the foetus. In the UK, abortion is legal up to the 24th week of the pregnancy. After that time an abortion can be carried out if there is a serious threat to the life of the mother or the **foetus** is severely disabled. According to the law, at present a woman must have the agreement of two doctors for the termination. The 24-week rule was introduced in 1991, as it was established then that babies born at 24 weeks are viable and with intensive care can survive. The principle behind this ruling is that, whatever the reasons for an abortion, a foetus should be given legal protection if it is possible for it to survive outside the womb. Medical science has now moved on, and there is some pressure to lower the time to 20 weeks, but as yet this has not happened.

Abortion raises some important moral questions:

- What is a person?
- Is all human life intrinsically valuable/sacred?
- Is all intentional killing of people always wrong?
- Is it always a duty to preserve innocent life?
- When does life begin?

When does life begin?

This question is central to the abortion debate and throws up a number of different answers: at conception; some time after conception; at birth. The answer is vital, as once you have decided this is a human being, you need to give that individual rights and protection under the law.

At conception

According to the teaching of the Catholic Church, life begins at conception and at this moment the genetic material of both parents mix and form a biologically distinct entity. This is an attractive view as it is so clear-cut, and marks a definite moment when the foetus becomes a human being.

In 1869 **Pope Pius XI** in his encyclical *Casti Connubi* stated that the foetus is a human person from the moment of conception and the life of an unborn child is as sacred as that of its mother; this was reinforced by **Pope Paul VI** in his encyclical *Humanae Vitae* in 1968 and again stated in the *Catechism of the Catholic Church* (1994):

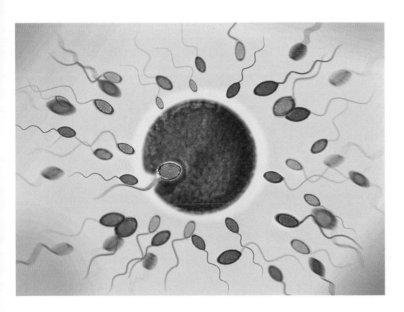

Sperm fertilising egg

Human life must be respected and protected absolutely from the moment of conception. From the first moment of his existence a human being must be recognised as having the rights of a person – among which is the inviolable right of every innocent being to life.

There are several biblical quotations which suggest that life begins before birth:

'Before I formed you in the womb I knew you.'

(Jeremiah 1:5b)

For it was you who formed my inward parts; you knit me together in my mother's womb.

(Psalm 139:13)

'For as soon as I heard the sound of your greeting, the child in my womb leaped for joy.'

(Luke 1:44)

After conception

As we have seen, according to the Human Fertilisation and Embryology Act of 1990, the foetus is given legal protection from 24 weeks if it is possible for it to survive outside the womb. Supporters of the argument that life begins at some point after conception say there is a difference between *potential* and *actual* life. Some would also add that life begins at the moment of implantation in the womb (about six or seven days after conception), others when the heart starts beating or there are signs of brain activity.

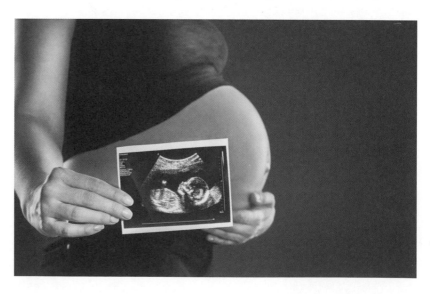

*Pregnant woman holding
ultrasound image of a
foetus*

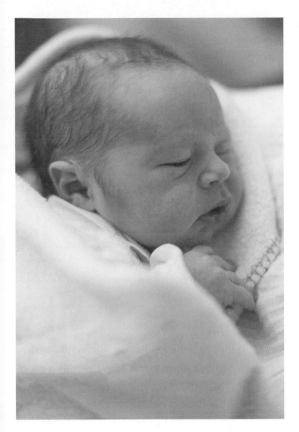

Newborn baby

At birth

Thus far there are two clearly defined views of when human life begins – at conception or some time after conception. However, for centuries it was established that birth was the point at which life began and the deliberate killing of a baby after birth was regarded as murder. Some still follow this line; for example, **Mary Anne Warren** argues that birth is the time when the baby no longer relies totally on the mother for his survival. **Jonathan Glover** rejects this, as there are no major differences between a late foetus and a newborn or premature baby. He therefore argues for a more flexible time as the beginning of life.

THE SANCTITY OF LIFE

The teaching on the **sanctity of life** holds that all life is sacred, worthy of respect and reverence, and intrinsically worthwhile. People therefore have a duty to preserve life and yet we have very mixed reactions to this idea.

Jonathan Glover (1941–)

Jonathan Glover teaches ethics at King's College, London. He argued that to call a foetus a human person was to stretch the term beyond its natural boundaries. He is quoted as saying: 'Our entanglements with people close to us erode simple self-interest. Husbands, wives, lovers, parents, children and friends all blur the boundaries of selfish concern. Francis Bacon rightly said that people with children have given hostages to fortune. Inescapably, other forms of friendship and love hold us hostage too . . . Narrow self-interest is destabilized.'

Sanctity of life
The belief that human life is valuable in itself.

Ensoulment

The moment when the soul enters the body – in traditional Christian thought this was at 40 days for boys and 90 days for girls. The Church now believes that life begins at conception.

Do we actually see some lives as being more valuable than others? Within the Christian tradition the views may be roughly divided into strong sanctity of life arguments and weak sanctity of life arguments.

Thought Point

1   What would your reaction be to the following:
    - A suicide bomber who kills many people in a crowded marketplace.
    - A man who shoots an intruder in his house.
    - A soldier who kills in war.
    - A compulsive serial killer.
2   Do we think some lives are more valuable than others? (E.g. how do we justify spending money on fertilisation treatment for a couple when the money could be used to improve the quality of life of the sick and elderly? Or allowing thousands to die of starvation in Africa? Or think it more tragic if a young person dies than if an old person dies?)

Those who hold a strong sanctity of life stance are often called *pro-life* and appeal to the biblical basis of their ideas: God is the giver and creator of life and people have no right to destroy what he has given. People are seen as created in the 'image of God – *imago dei* – so humans are set apart from other animals and have a 'spark' of divinity within them – the breath of life was breathed by God into Adam. The incarnation, according to Christian teaching, reaffirms the sanctity of human life as God himself became human:

So God created humankind in his image.

(Genesis 1:27a)

God blessed them, and God said to them, 'Be fruitful and multiply, and fill the earth and subdue it; and have dominion over the fish of the sea and over the birds of the air and over every living thing that moves upon the earth.'

(Genesis 1:28)

And the Word became flesh and lived among us, and we have seen his glory, the glory as of a father's only son, full of grace and truth.

(John 1:14)

And if God is the creator of life it is down to him to say when it should start and end. A person does not have the freedom to decide to end his own or anyone else's life.

He said, 'Naked I came from my mother's womb, and naked shall I return there; the Lord gave, and the Lord has taken away; blessed be the name of the Lord.'

(Job 1:21)

Throughout the Bible there is also the command not to take life, and the biblical writers saw this as part of the covenant with God and his people: 'You shall not murder' (Exodus 20:13).

This idea of the sanctity of life is also part of the teaching of *Natural Law* which underlies the ethical teaching of the Catholic Church. Taking life is seen as intrinsically evil and unborn life must be protected. Natural Law states that preserving the innocent is a primary precept and there are no exceptions which make it right.

However, abortion may be justified using the **doctrine of double effect**; for example, in the event of an ectopic pregnancy (where the **embryo** has not implanted in the womb but is developing in the fallopian tubes) it is considered all right to remove the embryo, as the intention is to save the life of the mother rather than to kill the foetus.

This principle is also held by those who hold a weak sanctity of life stance. They realise that the advances of medical science have meant that the boundaries between life and death are far more flexible than previously thought and so would allow exceptions to the general sanctity of life position. They would appeal to **extraordinary means** as a justification for killing, and would apply the Christian principle of love and compassion. However, a major criticism of this view is that, like the doctrine of double effect, it is difficult to assess or know true intentions.

Weak sanctity of life is also the basis for other Christian responses to abortion; for example, the Church of England's report of 1965, *Abortion: An Ethical Discussion,* expresses overriding compassion for the needs of the mother, especially where there is a threat to her mental or physical health. This view was reinforced in a more recent document, *Abortion and the Church,* in 1993:

We do not believe that the right to life, as a right pertaining to persons, admits of no exceptions whatever; but the right of the innocent to life admits surely of few exceptions indeed. Circumstances exist where the character or location of the pregnancy renders the foetus a serious threat to the life and health of the mother, in such circumstances the foetus could be regarded as an 'aggressor' on the mother. The mother would be entitled to seek protection against the threat to her life and health which the foetal life represented.

Doctrine of double effect
An action where the main intention is to do good, but which may have a bad side-effect. The good intention makes the action right.

Embryo
The developing bundle of cells in the womb up to eight weeks' gestation.

Ordinary and extraordinary means
According to Natural Law moral duties apply in ordinary situations. A patient may refuse certain treatments on the grounds that they are 'extraordinary' (i.e. over and above the essential).

Strengths of the sanctity of life

- It values *all* human life equally, regardless of status or gender.
- It states clearly that killing is always wrong and respects the individual's future.
- It gives everyone equal dignity.
- It avoids too much group pressure and power (e.g. to abort a disabled foetus).

Weaknesses of the sanctity of life

- **Charles Darwin** challenged the biblical view of *imago dei* with his theory of natural selection.
- **Kant** saw no reason to link vital signs to valuing life – but he did link the possession of reason to valuing life.
- **Peter Singer** stated that to treat human life as having a special priority over animal life is 'speciesism'.
- So we ought to value all life and not just human foetuses.
- The sanctity of life cannot cope with conflicts of duty – which life is more sacred: that of the mother or that of the foetus?

THE QUALITY OF LIFE

Quality of life

The belief that human life is not valuable in itself; it depends on what kind of life it is.

Some scholars think that those who hold a sanctity of life position as regards abortion only make it work by including **quality of life** arguments. The quality of life view allows the value of life to vary with its quality and may factor in the imminence of death, constancy of pain, an ability to think, an ability to enjoy life and make rational choices. However, when considering the foetus there is always the question of who benefits and whose quality of life is being judged: that of the foetus, the parents or society as a whole? There is a danger here of 'playing God' and the quality of life approach may be seen as paternalistic, as it allows others to make decisions. Above all there is the fear that it fails to treat the foetus with dignity and will inevitably lead down a 'slippery slope' to the Holocaust.

However, **Peter Singer** and **Helga Kuhse** both say that there is confusion, and that it would be better to drop the sanctity of life teaching and work out a quality of life ethic instead. This idea is based on what it means to be a person.

The sanctity of life

God is the creator of life

People are made in *imago dei*

Taking life is intrinsically evil

Unborn life is to be protected

The quality of life

Is the foetus a person? Does the foetus have a right to life?

Consciousness
Awareness of self as an independent being, the ability to feel pain and pleasure.

Personhood
Definition of a human being as a person – having consciousness, self-awareness, ability to reason and self-sufficiency.

Thought Point

What do you think makes a human life a person?

This question is vital as the answer depends on whether or not it is right to end the life of the foetus and the answer is crucial for evaluating the following argument:

- The foetus is an innocent person.
- It is wrong to end the life of an innocent person.
- Therefore, it is wrong to end the life of a foetus.

So is a foetus a person, at which stage does it become a person and what are the necessary criteria for personhood?

It has been argued that a person has to possess a concept of self – a person is self-aware; however, young babies are not self-aware and most people would agree that killing babies is killing human beings.

Viability
Where a foetus is considered capable of sustaining its own life, given the necessary care.

Other possible criteria also need to be considered:

- A person has to be conceived by humans.
- A person has to have a human genetic structure.
- A person has to look like a human.
- A person has a soul.
- A person is viable – they can survive birth.
- A person has a future like ours.

Mary Anne Warren suggests the following criteria:

- **Sentience –** the ability to have conscious experiences.
- **Emotionality –** the ability to feel happy, sad, loving.
- **Reason –** the ability to solve new and complex problems.
- **The capacity to communicate.**
- **Self-awareness –** awareness of oneself as an individual and as a member of a social group.
- **Moral agency –** the ability to regulate one's actions through moral principles.

She goes on to say that it is not necessary to have all these attributes – many people do not meet all the criteria for personhood and are still considered persons. A foetus, however, does not have any of these attributes and is not a person, though some do develop in later foetuses (e.g. the ability to feel pain). One solution she considers is to regard the foetus as a *potential person*; she rejects this as a basis for giving the foetus a right to life.

Others think this is a significant idea, as if you kill a person the most important thing you take away from them is their future, and the same could be said for a foetus – they and others will never be able to enjoy and benefit from their potential talents. Looking at the foetus as a potential person also removes the difficult speculations about when the foetus has a soul or develops consciousness. But at what point does a foetus become a potential person? In addition, is it right to judge a foetus by what it might be?

It is also possible to argue that even though the foetus is a person, abortion may be morally justified. This is the view of **Judith Jarvis Thomson**, who disputes the idea that 'It is wrong to end the life of an innocent person.' She says that even if a foetus has the same right to life as any other human being, women are not morally obliged to complete every unwanted pregnancy. She bases her argument on the following analogy:

> But now let me ask you to imagine this. You wake up in the morning and find yourself in bed with an unconscious violinist. He has been found to have a fatal kidney ailment, and the Society of Music Lovers has canvassed

all available medical records and found that you alone have the right blood type to help. They have therefore kidnapped you, and last night the violinist's circulatory system was plugged into yours, so that your kidneys can be used to extract poisons from his blood as well as your own. The director of the hospital now tells you 'Look we're sorry, the Society of Music Lovers did this to you – we would never have permitted it if we had known. But still, they did it, and the violinist now is plugged into you. To unplug him would be to kill him. But never mind, it's only for nine months. By then he will have recovered from his ailment, and can safely be unplugged from you.' Is it morally incumbent on you to accede to the situation?

(*A Defence of Abortion*)

This story raises a number of moral issues about rights and duties, but Judith Jarvis Thomson concludes that unwilling persons should not be required to be extremely Good Samaritans, whether towards violinists or towards foetuses, and suggests that there is a great gap between the claim that a human being has a right to life and the claim that other human beings are morally obliged to do whatever is necessary to keep him or her alive.

Thought Point

1   Do we become an individual with rights only at birth?
2   Is the foetus a separate individual like the violinist or is it part of the woman's body?
3   Would unplugging the violinist be the same as actively killing him?
4   The violinist was forced on the woman against her will; does this mean that this argument only supports abortion in cases of rape?
5   Is there a point at which a foetus is not a human being?
6   Does a person's right to life outweigh your right to decide what happens in and to your body?

As we have seen, a potential life cannot have rights and obligations – sperm has the potential to become a human being, yet nobody would claim that a sperm is a human being and should be treated as such. However, when a couple voluntarily cause an egg to be fertilised by a sperm with the intent of creating another life, there is a right to be born. What if the fertilisation was involuntary (rape) or accidental? This is what Judith Jarvis Thomson is examining – even if it is agreed that the embryo has the right to be kept alive, the mother cannot be obliged to carry this unwanted embryo. In addition, does the embryo have the right to use the mother's body and resources in order to sustain its own life?

A further problem about when a foetus becomes a person is the question of twins and the stage at which an embryo might divide into two or more individuals. Conception is not a single act but a process, and until about the 14th day it is not possible to say whether there will be a single or a multiple birth. Is it, then, possible to say that the single genetic identity established at conception is the basis for personhood? The Warnock Committee, whose recommendations were the basis for the 1990 Human Fertilisation and Embryology Act, chose the 14th day to distinguish the individual human embryo from a collection of cells and allowed them to be used for experimentation up to this stage. **Jonathan Glover** also argues that to call a foetus a person from conception stretches the term beyond normal boundaries.

APPLYING ETHICAL THEORIES TO ABORTION

Utilitarianism

Basic principle – the greatest good for the greatest number.

Utilitarianism does not accept the principle that human life has absolute value and that this should be upheld whatever the consequences, but attempts to assess each individual situation on its own merits to promote the greatest happiness for those concerned.

However, Utilitarianism only works if it is actually possible to assess the results of an abortion and decide whether they favour all concerned. In practice this is difficult as we cannot predict all consequences – the mother may react badly to the operation, which may go wrong, leaving her unable to have further children and so on.

Preference Utilitarianism might be a better approach to abortion, as it considers the preferences of the mother, the harm to other family members and so on.

Utilitarianism does not have one blanket answer to the question of abortion, but looks at the merits of each individual situation – it is easy here to make a judgement that depends primarily on an emotional response to a difficult situation.

Natural Law

Basic principle – everything is created for a purpose and when this is examined by human reason, a person should be able to judge how to act in order to find ultimate happiness.

Natural Law does not look at the people involved in a decision about abortion, or the consequences of the action; instead, Natural Law considers the act of abortion itself. Reproduction is a primary precept and abortion goes against this, as it stops the purpose and outcome of procreation. In addition, if you consider the foetus to be a human person from conception, then abortion also goes against the primary principle to preserve innocent life.

Kantian Ethics

Basic principle – the categorical imperative: universal maxims; treating others as ends in themselves and living in a Kingdom of Ends.

Immanuel Kant argued that reason enabled people to impose such laws upon themselves and when the categorical imperative is applied to abortion there are immediate difficulties. Abortion would be hard to universalise, as there are so many different situations and motivations for obtaining an abortion – all consideration of emotions is to be disregarded and yet abortion is an emotional decision, especially in situations where the mother has been raped, is very young or is carrying a severely disabled foetus. Kant would also take no account of the stage of pregnancy at which the abortion is to take place.

There is also the emphasis on treating people as ends in themselves and not as a means to an end – abortion would go against this if the foetus is considered to be a person.

Kant's stress on acting out of duty alone, with no account taken of compassion or love, means that all consequences are ignored whatever they may be. However, one could say that Kant does consider the human rights of the foetus.

THE RIGHT TO A CHILD

The first ever 'test-tube baby', Louise Brown, was born in the UK in 1978, and since then this issue has become more important in ethics as reproductive techniques have developed. This chapter needs to be read alongside Chapter 9, which considers the issue of embryo research.

What are rights? Generally rights are legal, social or ethical principles of freedom and are seen as stressing the dignity of all humans. They are usually referred to as human rights – rights that entitle people to life, freedom of speech, freedom from enslavement, etc. It is, however, unclear as to what exactly is meant by the term 'rights' as it is used by different groups for different purposes – rights are claimed for a variety of different things such

AI (artificial insemination)
The injection of sperm into a woman.

IVF (in-vitro fertilisation)
The procedure by which sperm and eggs from a couple are fertilised in a laboratory dish (in vitro = in glass; test-tube babies).

as the right to life, to vote, to work, to strike, to asylum, to equal treatment for both sexes. Rights even vary from country to country, such as the right to carry a gun. It is also difficult to say who has these rights: animals? workers? children?

It is not possible to talk about the right to a child in the same way as the right to work or to vote – the right to a child is of a different order.

Most of the debate about the right to a child is concerned with fertility treatments and who is eligible for them, with many of those arguing for the right to a child suggesting that fertility treatment should be available to all who require it; so a right seems to become confused with allocation of resources within the health system. When considering the right to a child it is better to consider the ethical issues involved.

Discussions about the right to a child cover issues such as whether a child is a gift or a right, whether it is right to obtain sperm samples by masturbation, whether it is right to pay someone to carry a baby and what the moral status of the foetus is on its journey from zygote to newborn baby. The process of **IVF** itself also raises ethical questions, as many more embryos are made than are needed.

There is also the problem of the fact that some of these techniques involve a third party in the sexual relationship – possibly posing physical risks to the resulting baby and replacing normal sexual activity as a method of reproduction.

IVF has the intention of overcoming the common problem of infertility, and may be seen as a practical solution to a medical problem. However,

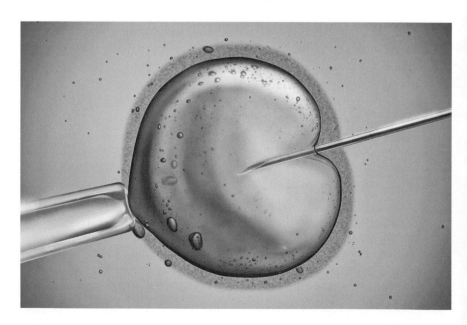

Human fertility: IVF

does this mean that the rights of the infertile to reproduce are of prime importance? This is clearly different from the right to have children, as the latter may simply lead the infertile to demand more liberal adoption laws, which this does not seem to be the case. One of the questions to consider in this chapter is whether there is a *right* to reproduce.

What is IVF?

There are different forms of reproductive technologies – called IVF for the purpose of this chapter.

*   AIH = artificial insemination by the husband, where the husband's sperm is injected into the wife's reproductive tract.
*   AID = where donor sperm is used.
*   IVF = in-vitro fertilisation – outside the human body using the sperm of a husband or donor, and the egg of the wife or a donor egg.

Ethical questions raised by IVF

*   When does human life begin and what is the status of the embryo? This involves considering whether human life only starts at implantation in the uterus, and if, as is most likely in the future, artificial wombs are developed, will the resulting human beings be human?
*   IVF is supposed to be for treating infertility, but what about the spare embryos that may be kept for up to fourteen days for experimentation?
*   The screening of embryos before implantation means that any imperfections can be weeded out. Will this lead parents to choose to remove undesirable traits and who is to decide what is undesirable?
*   Custom-made or 'designer' babies. In India, already, all IVF clinics allow sex selection and nearly all discarded embryos are female. In the future even the genetic make-up of a child could be chosen.
*   Older women, past child-bearing age, will be able to have children. This is already the case and in 2006 a 66-year-old Spanish woman had twins in this way. Women who want to follow a career will possibly be able to store eggs when young and fertile and use them later, achieving pregnancy through IVF.
*   IVF means that a quick, if not easy, fix has been found to the problem of infertility and miscarriages, so there is less research into the causes of infertility with a view to prevention.
*   Embryos are treated as properties.
*   IVF is not very successful. It is expensive and the hormone drugs used to increase fertility are potentially dangerous.

Does an individual have a right to a child?

In 1948 the UN Declaration of Human Rights stated that there is 'a right to marry and found a family free from constraint', but this does not clearly state that there is a right to reproduce. The right to reproduce seems to have followed the technological advances in assisted reproduction. It could, however, be argued that reproduction is fundamental to our freedom to act – but society already places restrictions on this; for example, incestuous reproduction. It could be argued that the right to reproduce is simply a basic need or desire – or do we just have a basic sexual drive rather than a need to continue the human race with our own genes? Reproduction may be seen as contributing to an individual's quality of life and may give her life meaning. Reproduction is seen as a fundamental choice that individuals must be allowed to make, and the lengthy, often unsuccessful and costly treatments reinforce the view that women are 'desperate' to reproduce and so have the right to do so.

Another factor that requires ethical consideration is the increase in foetal screening. This is aimed not only at genetically selecting embryos to aid sick siblings but also at making sure that technology is used to produce only 'perfect' children and to screen out any disabilities.

Who has the right to a child?

Married couples and possibly unmarried couples would head the list. However, what if the couple divorced or separated or, as in the case of Diane Blood, one partner died? Does the right then no longer exist?

The question is made even more complex when surrogate motherhood is considered. This was shown in the case of baby M in the USA – in the court case that followed, the ruling was that the Stern couple had a right to reproduce by whatever means. Mary Beth Whitehead was referred to as the surrogate mother as if Elizabeth Stern was the 'real' mother, despite the fact that the child was not carried by her and nor was it in any way genetically related to her. The court was actually defending the right of William Stern to reproduce – by whatever means. IVF would not have helped William Stern, so do men have as much right to reproduce as women?

IVF uses considerable medical resources that could otherwise be used to treat those with more serious illnesses, and so one solution might be to limit the use of IVF to those whose reproductive ability has been damaged by medical treatments or by exposure to dangerous working conditions.

Thought Point

1   Should IVF be available to all?
2   How should it be paid for? Is IVF a waste of money?
3   What restrictions would you place on it?
4   Who should be allowed to have IVF – married couples? unmarried couples? homosexual couples? single people?
5   Should surrogate mothers be allowed?
6   Why should a child created by sperm or egg donation be allowed to trace their biological parent?
7   What should be done with spare embryos?
8   Is IVF demeaning to women?
9   Is IVF 'playing God' or 'co-operating with God'?

APPROACHES TO IVF AND THE RIGHT TO A CHILD

Religious Ethics

Nine years after the birth of the first 'test-tube' baby, Louise Brown, the Catholic Church published the document *Donum Vitae* (1987). The Church welcomed Louise Brown as a gift and as a unique person, but expressed doubts about the process of IVF and the resulting science of human embryology. The creation of a surplus of human embryos in a laboratory made it possible to experiment on them – many embryos would never be transferred to a womb as Louise was.

The Catholic Church sees human life as sacred, with the parents as co-creators of new life – the baby is the result of the love the couple have for each other. IVF takes the new baby away from that expression of love and becomes simply part of a process:

> IVF and ET [embryo transfer] is brought about outside the bodies of the couple through actions of third parties whose competence and technical activity determine the success of the procedure.
>
> *(Donum Vitae)*

The Church sees the life of the embryo as entrusted to doctors, and technology as dominant in creating new life. The Catholic Church also sees every human life from the first moment of conception and at every stage of development, however early, as worthy of protection.

The Catholic Church does not approve of IVF, nor of the destruction of human embryos, nor of the freezing of embryos, nor of surrogacy; however, the Church does not disapprove of experiments on human embryos that are therapeutic and will assist the embryo to overcome the effects of disease.

Protestant ethics see the question of IVF differently. Paul Ramsay has a Christocentric approach and opposes AID, as it 'means a refusal of the image of God's creation in our own'. Reproduction should only be within marriage, as that is the only way to remain faithful to God, since the love between husband and wife should reflect the love of Christ for the Church.

Joseph Fletcher, on the other hand, was not negative towards IVF or even AID. His Situation Ethics was person-centred and saw that there were higher values in a couple's relationship than their biological relationship to their children. Fletcher did not see a third person as personally involved in the sexual relationship – what mattered was the outcome: pregnancy. Using IVF means that humans are using their technologies and creative skills for compassionate reasons.

Natural Moral Law

Natural Law would have many problems with IVF. First of all, there would be the problem of masturbation in order to obtain the necessary sperm – this would be a misuse of the genitalia and would not be following the natural function. IVF also results in the destruction of embryos and the first primary precept demands the protection of innocent life.

Natural Law is an absolute theory and does not take into account any consideration of the outcomes of an action, whether these be the creation of new life or the health benefits from research on spare embryos.

Utilitarianism

The Utilitarian approach to this issue would consider the pleasure/pain principle and measure the pain of the unused embryos against the pleasure of the parents and the baby that was created. A Utilitarian would also consider the low success-rate and the effect this may have on the happiness of the couple, their family and friends. Utilitarianism does not protect the rights of the embryo, nor does it see it as sacred in any way.

Finally, there is the problem of the cost to the health service and whether the money could be better spent saving more lives and so increasing the happiness of the majority. In addition, in considering the population problems the world is facing and the resulting poverty, a Utilitarian would ask whether it is ethical to spend money on assisting reproduction for a few and so adding to the population of the world and the pain of the many.

Kantian Ethics

Kantian Ethics, following the categorical imperative, would require that people are treated as ends in themselves. If the embryo is considered a person, a follower of Kantian Ethics would need to ask whether the destruction of so many embryos in order to create one life is justified. There is also a danger of treating the creation of human life as just another consumer good. Selecting an embryo as a genetic match to cure another sibling could also be seen as using the embryo as a means to an end, as would using a surrogate mother. It would also consider the question of universalisation and whether IVF is to be offered to every infertile couple.

REVIEW QUESTIONS

Look back over the chapter and check that you can answer the following questions:

1 Explain the importance of the question 'When does life begin?'.
2 What is meant by the idea of the sanctity of life and what Bible teachings would you use to explain the sanctity of life?
3 Is the sanctity of life a convincing argument against abortion or the right to a child? Explain your reasons.
4 Make a chart applying ethical theories to abortion.
5 Explain whether you think a child is a right or a gift. Give reasons.
6 List the main ethical problems raised by IVF.
7 Make a chart applying ethical theories to the right to a child.

Terminology

Do you know your terminology?

Try to explain the following ideas without looking at your books and notes:

1 Consciousness
2 The doctrine of double effect
3 Ensoulment
4 Personhood

Examination Questions Practice

Be careful not to be side-tracked by the question and just write everything you know about abortion.

Remember: (a) assesses AO1 and (b) AO2. To help you improve your answers look at the AS Levels of Response. See: http://www.ocr.org.uk/qualifications/as-a-level-gce-religious-studies-h172-h572/.

SAMPLE EXAM STYLE QUESTIONS

(a) Explain how a follower of Natural Law might approach the issue of abortion. (25 marks)

You would need to explain the theory of Natural Law as associated with Aquinas, influenced by Aristotle. Key points to include would be:

- Natural Law is absolutist and deontological, depending on the idea that God created things to fulfil a purpose.
- Human reason should be used to work out how to act morally.
- This should then be applied to the question of abortion by explaining how in Natural Law the preservation of the innocent is a primary precept and that the foetus deserves the same status as a born human.
- The concept of primary and secondary principles.
- The doctrine of double effect could also be applied to abortion, explaining how Natural Law would allow this.

(b) 'A woman has the right to choose an abortion.' Discuss. (10 marks)

- You could consider the rights of the foetus as against those of the mother, any other children and the rights of the father.
- Potential life may be considered as against that of the mother.
- On the other hand, you might include sanctity of life arguments and the question of personhood and the concept of soul.
- This could be contrasted with the woman's rights over her body, her choice to have sexual intercourse and whether her life is threatened.

SAMPLE AS EXAM STYLE QUESTIONS

(a) Explain how the principles of Natural Law might be applied to decisions about fertility treatment.

(b) 'Every adult has the right to become a parent.' Discuss.

(a) Explain the argument that all women have the right to a child.

(b) 'The right to a child should not be an absolute right.' Discuss.

(a) Explain the arguments against moral absolutism.

(b) How useful is absolute morality in dealing with the issues surrounding the right to a child?

(a) Explain the main strengths of a Utilitarian ethical system.

(b) To what extent is Utilitarianism a useful method for making decisions about abortion?

(a) Explain the main features of moral absolutism.

(b) Discuss the claim that an absolutist morality is the best way of preserving the sanctity of life.

(a) What is Virtue Ethics?

(b) Discuss the view that it is never virtuous to obtain an abortion.

(a) Explain how a follower of Natural Law might respond to issues raised by abortion.

(b) 'A Natural Law approach is the best approach to abortion.' Discuss.

FURTHER READING

Glover, J. *Causing Death and Saving Lives*, London, Penguin, 1990.

Hinman, L. 'Ethics Updates', available at http://ethics.sandiego.edu/.

Kuhse, H. 'Why Killing Is Not Always Worse – and Sometimes Better – than Letting Die', in *Bioethics – An Anthology*, Kuhse, H. and Singer, P. (eds), Oxford, Blackwell, 1999.

Lafollette, H. (ed.) *Ethics in Practice – An Anthology*, Oxford, Blackwell, 2002 (contains articles by Judith Jarvis Thomson, Mary Anne Warren and Rosalind Hursthouse on abortion).

Macquarrie, J. and Childress, J. *A New Dictionary of Christian Ethics*, London, SCM, 1986.

Singer, P. *Rethinking Life and Death*, Oxford, Oxford University Press, 1994.

8   Medical Ethics 2
Euthanasia and the Right to Life

WHAT YOU WILL LEARN ABOUT IN THIS CHAPTER

*   Definitions of the different types of euthanasia.
*   The idea of the sanctity of life and how it applies to euthanasia.
*   Personhood.
*   Suicide.
*   Ideas of autonomy.
*   The difference between killing and letting die/acts and omissions.
*   The approaches of different ethical theories to euthanasia.

KEY SCHOLARS

*   Thomas Aquinas (1225–1274)
*   Immanuel Kant (1724–1804)
*   Jeremy Bentham (1748–1832)
*   John Stuart Mill (1806–1873)
*   Germain Grisez (1929–)
*   Jonathan Glover (1941–)

*   James Rachels (1941–2003)
*   Peter Singer (1946–)
*   Helga Kuhse (1940–)
*   Joseph Boyle (1942–)
*   Daniel Maguire (1931–)

THE OCR CHECKLIST

Candidates should be able to demonstrate knowledge and understanding of:

*   the concept of the 'Sanctity of Life' and how it applies to euthanasia;
*   the concept of the 'Quality of Life' and how it applies to euthanasia;

- the right to life as applied to euthanasia;
- the application and the different approaches of the ethical theories listed below to euthanasia.

The ethical theories:

- Natural Law;
- Kantian Ethics;
- Utilitarianism;
- Religious Ethics.

Candidates should be able to discuss critically these issues and their strengths and weaknesses.

From OCR A Level Religious Studies Specification 7877.

Study hint

Many of the issues of medical ethics are progressing all the time as science and technology move forward. To stay abreast of these issues it is a good idea to keep a folder of relevant newspaper cuttings and annotate them with how you think the different ethical theories would react to the issue.

WHAT IS EUTHANASIA?

'Euthanasia' comes from the Greek *eu* meaning 'well' and 'easy', and *thanatos* meaning 'death'. Euthanasia is the intentional premature ending of another person's life either by direct means (active euthanasia) or by withholding medical treatment, food and hydration (passive euthanasia), because the patient asks for it (voluntary euthanasia) or without their express request (involuntary euthanasia).

Active euthanasia involves an actual act of mercy killing. For example, if a doctor decides that it is in the patient's best interest that they die, and so kills them for that reason, this is active euthanasia. This may be done by lethal injection by another person, but the patient would not die as quickly on their own. It is illegal in this country and many others.

Passive euthanasia involves helping someone die because it is judged that it is better for the person to be dead. This may be when a doctor withholds life-saving treatment with the intention that the patient dies – but it has to be done because of concern for the patient, not to free up hospital beds, etc. It is practised in the UK, and many of those who oppose active euthanasia see no problem with it.

The ethical question that these two forms of euthanasia raises is whether it is the same thing to kill someone as it is to let them die.

Voluntary euthanasia is carried out at the request of the person. This is illegal in the UK, but it is legal in the Netherlands under medical supervision. There is campaigning in this country for the same law here. In this country there are Do Not Resuscitate orders – DNRs – which can be seen

Active euthanasia
The intentional premature termination of another person's life.

Passive euthanasia
Treatment is either withdrawn or not given to the patient in order to hasten death. This could include turning off a life-support machine.

Voluntary euthanasia
The intentional premature termination of another person's life at their request.

as a chosen form of passive euthanasia. However, they are controversial as there have been cases of DNRs being written into a patient's notes without their consent. Guidelines issued by the British Medical Association say that DNR orders should only be issued after discussion with the patient and/or their family.

Involuntary euthanasia occurs when it is impossible to get the patient's consent – perhaps they have lost the ability to make a decision or are still an infant. Involuntary euthanasia is carried out against the wishes of the patient and few people would defend this approach. However, it is possible for someone to be the victim of involuntary euthanasia – such as having a DNR order applied regardless of the patient's wishes.

The ending of a life by euthanasia may thus be either through acts of omission or through intentional acts. Note: the active/passive distinction cuts across the voluntary/non-voluntary, involuntary distinctions. There can be passive and active versions of each.

The debate about euthanasia includes the following issues:

- The sanctity of life and the idea that it is God-given.
- The maintenance of life as an absolute.
- Is the act in itself wrong or do the consequences make it wrong?
- The question of personal autonomy.
- The motives that lead to euthanasia.
- The difference between killing and letting die.

EUTHANASIA, PERSONHOOD AND THE SANCTITY OF LIFE

There is an explanation of the sanctity of life and personhood in Chapter 7 on abortion, but we also need to consider its particular application to the question of euthanasia. Human life is recognised by most people as 'something sacred', and believers also see it as a 'gift from God'. There are, however, different views on what it is that makes us human: many believers would say that we are human from conception or at the latest from birth, whereas others might say that we can only be considered human when we think and act as conscious human beings. According to the first viewpoint, we are fully human whether we are embryos or comatose patients – immature or damaged, we are still persons, whereas others may argue that a patient who is in a **persistent vegetative state (PVS)** may be a human but is not really a person because he or she is unable to be so; thus in all important aspects they are already dead. If this view of personhood is taken to its logical conclusion, all sorts of people, including the mentally disabled and the paralysed, could also be considered as incomplete persons and so already dead.

Involuntary euthanasia
This term is used when someone's life is ended to prevent their suffering, without their consent, even though they are capable of consenting.

PVS (persistent vegetative state)
When a patient is in this condition, doctors may seek to end their life. The relatives have to agree and usually the patient must be brain-stem dead.

The sanctity of life is central to the Catholic position, set out in the *Declaration on Euthanasia* (1980), which defines euthanasia as 'an act or an omission which of itself or by intention causes death, in order that all suffering may in this way be eliminated'. To do this to another or to ask it for oneself is not allowed – in accordance with Natural Law; the first primary precept is self-preservation and so death should not be hastened by euthanasia. The document does, however, recognise that while a time to prepare for death is useful, suffering can be so great both physically and psychologically that it can make a person wish to remove it whatever the cost. It accepts that very few can follow the path of Mother Teresa of Calcutta and limit the dose of painkillers so as to unite themselves with the sufferings of Christ, but it also says that 'suffering has a special place in God's plan of salvation'.

The doctrine of double effect plays an important part in Catholic thinking about euthanasia according to the teaching of Pope Pius XII, which distinguishes between painkillers that have a secondary effect of shortening life and drugs used to hasten death with a secondary effect of killing pain. It is the intention which is all important. The document says that it is 'important to protect, at the moment of death, both the dignity of the human person and the Christian concept of life against a technological attitude that threatens to become an abuse'. The document refers to 'ordinary' and 'extraordinary' means – ways of attempting to save life which are disproportionate to the pain suffered. A major problem here is how 'extraordinary' means are to be measured – there is a lack of clarity here, as 50 years ago a patient kept alive today on a life-support machine would have died. Issues of quality of life are now being seen as important, and when death is imminent a patient may refuse unnecessary treatment so long as 'the normal care due the sick person is not interrupted'. The introduction of proportionalism is significant, but not all Catholic scholars would agree with this.

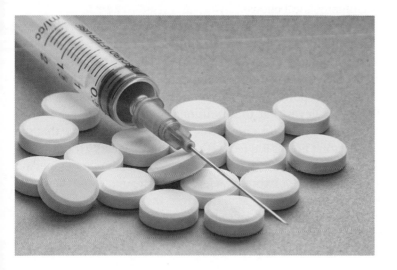

Germain Grisez and **Joseph Boyle** stress the importance of personhood and reject the view that one can cease to be a person and yet be bodily alive – they do not accept that a patient in a persistent vegetative state has lost that which makes them distinctively human: a human being is a whole, and bodily life is seen as a good in itself. Grisez and Boyle say that there are certain basic goods necessary for human well-being, including play and recreation, knowledge of the truth, appreciation of beauty, life and health, friendship and integration. They do not require this list to be in any particular order but they would absolutely reject euthanasia, as it attempts to achieve one good, such as freedom and dignity, by putting it in direct conflict with another: life and health. These basic goods cannot be compared or balanced off each other, and the key issue for them where euthanasia is concerned is that it is against the basic good of life.

The question of personhood, however, lies at the heart of the proportionalist position held by **Daniel Maguire**. This view states that life is a basic but not an absolute good and, while it is important to respect and value life, nobody should always be obliged to prolong it in every situation. Maguire rejects the idea that God alone has the power over life and death and that God alone should decide the time of death for each person; this seems to imply that we belong to God and are his property. He points out that we do, in fact, intervene to save life and to preserve it, and that there is no real difference between ending life and preserving it so long as the principle of achieving a good death is adhered to. Maguire uses the ideas of weighing up the proportional values of living in any condition and choosing a good death in certain specific circumstances. He recognises that this is a departure from the traditional Christian ethic of 'not destroying innocent life', and that making judgements between conflicting values is difficult and can lead to mistakes, but ethical reflection can lead to euthanasia being on some occasions a legitimate moral choice.

Euthanasia may also be seen as legitimate once the dying process has begun – this view still maintains the sanctity of life and respects life, but the dying process shows that life has reached its limit. The use of euthanasia to shorten the time taken to die by not prolonging life is considered legitimate, as humans can still have power over this without denying the sanctity of life.

Peter Singer believes that the traditional sanctity of life ethic must collapse and we need to develop a new ethic, as people now believe that the low quality of a person's life, as judged by the person, can justify them taking their life or justify someone else doing it for them. In cases where a person cannot make a judgement or express a view about the quality of their own life, someone else should do it for them. However, there is so much more that contributes to the quality of a person's life than that which can be measured medically, and Singer also fails to consider that a person's life has a value to the wider community as well as to the individual.

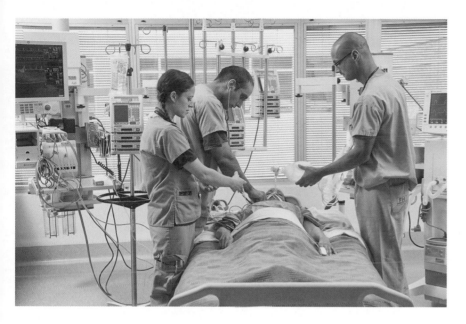

Consideration of the quality of life looks at whether the use of extra-ordinary means would usefully improve the quality of life of the patient. This idea is basically Utilitarian, as doctors consider the possible length of life of the patient, their state of mind, how the procedure would enhance their life, the resources needed and even the resources available – essentially the QUALYS (quality adjusted life year schedules) used in the USA. This is very different from the Catholic view, which allows the patient to refuse treatment if there is 'an acceptance of the human condition, or a wish to avoid the application of a medical procedure disproportionate to the results that can be expected, or a desire not to impose excessive expense on the family or the community'. No one is obliged to have a medical procedure that is risky or burdensome.

EUTHANASIA AND THE RIGHT TO LIFE

A person's right to life corresponds to the duty of others not to kill that person. The idea of a duty not to kill seems to rule out any form of euthanasia – but we do not see the duty not to kill as absolute, as we think some wars can be justified, or killing in self-defence or in the defence of others can be justified; even capital punishment is justified by some people. It is, in fact, easier to justify killing in voluntary euthanasia, where the person chooses death, than in these other cases, where the person who dies does not choose to do so. Life is a person's most valued and precious possession; can this then be just overturned if the person no longer wishes to live? Can the right to life, like any other right, be overturned or renounced? If that happens, can others say that they have a duty to kill him? If the person asks for voluntary euthanasia, is he then actually asserting his right to be killed in a particular way? However, who then has the duty to kill him? Many doctors who are happy to let people die, withdraw treatment or even assist suicide may not be so happy about having a positive duty to kill at a patient's request.

Thought Point

1   Is the sanctity of life ethic out of date? What could replace it?
2   What problems do you see in the doctrine of double effect?
3   Is there any point to suffering and can it help a person to become nearer to God?
4   What problems do you foresee in stressing the quality of life?
5   Is it wrong to help humans to die when they are actually dying? How do we decide when the dying process has begun?

EUTHANASIA AND SUICIDE

Assisted dying/suicide
When a person takes their own life with the assistance of another person. When the other person is a doctor, it is called physician-assisted suicide.

Suicide is the deliberate terminatation of one's own life, and many people, not only those who are religious, are appalled that people could even think of choosing death over life. They feel it demeans life and denies its meaning. All sorts of things give our life meaning – it may be 'God's plan' or it may be family or career – and suicide makes all this meaningless and trivial, as the act is not natural and breaks the timeless cycle of birth and death.

Henry Sidgwick said that only conscious beings can appreciate values and meanings, and so they see life as significant and part of some eternal plan, process or design. Suicide, therefore, is a statement by an intelligent, conscious being about the meaninglessness of life, but it is a statement that society rejects, and in the past suicide was seen as a criminal act.

Suicide, then, breaks the social contract, but it also breaks the bond between God and man – Thomas Aquinas also saw suicide as an unnatural act and a rejection of God's gift of an immortal soul. This view lay at the heart of the old legislation about suicide, which the state had a right to prevent and punish.

Today suicide is no longer illegal but the state still attempts to treat people as possessions and not allow them full autonomy and freedom – so the 'nanny state' protects drug addicts, alcoholics, smokers and the obese from themselves.

However, suicide is subject to a double moral standard: self-sacrifice in the form of martyrdom either for religious or political beliefs is admired, and for a believer such a death is seen as part of a journey leading to life with God; to die on the battlefield is courageous, and many people are involved in life-threatening occupations such as the fire and rescue service, the armed forces and the police; certain industries such as the manufacture of cigarettes, alcohol and armaments increase the mortality rate. Death here is controlled by religion, the state and political parties, whereas suicide is a free act and does not serve any social ends or uphold group values and structures.

- Is it morally justified to commit suicide to avoid forthcoming pain, loss of self-control or coma?
- Is it morally justified to ask others to help you commit suicide if you are incapable of doing it yourself?

EUTHANASIA AND PERSONAL AUTONOMY

John Stuart Mill (*On Liberty*, 1859) writes that in matters that do not concern others, individuals should have full autonomy. Those who support voluntary euthanasia believe that personal autonomy and self-determination are paramount and any competent adult should be able to decide on the time and manner of their death.

A house in Switzerland run by the medically assisted suicide organisation Dignitas

The right to have one's life ended by euthanasia is the subject of ethical, social and legal limitations. In some countries such as the Netherlands and Belgium it is allowed and socially acceptable to have a doctor end one's life if death is imminent and the quality of life is very poor. However, the patient has to be of sound mind and to request death repeatedly.

But what if the patient's wishes are based on faulty information about their illness, or depression clouds their judgement? What if a cure is found just after the patient's death? What if the request for euthanasia is easier to respond to than providing good palliative care?

Personal **autonomy** is an important value but it is often in conflict with other equally important ones – how do we work out which value overrides another and which are the true basic goods?

Autonomy

In ethics this means freely taken moral decisions by an individual.

KILLING AND LETTING DIE

Many doctors will argue that euthanasia goes on already, as they will give patients painkillers in such doses that death will be hastened, and in the case of the brain-dead or those in persistent vegetative states they will withdraw or withhold treatment to bring about death.

However, we do see a difference between killing (taking life) and letting die (not saving life). There is a right not to be killed, but no right to have one's life saved.

James Rachels saw no distinction between active euthanasia (killing) and passive euthanasia (letting die). If anything, he believes that passive euthanasia is worse, as it is cruel and inconsistent and the process of dying may be long and drawn out, bringing about more suffering than is necessary. The result is the same – the patient is dead.

Many arguments concerning euthanasia, whether active or passive, are influenced by the fear that allowing one kind of euthanasia will be the first step on a **slippery slope**, and the value of human life will be depreciated and made subordinate to economics and personal convenience. **Helga Kuhse** challenges this 'slippery slope' view and concludes that the situation in the Netherlands is not following the example of Nazi Germany in making some lives valueless for reasons other than mercy or respect for autonomy.

James Rachels (1941–2003)

James Rachels taught at the University of Richmond, New York University, the University of Miami, Duke University and the University of Alabama at Birmingham, USA. Rachels argued for moral vegetarianism and animal rights, preferential quotas, and the humanitarian use of euthanasia.

Slippery slope

This means that when one moral law is broken others will also be gradually broken and there will be no moral absolutes.

APPLYING ETHICAL THEORIES TO EUTHANASIA

Utilitarianism

Basic principle – the greatest good for the greatest number.

One of the first questions we need to ask when considering Utilitarianism and euthanasia is: what counts as a good consequence? One answer is that given by **John Stuart Mill**: good consequences are simply happiness, and happiness is pleasure and freedom from pain – not only physical but also mental and psychological pain. In his *Essay on Liberty,* Mill states that good consequences depend not only on the quantity of the pleasure but on the quality as well – this higher happiness stresses self-development and develops people's rational nature. Mill's notion of victimless crime may also be applied to voluntary euthanasia: as there is no victim of crime since the patient wishes to die. However, even though the patient has their wish and the doctor is merely carrying it out, there are still the effects on society and on the doctor–patient relationship, making society itself the victim as human life loses its value.

Both **Jeremy Bentham**'s hedonistic Utilitarianism and Mill's view argue that euthanasia is right. Bentham would say that if a person's continued existence brings more pain than suffering, both to them and to their family, then their life could be ended. Utilitarianism would also consider the resources that are being spent in keeping them alive and argue that more happiness could be produced if these resources were used in other ways. The idea of 'death with dignity' through voluntary euthanasia also fits Mill's Utilitarianism, as it is possible to claim that the good they seek is not just the absence of pain but the preservation of dignity and the exercise of personal autonomy.

However, there is a problem with the way Utilitarianism can be used to justify euthanasia, as it seems to justify too much – if enough people gain happiness and quality of life from the death of one person, then such an action is justified. There is no protection for the individual against the majority and no safeguarding of the individual's rights.

Peter Singer takes this further and believes that the traditional sanctity of life ethic must collapse and we need to develop a new ethic, as people now believe that the low quality of a person's life, as judged by the person, can justify them taking their life or justify someone else doing it for them. In cases where a person cannot make a judgement or express a view about the quality of their own life, someone else should do it for them. However, there is so much more that contributes to the quality of a person's life than that which can be measured medically, and Singer also fails to consider that a person's life has a value to the wider community as well as to the individual.

Natural Law

Basic principle – everything is created for a purpose and when this is examined by human reason, a person should be able to judge how to act in order to find ultimate happiness.

Natural Law does not look at the people involved in a decision about euthanasia, or the consequences of the action – instead Natural Law considers the act of euthanasia itself. Protection of life is a primary precept and euthanasia goes against this. It would seem, therefore, that for a follower of Natural Law euthanasia is always wrong. However, the doctrine of double effect will allow a form of indirect euthanasia as it is permissible to give someone pain relief even if the action leads to death. Death in this case is a by-product of another action and seems to be almost proportionate, leading many Natural Law thinkers to find the doctrine of double effect hard to reconcile with the precepts of Natural Law.

Natural Law does allow a patient to refuse treatment if it is over and above what is needed for existence – extraordinary means. Proportion is important in Natural Law and actually enables each situation to be looked at individually so that the action that is proportionate to the needs of the patient is chosen. The weak sanctity of life argument says that where death is inevitable the doctor treats the patient with care and compassion: 'Thou shalt not kill; but need not strive officiously to keep alive.' Arthur Clough's poem *The New Decalogue* sums up this view.

Kantian Ethics

Kant would value personal autonomy, but for Kant the outcome of an action is not relevant to whether it is right or not. He also disagreed with making moral choices out of compassion, kindness or any other emotion – only reason leads to right actions. However, applying the categorical imperative to euthanasia does not give a clear response. One could say that euthanasia on a universal scale would not be right as can be seen from his writings on suicide:

> Firstly, under the head of necessary duty to oneself: He who contemplates suicide should ask himself whether his action can be consistent with the idea of humanity as an end in itself. If he destroys himself in order to escape painful circumstances, he uses a person merely as a means to maintain a tolerable condition up to the end of life. But a man is not a thing, that is to say, something which can be used merely as means, but must in all his actions be always considered as an end in

himself. I cannot, therefore, dispose in any way of a man in my own person so as to mutilate him, to damage or kill him.

(Kant, 'Groundwork of a Metaphysics of Morals' in
The Moral Law, 2005, p. 34)

Kant believes that human life should only be treated as an end in itself and never as a means to an end – suicide for Kant cannot be morally justified, and logically one could say the same about euthanasia. However, we are merely interpreting what we believe Kant said and some modern followers of Kant could argue that a person's ends are best served by ending their suffering.

Thought Point

In pairs or groups research one of the following and apply ethical theories to it:

1   Tony Bland and his doctor, Jim Howe.
2   Diane Pretty.
3   Annie Lindsell.
4   Baby Charlotte Wyatt.
5   Mary Ormerod.
6   Terri Schiavo.
7   Dr Anne Turner and Dignitas.

Further research

Dr Andrew Fergusson – chairman of Healthcare Opposed to Euthanasia (HOPE)
Dame Cecily Saunders – founder of the modern Hospice Movement
Baroness Warnock
Euthanasia in the news

REVIEW QUESTIONS

Look back over the chapter and check that you can answer the following questions:

1   (a) Explain the link between euthanasia and the sanctity of life.
    (b) Explain the link between euthanasia and the quality of life.

continued

2   What is the difference between killing and letting die? Does it matter?

3   What are QUALYS?

4   Make a chart applying the different ethical theories to euthanasia.

Terminology

Do you know your terminology?

Try to explain the following ideas without looking at your books and notes:

* Autonomy
* Active euthanasia
* Involuntary euthanasia
* Voluntary euthanasia
* Passive euthanasia
* Slippery slope

Examination Questions Practice

Read the question carefully – if it asks you to write about voluntary euthanasia, do not write about other sorts just because you know about them. Do not just reproduce 'My euthanasia essay'.

Remember: (a) assesses AO1 and (b) AO2. To help you improve your answers look at the AS Levels of Response. See: http://www.ocr.org.uk/qualifications/as-a-level-gce-religious-studies-h172-h572/.

SAMPLE EXAM STYLE QUESTIONS

(a) Explain what is meant by the sanctity of life. (25 marks)

You will need to include some of the following concepts:

* This teaching means that life is special and sacred, ordained by God.
* Life begins at conception and continues until natural death.

To write a good answer you need to include biblical teaching and/or link the sanctity of life to the precept to preserve innocent life in Natural Moral Law.

You could also explain that this view rejects autonomous or secular ethics and contrast the idea of the sanctity of life with teleological and quality-of-life arguments.

(b) 'The concept of the sanctity of life is not helpful in understanding the issues surrounding euthanasia.' Discuss. (10 marks)

- A common argument is to contrast the sanctity of life with the argument for autonomy and quality of life.
- You could also argue that the sanctity of life argument leaves no room for compassion and consider a relative theory of ethics such as Situation Ethics as an alternative.
- You may put the alternative point of view and argue in support of the sanctity of life, possibly linking it to the precept to preserve innocent life in Natural Moral Law.
- It is a good idea to use biblical teaching to back up your argument.

SAMPLE AS EXAM STYLE QUESTIONS

(a) Explain Kant's theory of ethics.
(b) How helpful would this theory be when faced with the problem of dying without dignity?

(a) Explain the main differences between the Utilitarianism of Bentham and Mill.
(b) Evaluate the claim that Utilitarianism is a useful method in judging issues of voluntary euthanasia.

(a) Explain the main features of Natural Law.
(b) Discuss Natural Law in relation to voluntary euthanasia.

(a) Explain how Utilitarianism might be applied to euthanasia.
(b) 'One set of moral principles should apply to all societies.' Discuss.

(a) Explain how a follower of Natural Law might respond to issues raised by voluntary euthanasia.
(b) 'A Natural Law approach is the best approach to voluntary euthanasia.' Discuss.

(a) Explain religious objections to euthanasia.
(b) 'Religious objections to euthanasia ignore human dignity.' Discuss.

FURTHER READING

Cook, D. *The Moral Maze*, London, SPCK, 1983.
Glover, J. *Causing Death and Saving Lives*, London, Penguin, 1990.
Hinman, L. 'Ethics Updates', available at http://ethics.sandiego.edu/.
Kuhse, H. and Singer, P. (eds) *Bioethics – An Anthology*, Oxford, Blackwell, 1999 (contains articles by Jonathan Glover, Germain Grisez and Joseph Boyle, James Rachels and Helga Kuhse).
Lafollette, H. (ed.) *Ethics in Practice – An Anthology*, Oxford, Blackwell, 2002.
Macquarrie, J. and Childress, J. *A New Dictionary of Christian Ethics*, London, SCM, 1986.

Singer, P. *Practical Ethics,* Cambridge, Cambridge University Press, 1993.
Singer, P. *Rethinking Life and Death*, Oxford, Oxford University Press, 1994.
Warnock, M. *An Intelligent Person's Guide to Ethics*, London, Duckworth, 1999.
Wilcockson, M. *Issues of Life and Death*, London, Hodder & Stoughton, 1999.

9 Medical Ethics 3
Genetic Engineering and Embryo Research

WHAT YOU WILL LEARN ABOUT IN THIS CHAPTER

- An understanding of genetic engineering and embryo research, and the issues involved.
- The idea of the sanctity of life and how it applies to embryo research.
- Religious approaches to genetic engineering and embryo research.
- 'Designer babies'.
- The ethical implications of our knowledge of the human genome.
- Testing and genetic screening.
- Stem cell research.
- Genetically engineered crops.
- The approaches of different ethical theories to genetic engineering and embryo research.

KEY SCHOLARS

- Thomas Aquinas (1225–1274)
- Immanuel Kant (1724–1804)
- Jeremy Bentham (1748–1832)
- John Stuart Mill (1806–1873)
- Peter Singer (1946–)
- Celia Deane-Drummond
- Joseph Fletcher (1905–1991)
- Jonathan Glover (1941–)
- Paul Ramsay (1913–1988)
- Robert Song (1962–)

THE OCR CHECKLIST

Candidates should be able to demonstrate knowledge and understanding of:

- the ethical questions raised by the different types of genetic engineering to humans, animals and plants; human embryo research;
- the application and the different approaches of the ethical theories listed below to genetic engineering.

The ethical theories:

- Natural Law;
- Kantian Ethics;
- Utilitarianism;
- Religious Ethics.

Candidates should be able to discuss critically these issues and their strengths and weaknesses.

From OCR A Level Religious Studies Specification H172.

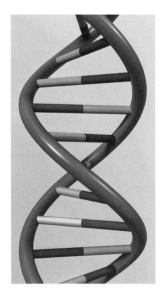

DNA helix

WHAT IS GENETIC ENGINEERING?

Genetics is about our genes, which are made of DNA and are the basic building blocks of life. Every cell has a full set of genes, carried in strands of DNA which are chromosomes. When new cells are replicated, each new cell has characteristics passed on by the DNA – genes are like a blueprint of life. In humans the genes decide the characteristics inherited from each parent.

It was in the mid-1970s that scientists first discovered how to move pieces of genetic material from one species to another – this came to be called **genetic engineering**. Some said that this was simply an extension of what breeders of plants and animals had been doing for hundreds of years and what nature did through evolution and natural selection, but others claimed that it was 'playing God' and was unnatural. Genetic engineering, however, continued to develop, and the technology was extended from plants to animals and finally to human cells. Today genetically altered crops, such as soybean and maize, are grown extensively, especially in the USA, and marketed all over the world. Scientists working for pharmaceutical companies use altered genes to produce 'designer' drugs, and research is gathering pace to treat certain inherited diseases by gene therapy.

The ethical questions first aired in the 1970s continue to be raised, both about the process itself and about the results. Others will say that humans have always altered their environment to benefit themselves, and this new biotechnology could help fight hunger and disease.

WHAT IS EMBRYO RESEARCH?

Embryo research has as its aim to find cures for serious illnesses using tissue or cells from **embryos**. Most of this research concentrates on **stem cells** and the field of regenerative medicine – the repair of damaged organs and body parts. Stem cells can change into other types of cells such as heart cells, muscle cells, nerve cells or skin cells. The ultimate stem cells are the system cells in the early embryo because they can develop into every single cell type. There is very little debate over the use of adult stem cells which can be taken from body tissue without harming the patient; so far these are the only ones that have successfully helped patients. Embryonic stem cells are removed from early embryos in a process that destroys the embryo – this makes it inherently problematic as far as ethics is concerned. These embryonic stem cells may be taken from embryos left over from IVF treatment or created in a laboratory from donated sperm and eggs. At the present state of the science no cure has been achieved using embryonic stem cells and they will always cause problems, as they do not have the same genetic make-up as the patients and will be rejected unless anti-rejection drugs are used. So the best option, at present, is to make new embryos by **therapeutic cloning** – the same method as used to create Dolly the sheep. This of course gives rise to another problem – the potential of this development is limited by the supply of human eggs and possible exploitation if poor women are to be paid for eggs.

Reproductive cloning has been tried in animals and there have been some successes after many, many failures. The only dividing line between therapeutic cloning and reproductive cloning is the intention of the scientists.

In the UK the law is clear: embryos may not be experimented on past fourteen days; a human embryo cannot be placed in an animal; human cloning is not allowed; the genetic structure of any cell cannot be altered while it is part of an embryo.

The Human Fertilisation and Embryology Authority allows embryo research for the following purposes only:

- to promote advances in the treatment of infertility
- to increase knowledge about the causes of congenital disease
- to increase knowledge about the causes of miscarriage
- to develop more effective techniques of contraception

Genetic engineering
The technology involved in cloning, gene therapy and gene manipulation.

Embryo
The developing bundle of cells in the womb up to eight weeks' gestation.

Stem cell
A 'master' cell that can become any kind of material.

Therapeutic cloning
A method of producing stem cells to treat diseases such as Alzheimer's.

Cloning
A form of genetic engineering by which a plant, an animal or a human is created with the same genetic identity as another.

- to develop methods for detecting the presence of gene or chromosome abnormalities.

For the purpose of this book we will look at genetically engineered crops, genetic selection, genetic testing and screening, the alteration of human genes, stem cell research, and whether the Human Genome Project understands humans primarily in terms of their genetic inheritance.

GENETICALLY ENGINEERED CROPS – 'FRANKENFOOD'?

The production of genetically modified (GM) crops has led to very strong reactions. In the UK press they were called 'Frankenfoods' after Mary Shelley's scientist and his manufactured monster.

These GM crops have certain obvious advantages: the food has better taste and quality and a greater resistance to pests and diseases; it is environmentally friendly in that it does not require chemical pesticides and will conserve soil, water and energy. The most talked-about advantage is that these GM crops offer the world's best chance to end or at least greatly reduce hunger and malnutrition through greater yields and sturdier crops.

However, critics say that these GM crops threaten the environment and may cause havoc through cross-pollination. Genetically engineered crops could have, as yet ,unknown effects on human health by causing unexpected allergic reactions, and eventually reducing resistance to disease and transferring antibiotic resistance markers. A potentially more serious criticism does not concern the effects on the developed world, which can protect itself, but on the developing world: many poor farmers are encouraged to grow GM

crops. Giant multinationals such as Monsanto and Novatis own patents on these altered crops and demand that farmers buy new seeds each year at great expense instead of reusing seeds from the previous year's crop. One country that has stood out against this is Zambia, which does not have enough food of its own but refuses to import from the USA and rejects any seeds or foods that have been genetically modified. This decision is partly to protect its export of vegetables to Europe, and partly a response to health warnings and damage to the environment; it is also concerned that this new biotechnology is part of a globalised system of agriculture that favours large producers, and argues that it is more important to retrain small farmers to farm organically as they did in the past.

Finally, GM food cannot be seen as the sole solution to world hunger – that problem is far more complex, and questions of injustice in the social situations of today's world need to be examined.

SELECTING HUMAN GENES – 'DESIGNER BABIES'?

The ethical debate surrounding the selection of human genes is even more complex than that over GM foods. There are a number of reasons why embryos are selected: to screen for genetically inherited diseases such as Huntington's disease, Tay-Sachs and cystic fibrosis or for genetic conditions such as Down's syndrome; to create a healthy baby to treat a sick sibling; or to select the sex of the child (this is illegal in the UK).

In order to do this, embryos are created by in-vitro fertilisation and a single cell is removed from each for genetic testing; one embryo is selected for implantation and the rest discarded.

Case studies

In 2002 a British couple, Michelle and Jayson Whittaker, asked the Human Fertilisation and Embryology Authority if they could genetically select an embryo that would be a match for their son Charlie, who had a life-threatening blood disorder. They were refused permission and went to the USA for IVF treatment.

In 2003, however, the Hashmis, who also had a son with a rare blood disorder urgently needing a bone-marrow transplant, were granted permission to select an embryo after many months of wrangling in the courts.

- Is this just a brilliant way of saving a child's life?
- Are scientists 'playing God'?

- What about the motivations of the parents?
- How could different ethical theories approach these situations?

Sex selection

The Mastersons have sons, but their only daughter died, and they want to use sex selection to have another daughter.

- If they want a daughter so badly, will they just want her to be like the daughter they had? Will this damage her?
- Can we even begin to know their motives?
- Would we feel differently if the sex selection was for medical reasons (e.g. to select a female to have a baby free from the haemophilia gene)?

Genetic screening, and the idea of 'designer babies', involves destroying unwanted and unsuitable embryos. If the embryos are seen as persons from the moment of conception and, therefore, as having an intrinsic dignity and value that cannot be compromised in the name of other values, then any destruction of embryos would be opposed. However, fertilisation is a process that takes about 24 hours to complete and so there is no specific moment when personhood may be said to be conferred. **Peter Singer** points out that up to 14 days after conception the fertilised egg has the capacity to divide into two and become identical twins. In some cases it has been observed that such divided eggs blend back together into one **blastocyst**. If the egg is fertilised in vitro, one cell can be removed to have its genetic structure tested and the developmental process is unharmed. In fact, all the cells of the blastocyst can be separated and each has the capacity to become a whole human being – this is important as the blastocyst does not have true individuality. Without individuality it is difficult, according to Singer's argument, to see how the organism can be a person. However, even if the early embryo is not a person with full human rights, we do not yet have enough knowledge of early brain activity to know whether an early embryo feels pain.

Some people are concerned that the newborn baby will be subject to painful medical procedures to help a sibling, but, in fact, the necessary cells are taken from the umbilical cord. There are also concerns that, in an increasingly materialistic society, the baby is being treated as a commodity – just made to be a donor or to fulfil parental desires. As it is so difficult to assess the motives of others, some may say that embryo selection is the beginning of a 'slippery slope', with babies ultimately being chosen for eye colour or intelligence. However, we have been doing the same to animals for hundreds of years – would the selection or enhancement of humans be any different?

Blastocyst
A fertilised egg at about four to five days of development.

Zygote
A 'proto-embryo' of the first two weeks after conception – a small collection of identical cells.

TESTING AND GENETIC SCREENING

Genetic testing

Scientists have created tests for various genetic diseases – for example, whether a patient is carrying the gene which produces breast cancer or sickle cell anaemia. Patients have to agree to the tests and understand the implications of the test should they prove positive. One of the main ethical questions is whether the tests should remain private or whether the results should be divulged to employers or insurance companies. If the government goes ahead with plans for an identity card that carries genetic information, it would be difficult to keep such information private and could lead to discrimination. Genetic problems could also affect other family members – should they be informed if they have not given consent? Gene testing usually gives only a probability of developing the disorder and a limitation of all medical testing is the possibility of laboratory error.

Genetic screening

Genetic testing is done on sections of the population who are known to be at risk – this may be done on an adult, a child or a foetus. There are some advantages in knowing, in that the person can be encouraged to change their lifestyle to reduce the danger of developing the disease. However, it may

lead to discrimination against certain groups, such as the wish of a Jewish committee in New York to prevent Ashkenazi Jews who carry the Tay-Sachs gene from marrying each other. It may also lead to aborting a foetus which has a genetic flaw, which may prevent the child from pain and suffering but which also raises questions about how we as a society define 'normal' and 'abnormal'. If, for example, scientists were to discover a gene for being born violent, should we test everyone to see if they are carrying the gene and then eliminate them to make society a safer place?

Gene therapy

A further problem involves the use of gene therapy to correct, alter or replace genes. This has proved successful in some areas but also causes problems, as in the case of sickle cell anaemia which is prevalent among Afro-Caribbeans – this gene affects a few in a terrible way but it is the same gene that gives natural immunity from malaria.

There is also the issue of the allocation of health resources and how they are used. Can genetic screening be justified for a few individuals? Can it be justified if there is no cure available, e.g. Huntington's disease? How do we even know what to test for as more and more diseases are discovered to have genetic links?

THE ALTERATION OF HUMAN GENES

Human genome
A map of the human genes.

Germ line engineering
Changes in the parent's sperm or egg cells with the aim of passing on the changes to their offspring.

Somatic cell engineering
Changes in somatic (body) cells to cure an otherwise fatal disease. These changes are not passed on to a person's offspring.

Gene therapy aims to cure or ultimately prevent disease by changing genes. The science is only in its infancy and primarily experimental. Gene alteration can be targeted to somatic (body) cells, in which the patient's **genome** is changed, or to germ (egg and sperm) cells, in which the parent's egg and sperm cells are changed with the aim of passing on the changes to future generations. **Germ line** therapy is often confused with genetic selection, but it is not, in fact, being actively investigated in larger animals or humans. Ethically this therapy is questionable, as it could ultimately change the whole of humanity and what it means to be human – we take charge of our own evolution.

The alteration of genes in a patient's **somatic cells** was first used successfully in 1990 – this type of genetic therapy raises the fewest ethical questions, especially when it is used to treat a life-threatening disease. However, gene therapy given to a foetus before birth could again mean that we decide which genetic predispositions are to be altered – for example, at present, conditions such as obesity, below-average intelligence and poor eyesight are seen as normal inheritable characteristics, but in the future may be considered to be grounds for alteration or even abortion. Some people feel that there is no difference between gene alteration to prevent a minor disability and paying school fees so that children get a first-class education. This may of course create a further ethical issue whereby a division is created between the genetically rich and everyone else.

However, most diseases involve the interaction of many genes and the environment. Many people who develop cancer not only inherit the disease gene, but also may not have inherited particular tumour-suppressing genes. Diet, exercise, smoking and other environmental factors may all have contributed to their disease. Studies of identical twins show that individuals with the same genetic make-up do not develop the same diseases – environment plays a part.

STEM CELL RESEARCH

Stem cells are cells that can change into other types of cells – in the very early embryo they are *totipotent*: they can become any kind of body cell; in the adult they are *pluripotent*: they have the capacity to become a variety of cells, but not all. Adult stem cells can be taken from an adult, a child or even from the placenta of a newborn baby without harming the patient, but those removed from early embryos destroy the embryo. There are also foetal stem cells which are taken from aborted foetuses and are believed to have almost the same potential as embryonic stem cells.

Scientists hope that stem cells can be used to cure many disorders such as Parkinson's disease, diabetes, spinal cord injuries, heart disease and cancer – but all this is a long way off, decades in the future. In 2006 it was reported in the *Lancet* how, five years previously, patients' own cells had been used to grow and replace bladders in seven children who suffered from spina bifida. These were not stem cells, but more specialised cells which can only grow into bladder cells. This has improved the lives of these children beyond measure, and they do not have to take anti-rejection drugs, as the bladders are made from their own cells. A bladder is a much simpler organ than a liver or a kidney, but they are now testing kidneys successfully in cows. This is a very different situation from the use of embryonic stem cells, which necessitates the destruction of embryos for the benefit of others, which goes against the teaching on the sanctity of life.

Embryonic stem cell research is the threshold of cloning – first developed at the Roslin Institute by Ian Wilmot in 1997, when Dolly the sheep was cloned. Human cloning is illegal in the UK, but several rogue scientists have attempted it elsewhere. Scientists simply say that it is unsafe for the cloned child, as, from the experience of cloning other mammals, producing one child might need hundreds of pregnancies and many abnormal late-term

Two diagrams of stem cell
research

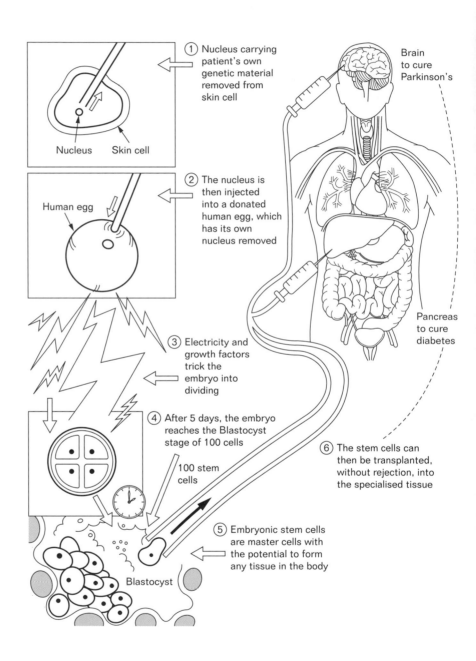

① Nucleus carrying patient's own genetic material removed from skin cell

Nucleus   Skin cell

② The nucleus is then injected into a donated human egg, which has its own nucleus removed

Human egg

③ Electricity and growth factors trick the embryo into dividing

④ After 5 days, the embryo reaches the Blastocyst stage of 100 cells

100 stem cells

Blastocyst

⑤ Embryonic stem cells are master cells with the potential to form any tissue in the body

Brain to cure Parkinson's

Pancreas to cure diabetes

⑥ The stem cells can then be transplanted, without rejection, into the specialised tissue

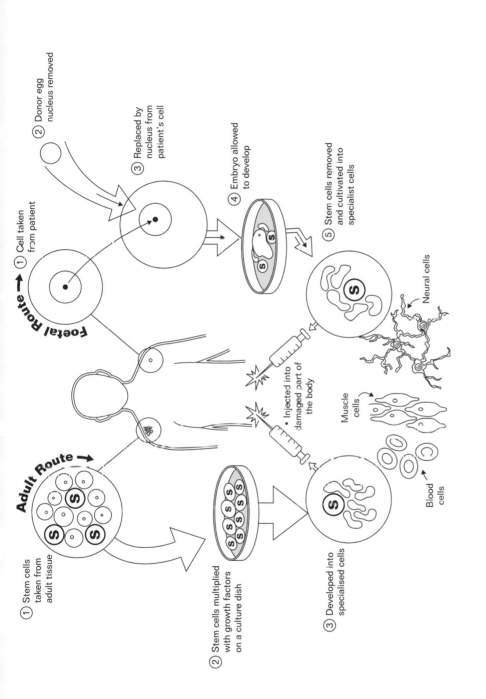

Foetal Route

① Cell taken from patient

② Donor egg nucleus removed

③ Replaced by nucleus from patient's cell

④ Embryo allowed to develop

⑤ Stem cells removed and cultivated into specialist cells

Adult Route

① Stem cells taken from adult tissue

② Stem cells multiplied with growth factors on a culture dish

③ Developed into specialised cells

• Injected into damaged part of the body

Neural cells

Muscle cells

Blood cells

foetuses could be produced. Others oppose human cloning on the grounds that it would produce confusion in family relationships and encourage parents to see cloned children as objects rather than independent human beings. However, the problems will eventually be overcome and many will argue that cloning is a possible solution for infertile couples, and that clones would simply be like identical twins, which are natural clones of each other.

Many scientists now say that it is unnecessary to use embryonic stem cells in their search for cures:

- Embryonic stem cells are very 'plastic', which means they can be unstable and become malignant, causing cancer.
- Adult stem cells are found in umbilical cord blood and placenta blood, as well as virtually every major organ of the human body.
- Adult stem cells have already been successfully used in treatments, while embryonic stem cells are still at the theoretical stage.
- The benefits of embryonic stem cells are a long way off.
- Adult stem cells overcome the problem of immune rejection.
- With the rise of animal rights activists and the problems involved in using adults to test drugs, it is likely that embryos will be used less for actual research and more for testing by pharmaceutical companies.

THE HUMAN GENOME PROJECT – A LIMITED VIEW OF HUMANITY?

Robert Song asks whether the human genome project and the resulting advances in biotechnology simply reduce human beings to their genetic inheritance. He does not criticise the science itself, nor does he say that the new genetics is intrinsically reductive in itself. He sees the developments in genetics as shaped by what he calls the 'Baconian Project' – the aim to eliminate suffering and maximise choice. This view may be traced back to the rise of the natural sciences in the seventeenth century (and also follows Francis Bacon's emphasis on the necessary social use of scientific knowledge), the Utilitarianism of the eighteenth century and the Romantic emphasis on individual fulfilment and autonomy. The result of this is that all suffering is seen as pointless (the rise in a desire to legalise euthanasia could follow from this), which has brought about an increase in the number of medical interventions and an understanding of our bodies as things to be changed according to our individual tastes through plastic surgery and so on. The human genome project has given us not just the knowledge of the 'basic building blocks' of the body and how it is constructed, but also the knowledge of how it may be reconstructed.

APPLYING ETHICAL THEORIES TO GENETIC ENGINEERING AND EMBRYO RESEARCH

Religious Ethics

The sanctity of life is a key theme with which to approach the questions of genetic engineering and embryo research. The Bible teaches that God created the human in his image and so human life has intrinsic value. Using an embryo for the sake of another human is wrong, as the embryo has intrinsic worth. Any technology that creates spare embryos to be used or discarded is wrong.

However, there are not the same objections to using adult stem cells or to the modification of animals or plants.

Catholic ethics are based on Natural Law and so are positive about advances in science that improve human life, but never at the expense of human life, which is sacred from the moment of conception. The Catholic Church also expresses concern about who is investing in the research and who will benefit from it. However, the Catholic Church recognises the need for humans to use their God-given intelligence to transform and humanise the world. This was the view of Pope Pius XII when he justified the use of painkillers: 'Man preserves, even after the Fall, the right of dominating the forces of Nature, of using them in his service, and of employing the resources so offered to him to avoid or suppress physical suffering.'

Catholics claim that certain actions are intrinsically evil, as they go against what it is to be human. Evil is seen as falling short of what humans are intended to be and is a result of free will. They make a distinction between *doing evil* and *suffering an evil*. Humans that are physically impaired (e.g. are blind or have Down's syndrome) are suffering an evil because they fall short of what it is to be fully human. Correcting these impairments is therefore a good thing – but the use of genetic engineering to achieve this is still ruled out. There is also concern that too much stress is placed on being physically perfect and the spiritual side of what it means to be human is neglected.

The Catholic Church rules out embryo research as being unnatural and destroying life, but it approves of genetic engineering which respects human life and human rights on the basis of its help for the individual and society.

Other Christian churches may take a different view and follow a Situation Ethics line based on agape. An action is good if it is based on love and bad if it is based on selfishness. Two influential Protestant writers on bioethics were the Episcopalian **Joseph Fletcher** and the Methodist **Paul Ramsay**. Fletcher saw a human being as 'a maker and a selecter and a designer' who acts morally when in control of genetics. He was not opposed to IVF and therefore it could be concluded that embryo research is the most loving thing to do with spare embryos when the only other option is to destroy them, especially when such research could lead to cures for terrible diseases.

However, creating embryos for the direct purpose of stem cell research is difficult to justify as being the most loving action.

Ramsay opposed separating procreation from conjugal love and was pessimistic about our attempts to 'play God', but his arguments were always teleological and looked at the benefits of genetic engineering for humanity. He approved of genetic screening as doing 'more good than harm' and said it was important that 'the benefits from any course of action must be weighed up against any risk'.

Christians in general seem to look favourably at genetic medicine, while acknowledging both the risks and the limits that should be imposed on research in terms of respect for human life.

Natural Law

Basic principle – everything is created for a purpose and when this is examined by human reason, a person should be able to judge how to act in order to find ultimate happiness.

Natural Law has the primary precept of self-preservation and from this may be deduced the secondary precept 'no embryo research', as it destroys life. However, it could be argued that the research can be justified, as it preserves life by curing diseases.

Utilitarianism

Basic principle – the greatest good for the greatest number.

Utilitarianism does not accept the principle that human life has absolute value and this should be upheld whatever the consequences, but attempts to assess each individual situation on its own merits to promote the greatest happiness for those concerned.

However, Utilitarianism only works if it is actually possible to assess the results of genetic engineering and embryo research and decide whether they favour all concerned. In practice this is difficult, as we cannot predict all consequences. However, it is possible to say, from a Utilitarian point of view, that it is better to save many lives in the future by embryo research at the cost of a few embryos now.

Bentham's hedonic calculus can only be applied to those who suffer. Early embryos, it is assumed at the present stage of knowledge, do not have the capacity to feel pain and so cannot be measured according to the hedonic calculus. However, the benefits of genetic engineering and embryo research are justifiable using the hedonic calculus – the pleasures brought about by cures for diseases such as Parkinson's outweigh the cost to the embryos. However, the costs to the Health Service, as mentioned above, also need to be considered and the likelihood of success taken into account.

Kantian Ethics

Basic principle – the categorical imperative: universal maxims; treating others as ends in themselves and living in a Kingdom of Ends.

Kant argued that reason enabled people to impose such laws upon themselves and when the categorical imperative is applied to genetic engineering and embryo research there are immediate difficulties: both would be hard to universalise simply. For example, it would be possible to universalise the maxim 'use spare embryos left over from IVF for stem cell research' but not 'create embryos for stem cell research', as there would be no embryos left to reproduce and the human race would die out.

There is also the emphasis on treating people as ends in themselves and not as a means to an end – embryo research would also go against this if the embryo is considered to be a person. Kant was not clear on the moral status of embryos. However, the Kantian idea of respect for persons and the requirement for human rights to be respected, that informed consent should be obtained and so on will mean that genetic medicine, testing, screening and adult stem cell research will be truly humanising. Respect for autonomy and privacy is also essential to Kantian Ethics.

Kant's stress on acting out of duty alone, with no account taken of compassion or love, means that all consequences are ignored, whatever they may be.

REVIEW QUESTIONS

Look back over the chapter and check that you can answer the following questions:

1   Explain the differences between therapeutic and reproductive cloning.
2   How could genetic engineering be used to alleviate world hunger? What are the problems with this?
3   Explain the difference between adult and foetal stem cells – why is this important ethically?

continued

4   Take a current newspaper article about any form of genetic engineering or foetal research. Stick it on a piece of A3 paper and write brief notes around it on how different ethical theories would approach the issue.

5   List some of the ethical problems with genetic engineering and foetal research.

Terminology

Do you know your terminology?

Try to explain the following key terms without looking at your books and notes:

- Blastocyst
- Cloning
- Germ line engineering
- Somatic cell engineering

Examination Questions Practice

When writing answers about genetic engineering, make sure you know and understand the terminology and can explain the ethical implications of genetic engineering.

Remember: (a) assesses AO1 and (b) AO2. To help you improve your answers look at the AS Levels of Response. See: http://www.ocr.org.uk/qualifications/as-a-level-gce-religious-studies-h172-h572/.

SAMPLE EXAM STYLE QUESTIONS

(a) Explain how Utilitarianism might be applied to embryo research. (25 marks)

- You need to begin by explaining Utilitarianism – the amount of pleasure or happiness caused by an action.
- You should explain that Utilitarianism is teleological and focused on consequences – an action is right if it produces the greatest good for the greatest number.
- You should then apply this to embryo research – balancing good over evil and bringing benefit to sufferers of inherited diseases.
- You need to explain that a Utilitarian would look at the merits of each situation, but would also need to consider the costs involved.

(b) To what extent can embryo research be justified? (10 marks)

Here you need to contrast and analyse the different approaches:

*   You could defend embryo research, as it brings relief to sufferers and improves their quality of life, curing diseases that were once thought incurable.
*   On the other hand, you may question the techniques and the misuse of spare embryos.
*   You could explain that some people may object to interfering with nature using Natural Law theory.

SAMPLE AS EXAM STYLE QUESTIONS

(a) Explain the main strengths and weaknesses of Utilitarianism.
(b) Evaluate a Utilitarian approach to genetic engineering.

(a) Explain the differences between a relative morality and an absolute one.
(b) How useful is a relative morality in dealing with issues surrounding genetic engineering?

(a) Explain how the Religious Ethics you have studied might be applied to the issues raised by genetic engineering.
(b) 'Genetic engineering is ethically justified.' Discuss.

(a) Explain the Natural Law theory of ethics.
(b) How useful, if at all, is the theory of Natural Law in relation to embryo research?

(a) Explain how Natural Law could be applied to embryo research.
(b) 'A Natural Law approach to embryo research does society more harm than good.' Discuss.

(a) Explain Kant's theory of the categorical imperative.
(b) How useful is the categorical imperative when considering embryo research?

FURTHER READING

Deane-Drummond, C. (ed.) *Brave New World*, London/New York, T&T Clark, 2003.
Deane-Drummond, C. *Genetics and Christian Ethics*, Cambridge, Cambridge University Press, 2005.
Glover, J. *Causing Death and Saving Lives*, London, Penguin, 1990.
Hinman, L. 'Ethics Updates', available at http://ethics.sandiego.edu/.
Kuhse, H. and Singer, P. (eds) *Bioethics – An Anthology*, Oxford, Blackwell, 1999.
Lafollette, H. (ed.) *Ethics in Practice – An Anthology*, Oxford, Blackwell, 2002.
Macquarrie, J. and Childress, J. *A New Dictionary of Christian Ethics*, London, SCM, 1986.
Peters, T. *Playing God? Genetic Determinism and Human Freedom*, London, Routledge, 1997.
Song, R. *Human Genetics: Fabricating the Future*, London, Darton, Longman & Todd, 2002.

Essential terminology

Christian Realism
Jus ad bellum
Jus in bello
Jus post bellum
Just War theory
Pacifism
Proportionality
Realism

10 War and Peace

WHAT YOU WILL LEARN ABOUT IN THIS CHAPTER

*   The principles of Just War theory and its application.
*   Realism and Christian Realism as an approach to war.
*   The theories of ethical and religious pacifism.
*   Absolute Pacificism.
*   Religious Pacifism.
*   Contingent Pacifism.
*   Preferential Pacifism.
*   How different ethical theories approach issues of war and peace.
*   How Religious Ethics approaches issues of war and peace.
*   The strengths and weaknesses of these different approaches to issues of war and peace.

KEY SCHOLARS

*   Plato (428–347 BCE)
*   Ambrose of Milan (c.340–397)
*   Augustine of Hippo (354–430)
*   Thomas Aquinas (1225–1274)
*   Francisco de Vitoria (1480–1546)
*   Francisco Suárez (1548–1617)
*   Hugo Grotius (1583–1645)
*   Emerich de Vattel (1714–1767)
*   Jeremy Bentham (1748–1832)
*   John Stuart Mill (1806–1873)
*   Bertrand Russell (1872–1970)
*   Reinhold Niebuhr (1892–1971)
*   Dietrich Bonhoeffer (1906–1945)
*   Thomas Merton (1915–1968)
*   G.E.M. Anscombe (1919–2001)
*   Martin Luther King, Jr. (1929–1968)
*   Walter Wink (1935–2012)

THE OCR CHECKLIST

Candidates should be able to demonstrate knowledge and understanding of:

* the principles of 'Just War' and its application;
* the theories of ethical and religious pacifism;
* the application and the different approaches of the ethical theories listed below to war and peace.

The ethical theories:

* Natural Law;
* Kantian Ethics;
* Utilitarianism;
* Religious Ethics.

Candidates should be able to discuss critically these issues and their strengths and weaknesses.

From OCR A Level Religious Studies Specification H172.

WHAT IS WAR?

A war cemetery

Most people are now totally familiar with war. It used to be something you learned about in history books, but now we see its horror every day on television in our own homes. Except for disease and natural disasters there is nothing else that brings home human suffering so forcefully. It is hard to imagine that any country would want to go to war with the population of another country; that any sane individual would want to attack another country to seize its land or change its political processes. Therefore, there must be very powerful motivations for going to war.

People go to war for greed, for excitement and adventure, for religion and politics. War is a peculiar human activity and can bring out some of our best traits such as courage and self-sacrifice, and yet it can also lead men and women to commit acts of cruelty and barbarism.

War is conflict among states where armed forces confront the armed forces of another state. It is generally conducted within certain customs or laws. By common consent war is now generally seen as 'just' if it is in self-defence and if it is sanctioned by the UN. However, there were just wars prior to the formation of the UN and UN permission is not intrinsic to just war theory. It is difficult to argue the idea of 'just cause' if the war is against a state that poses no immediate threat, but which perhaps has an undemocratic regime.

Thought Point

1. What would make anyone want to go to war?
2. Under what circumstances would you be prepared to go to war?
3. Under what circumstances would you not be prepared to go to war?
4. Is the 'war against terrorism' truly a war?
5. Can you think of any circumstance in which someone would be justified in killing another person?
6. Why does it always appear that the enemy's justification for war is weaker than our own?

There are three main approaches to the issues surrounding war and peace:

Just War theory
The belief that war is morally justified if it meets certain criteria.

Realism
Normal moral rules cannot be applied to how states act in time of war.

Pacifism
The belief that violence is wrong.

1. **Just War theory** – states can have moral justification for going to war and sometimes war is morally right.
2. **Realism** – says that basically ethics has nothing to do with war. War is often necessary to promote security, survival and economic growth.
3. **Pacifism** – it is right to apply ethics to war and ask whether the war is just, but the answer will always be the same: war is always wrong and there is always some better solution than fighting.

JUST WAR THEORY

Just War theory is probably the most influential approach to issues of war and peace. It is constantly being refined and redeveloped and has even been codified into contemporary international laws governing armed conflict, such as the United Nations Charter and The Hague and Geneva Conventions. Just War theory, complete with a picture of Thomas Aquinas, was even discussed in *The Times* at the time of the first Gulf War.

The origins of Just War theory

The origins of Just War discussion go back to philosophers such as **Aristotle** and **Cicero**, who wrote that a war in self-defence was just. The first significant Christian development of Just War principles came with **Ambrose of Milan** and his student **Augustine of Hippo**. The political situation had changed rapidly and the Roman Emperor Constantine began to use the Roman state to support the Church. According to an influential bishop named Eusebius, Christian pacifism was from then on to be strictly for clergy, monks and nuns; lay Christians, however, were obliged to defend the country with force.

Ambrose and Augustine stipulated that war must only be waged by a legitimate governmental authority; it must be intended to restore peace and justice; it should be a last resort. There were also limits on the conduct of war: reprisal killings and massacres were forbidden. Augustine drew on the existing Roman idea of *justum bellum* (just war) and the Old Testament tradition where wars on behalf of Israel and God were clearly commanded by God.

Thomas Aquinas drew together the thinking on Just War and listed right authority, just cause and just intention as the most important aspects. In the *Summa Theologiae* Aquinas presents the general outline of what became the Just War theory, and he discusses not only war's justification, but also the kinds of activity that are permissible in war, who can fight a war and when a war can be fought. In spite of all this, he starts by saying that war in itself is sinful as it is contrary to peace.

In the sixteenth and seventeenth centuries **Francisco Suárez** and **Francisco de Vitoria** added the extra conditions of proportionality, last resort and reasonable chance of success.

Just War theory can be divided into three parts:

1 *Jus ad bellum* concerns the justice of resorting to war in the first place.
2 *Jus in bello* concerns the justice of conduct within the war.
3 *Jus post bellum* concerns the justice of peace agreements and the ending of the war.

These rules are addressed primarily to heads of state and governments, as they are the ones that set the wheels of war in motion. Just War theory demands that for war to be justified a state must fulfil each of the following six requirements.

St Ambrose (c. 340–397)

Ambrose was born in Trier and studied in Rome. He became Bishop of Milan in 374. Here he defended the Church against Arianism. He also received the future St Augustine into the Church. His feast day is 7 December.

Francisco Suárez (1548–1617)

Francisco Suárez was born in Granada on 5 January 1548. He taught theology and philosophy studies privately and also at Avila, Segovia and Valladolid. From 1580 to 1585 he taught at the Roman College in Rome. He was eventually appointed to the chair of theology at the University of Coimbra in Portugal. He died in Coimbra on 25 September 1617.

Francisco de Vitoria (1480–1546)

Francisco de Vitoria was born at Vitoria, Álava, Castile. He entered the Dominican Order and studied and lectured in Paris for sixteen years.

In 1523 he returned to Spain and lectured in

continued

Valladolid. In 1526 he was elected to the chair of theology at Salamanca. Vitoria is well known for his anti-colonial views; he doubted the justice of the Spanish conquest of the New World. He died on 12 August 1546.

Jus ad bellum

Justice in the decision to wage war.

Jus in bello

Justice in the conduct of war.

Jus post bellum

Justice in the ending of the war.

Hugo Grotius (1583–1645)

Hugo Grotius was born in Delft on 10 April 1583. He studied at the University of Leiden and then studied law at Orleans. In 1607 he was appointed Attorney-General of the province of Holland. One of his most significant works was *De Jure Belli ac Pacis* (On the Law of War and Peace) (1625). Following a shipwreck, he died in Rostock on 28 August 1645.

Jus ad bellum

1 Just cause

This is seen as the most important rule which sets the tone for all the others. There must be a good reason to go to war. So what makes a good reason? According to some of the most influential thinkers on the subject these are some of the reasons:

- **Augustine**, quoted by **Thomas Aquinas**, said: 'A just war is wont to be described as one that avenges wrongs, when a nation or state has to be punished for refusing to make amends for wrongs inflicted by its subjects, or to restore what has been seized unjustly' (*Summa Theologiae II–II* Question 40).
- For the Dominican **Francisco de Vitoria,** a nation has just cause when it tries to correct a violation of its rights.
- For the Jesuit **Francisco Suárez** the victim nation also has the right to punish those who are responsible for the injustice.
- For **Hugo Grotius** and **Emerich de Vattel** the prevention of injustice also constitutes a just cause. However, one has to be certain of the facts.

Based on these ideas it seems that just cause is essentially about the correction and/or punishment of an injustice that has been done, or about the prevention of an injustice that is about to happen. This is a little vague, as it does not explain what kind of injustice has to occur for the war to be just. It seems to involve *self-defence* and *defence of others*.

Is war justifiable only in response to armed attack, such as the German invasion of Poland in 1939 or the Iraqi invasion of Kuwait in 1990? Is it true that to know who was right and who was wrong in a war, you only need to know who fired the first shot?

An important point to consider when looking at just cause is whether it is permissible to launch a pre-emptive strike against anticipated aggression. After all, the presumed injustice has not yet taken place, so how can it be self-defence? The UN Security Council forbids pre-emptive strikes unless they have been clearly authorised in advance. This problem was highlighted in the run-up to the 2003 US-led pre-emptive strike on Iraq. The US still maintains it was right to strike first, in spite of there being no weapons of mass destruction, as part of its war on terror. Many other countries disagreed with this action.

Self-defence also allows the retaking of what has previously been wrongfully taken away.

According to Just War tradition, the 'other' does not need to be another state; it can also be a group of individuals belonging to another state whose fundamental rights are being violated. For Vitoria, Suárez and Grotius the

US troops prepare for military action in Iraq

concept of intervention for *humanitarian* reasons was not unknown and the idea that the responsibility of state leaders does not stop at their borders follows logically from their Natural Law perspective, that a universal moral code unifies all of humanity. This gives the right to intervene in the affairs of another state to protect the innocent citizens of that state. There are numerous examples of this in our recent history, when states massacred large numbers of their own citizens: Cambodia and Uganda in the 1970s, Rwanda in 1984, Serbia–Kosovo in 1998 to 1999 and the massacres in Sudan/Darfur which began in 2004 and seem to be still rumbling on today.

Nearly 2 million people died in Cambodia between 1975 and 1979

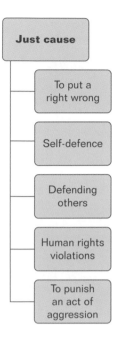

Just cause

- To put a right wrong
- Self-defence
- Defending others
- Human rights violations
- To punish an act of aggression

However, the situation is not as simple as it would seem, since when we intervene to provide humanitarian assistance we are violating the sovereignty of that state and so giving that state just cause in defending itself. In addition, how far should the intervention go? Should it be limited to humanitarian assistance or should the operation attempt to create an environment safe for democracy and human rights? **John Stuart Mill** advocated respect for the principle of self-determination: 'The members of a political community must seek their own freedom' and 'they cannot be set free by external force'. Others disagree and say that sometimes we simply do not do enough – it is not enough to feed people while allowing them to be killed.

Just cause is found on both sides of a conflict – nobody engages in war without thinking they have just cause. Just cause, then, cannot be an absolute principle, as the US Catholic bishops wrote in their pastoral letter *The Challenge of Peace, God's Promise, and Our Response* (1983): 'Every party should acknowledge the limits of its Just Cause and the consequent requirement to use only limited means in pursuit of its objectives.' Just War theory tells us not to exaggerate our own claims and to try to avoid the use of excessive force in pursuit of our own just cause.

2 Legitimate authority

A state may only go to war if the decision has been made by the appropriate authorities. When **Augustine** first framed the Just War principle, he associated it with the Roman Empire. In the Middle Ages, kings, nobles and cities claimed to have the authority to wage war, and throughout modern history revolutionary, secessionist and anti-colonial movements have challenged the right of established governments to be the only authority allowed to use legitimate force. After the Second World War the primary responsibility was given to the United Nations Security Council.

Just War principles have adapted to varying cultural and political needs.

3 Right Intention

The principle of Right Intention is closely related to the just cause principle and may be seen as its subjective element. Having a reason to go to war is not enough – the actual motivation must be moral. However, which intention is the right one? Reasons for going to war include the following:

- to kill and rob (barbaric wars)
- to seek glory in war (wars of chivalry)
- to promote commercial interests
- to promote colonial expansion
- to seize the land and resources of other countries
- for the sake of religion

- civil war
- revolution
- to retake something wrongfully taken
- to avenge a wrong
- in self-defence
- to prevent possible aggression in the future
- pre-emptive strikes
- to defend other states
- to protect people from genocide (humanitarian intervention).

Intuitively, most of us tend to think that some of the reasons in the above list are right and others wrong; for example, a war in self-defence is usually considered right. Intentions are often mixed and culturally influenced; for example, the Vikings would have found the intention to kill and rob perfectly acceptable, and a medieval knight would be happy to seek glory in war. So the principle of Right Intention needs to be based on more solid ethical grounds than our intuitions.

Augustine was the first to propose this principle, and for him just wars should be waged with the intention of achieving peace. He taught that if we go to war with the intention of achieving peace with the assistance of God, we would avoid such lower motives as revenge, cruelty and lust for power. However, the peace needed to be a just peace – wars, according to Augustine, were just when they aimed at restoring justice. This view is also criticised as being subjective, as it leaves people free to wage war because they believe they are following God's command. Augustine justified the use of force for the general good, but said that an individual Christian is not justified in using force for his own self-defence, for instance when being attacked by robbers. Augustine said that such an act is motivated by self-love and so is wrong.

Hugo Grotius opposed the Right Intention principle as too subjective, but it was interpreted again by the US Catholic bishops in 1983, who stated that good intentions in the use of force should aim at achieving a just cause, which is 'confronting a real and certain danger'. It is not always possible to know what the real intentions are of those who use military force and this principle is always open to abuse, so perhaps Grotius was right to be sceptical.

4 Likelihood of success

Deaths and injuries incurred in a hopeless cause are not morally justifiable. This idea was identified explicitly as a Just War principle by **Hugo Grotius** early in the seventeenth century. What is actually meant by success? For some it will mean victory, for others stopping the enemy near the border; it may even be respect for having fought with courage. The likelihood of success principle is closely linked to the following one: proportionality.

Proportionality

In war weapons should be proportionate to the aggression.

5 Proportionality

Proportionality is a relational principle; nothing is proportional by itself, but always in relation to something else. It is often said that punishment should be proportional (i.e. related in some way) to the crime.

When it comes to the *jus ad bellum* part of Just War theory, it is easy to find real and imaginary examples of disproportionality. It would be disproportionate for a nation to start a war because a few drunken soldiers went across a border, or over fishing rights. It is harder to find examples that are proportional – it is proportional when a relatively strong nation is attacked by an equally strong nation, and when a very strong nation responds to an attack by another relatively strong nation on a weak ally, such as in the 1990–1 Gulf War.

Does this mean that the good consequences of going to war must be equal to or greater than the bad? Is it possible to anticipate that the costs of war would be higher than the benefits? National pride can often get in the way, as can the excitement of war, or events may simply run out of control so that one step in the direction of war leads to another.

The principles of likelihood of success and proportionality are different principles, but they both share the idea of taking *everyone's* consequences into account and they are both difficult to apply. They both attempt to measure benefits and harms based on the just cause principle.

6 Last resort

According to Just War theory, the use of force can only be justified as a last resort, when all other means of resolving the conflict have been tried. This idea dates from **Cicero**, who said that, according to Roman legal practice, a certain time period should pass between the demand for reparations and the initiation of hostilities. **Thomas Aquinas** also thought of war as a kind of sanction for an injury in case there was no other way to right the wrong. Alternatives to war were explored by **Hugo Grotius**, who proposed peace conferences, arbitration and even favoured methods of solving conflict that seem odd today, such as drawing lots and individual combat. He considered that both sides should do all they can to avoid war.

Last resort is often risky – sometimes an unjust peace may be preferred to the horrors of war, but at other times it may be seen as a sign of weakness; for example, the policies of appeasement of Britain and France towards Nazi Germany just allowed Hitler to build up his armaments and strengthen his military position in Europe.

Economic sanctions are the favoured method of trying to persuade an offending state to alter its policies. They do not always work; for example, the economic sanctions against Iraq were insufficient to make Saddam Hussein remove his troops from Kuwait and they also failed to force the Iraqi government to comply with UN resolutions following the Gulf War. Sanctions may also go against the *jus in bello* principles of discrimination and proportionality as they usually have as bad an effect on the civilian population as war itself.

Just War theory insists that all six criteria must be fulfilled for any declaration of war to be justified. The criteria are a mixture of deontological and consequential requirements.

Jus in Bello

Jus in bello refers to justice in war, to right conduct in the midst of battle. In Western culture these rules can be traced back to Greek warfare, when there were a number of unwritten conventions covering things such as the ransoming of prisoners of war, the pursuit of a defeated enemy, and an agreement that battles should only be fought during the campaigning season (the summer).

Plato introduced the idea of not touching those who were not to blame for the conflict, in other words the non-combatants. However, these rules only applied to warfare among Greeks, not foreign enemies.

Today, responsibility for keeping the *jus in bello* rules is mainly that of the military commanders, officers and soldiers. They are accountable for any breaches and may end up being put on trial for war crimes.

There are several rules of *jus in bello,* but the first two are considered the most important.

1 Proportionality

In the context of *jus in bello,* the term 'proportionality' refers to soldiers using proportional force to achieve the end they seek. The issue is one of weighing the evil of war against the good results gained by war. According to this guideline, each act in a war, each battle, each campaign, must adhere to the principle of proportionality.

However, this does not give any direct guidance to those who have to make the decision in a time of war as to how to apply the principle of proportionality. Consider, for example, the bombing of Dresden during the Second World War: tactically the bombing accomplished little militarily, yet it did much to harm many people who had little or nothing to do with the German war effort. It is estimated that between 35,000 and 135,000 people were killed, many of whom were refugees fleeing the advance of the Soviet army. Tactically, then, the bombings were immoral. Some argued that a broader strategic look needed to be taken at the bombings of the German cities which could make these raids morally legitimate, as the principle of discrimination can be overruled by the principle of proportionality. However,

*After the bombing of
Dresden*

the Dresden raids happened so late in the war that they fail the strategic tests and were, therefore, immoral.

The principle of proportionality as a *jus in bello* criterion is in itself easy enough to understand, but it is difficult to employ in concrete situations. This is partly due to the uncertainty of war, and partly because rational calculations are difficult to make.

It is useful, however, as a restraint on some of the horrible effects of war, and it does encourage those who have to make decisions in the heat of battle to consider the costs and benefits impartially. It asks commanders not to forget the sufferings of those 'on the other side' and not just to look at immediate consequences. Thus to most people the use of nuclear arms on a large scale is seen as violating the principle of proportionality, because of the future effect of radioactive fall-out on the environment and on both present and future generations.

2 Discrimination and non-combatant immunity

Broadly speaking this means that those at war have an obligation to distinguish between appropriate and inappropriate targets of destruction, and between innocent civilians and those involved in waging the war.

Since the twentieth century the principle of Discrimination has focused on non-combatant immunity – usually to no avail, as civilian casualties, especially those of children, have been a painful feature of every conflict in the twentieth and twenty-first centuries. Such casualties are often referred to as 'collateral damage'. In 1983 the US Catholic bishops said: 'The lives of innocent civilians may never be taken directly. Regardless of the purpose alleged for doing so.' However, what exactly does 'taken directly' mean? In the Gulf War, the Iraqi military placed their command posts over schools so that the allied forces would have to kill children in order to destroy them – would this mean that innocent civilians were 'taken directly'? Again, is it morally right to bomb roads, bridges, airport runways, water supplies and power stations as Israel did in Lebanon in 2006?

A further complication is recognising who exactly is a non-combatant. Soldiers who are taken prisoner are no longer combatants, since they do not pose any threat, and nor are soldiers who are wounded. However, many wars in recent history have been fought by soldiers who do not wear uniforms or any distinctive signs. Guerrillas blend in perfectly with the civilian population, and guerrilla movements often rely on some measure of support from local people, as they try to avoid local casualties or attack local property in order to build up this support.

So who exactly are the 'innocent' in war? According to **Hugo Grotius**, if state A is justly fighting against state B, then all those in state A are innocent and all those in state B are guilty of aggression. This is now considered too simplistic, as wars do not always have the consent of the whole population. **Robert Holmes** suggests categorising people depending on their involvement in the war:

1   The initiators of the war: the government or leaders.
2   The agents of the war: the military commanders and the combatants.
3   Contributors to the war effort: those who work in munitions, military research or propaganda. This could also possibly include taxpayers whose taxes pay for it – though taxpayers do not have much say in how their money is spent.
4   Those who approved of the war without actually encouraging it.
5   Those who neither contribute to nor support the war: children, some elderly people, people in mental institutions or in prison.

However, this approach is also fairly simplistic, as it does not include the question of the conscription of those who have no wish to be soldiers but are forced to fight, or even the use of child soldiers.

Discrimination also concerns the question of nuclear weapons, which is dealt with below, but more important today is the problem posed by the proliferation of landmines. A UN report written in 2000 states that landmines have an appalling individual impact, and also create long-term economic and social destruction for generations to come, as they are active for years and the minefields are often unmarked.

A young landmine victim in Afghanistan

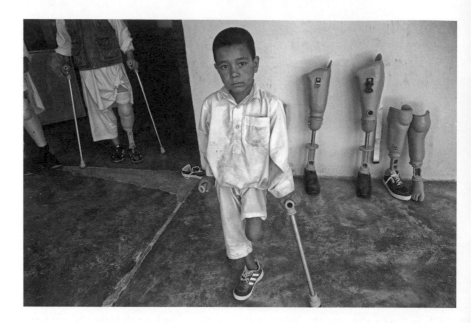

The principle of discrimination provides much guidance on approaching modern methods of warfare, including terrorism. Terrorism is always aimed at innocent victims (non-combatants), and the seeming randomness of terrorist attacks puts pressure on governments to yield to terrorists' demands. However, without even looking at other issues, the principle of discrimination will conclude that terrorism is unjustified.

3 Obey all international laws on weapons

There have been various attempts in the past to rule out certain weapons, ranging from crossbows to gas. In 1054 at the Council of Narbonne the Church decided certain days on which fighting could not take place. In 1139 the Lateran Council banned crossbows, bows and arrows and siege machines as unethical. However, these restrictions were rather like those of Plato and the Greeks, as they only applied to warfare between Christians. Chemical and biological weapons are forbidden by many treaties.

Nuclear weapons are not so clearly prohibited, but any use of them would be met by incredible hostility from the international community. As far as nuclear weapons are concerned, we need to weigh up the principle of discrimination against the principle of proportionality, and the principle of proportionality seems to dominate, which is why many support nuclear deterrence, even though they recognise that the threat to use nuclear weapons is a threat to cause non-combatant casualties. However, given the destructiveness of nuclear weapons, could their use ever be proportionate to the final goal?

A United Nations arms expert collects samples during an investigation into a suspected chemical weapons strike in Syria

4 Fair treatment of prisoners of war

Enemy soldiers who surrender or who are captured no longer pose a threat. Therefore, it is wrong to torture them or otherwise mistreat them. The Geneva Convention says they should be kept in benevolent quarantine, away from the battle until the war ends, when they should be exchanged for one's own POWs. The question is whether terrorists also deserve such protection, and controversy continues about the aggressive questioning of terrorist suspects held in US detention centres.

5 *No means* malum in se

Soldiers may not use weapons or methods of warfare which are *malum in se*, or 'evil in themselves', such as mass rapes, genocide or ethnic cleansing, forcing soldiers to fight against their own side, and using weapons whose effects cannot be controlled, such as biological weapons.

6 No reprisals

A reprisal is when country A violates *jus in bello* while at war with country B. Country B then retaliates with its own violation of *jus in bello*, seeking to make country A obey the rules. Reprisals do not seem to work, but just escalate violence and make the destruction even more indiscriminate.

Controversial US military prison for 'enemy combatants' in Guantanamo Bay

Jus in bello also requires a state to respect the rights of its own citizens, even though it is engaged in war. This includes issues such as conscription and censorship of the press. Some states have used the cover of war to engage in massive human rights violations, usually against some disliked minority group.

Jus post bellum

Jus post bellum refers to justice during the ending of war. It helps to ease the move from war to peace. This is a new approach to war and, if applied correctly, could lead to fewer wars.

1 Proportionality

The peace treaty should be reasonable and not seek to humiliate – so this rules out unconditional surrender. The settlement should not be able to be used as a source of revenge in the future.

2 Discrimination

A distinction needs to be made between the leaders, the soldiers and the civilians in the defeated country. Civilians should be protected, which rules out any economic sanctions after the war.

3 Rights vindication

The settlement should secure the rights to life and liberty, territory and sovereignty, especially any violations which may have been a trigger for the war. This means that the war and the subsequent peace treaty will actually have an improving effect on the country.

4 Punishment

Where necessary any leaders of an oppressive regime who engaged in massive human-rights violations should face international war crimes tribunals. Soldiers from all sides of the conflict should also be held accountable for their actions and face investigation and possible trials.

5 Compensation

Financial restitution may be necessary so that the defeated country can get back on its feet and repair its infrastructure: roads and transport links, hospitals, and schools and institutes of further and higher education.

6 Rehabilitation

The postwar environment provides an ideal chance to reform an aggressive regime. This may involve disarmament, the rehabilitation of the military, retraining of police, working with local people on new constitutions, education, helping people to see that the new order is better than the old and leaving the new regime to govern its own affairs when it is ready.

Ex-Bosnian Serb army leader Ratko Mladić at a war crimes tribunal

Finally, *jus post bellum* requires *time*; it cannot be achieved overnight or even in a few years, as the situation in Afghanistan shows, but it can be achieved in the end, as modern Germany and Japan testify.

Just War theory may be an ancient one, but it still provides rules to guide decision-makers on starting wars, conduct during war and the ending of war. It tries to ensure that wars are only started if they are just, that is, for a few defensible reasons, that they are fought in a responsible and controlled way and that the dispute is ended justly.

Strengths of Just War theory

- Just War theory defines the conditions under which violence may be used and it combines the wisdom of thinkers and philosophers from many centuries.
- It is a flexible theory, and grows and develops with the times.
- Just War theory recognises the necessity of action against an aggressor.
- Just War theory allows defence of the defenceless.
- Just War theory does not allow acts of war simply because they are thought to be in the interest of one nation.
- Weapons of mass destruction may change Just War theory, but we still need to consider their use within a moral framework.
- In spite of difficulties with the individual principles, Just War theory remains a universal theory.

Weaknesses of Just War theory

- Just War theory says that violence is permitted, but morality must always oppose deliberate violence.
- Just War theory is unrealistic, as the strong and powerful will always win.
- The conditions are too simplistic and ambiguous to apply in practice.
- Weapons of mass destruction demand a different approach, as they break all the basic rules.
- Terrorism demands a different approach, as terrorists take no notice of the rules.
- Many wars are only considered just in hindsight.

Thought Point

Is it morally defensible to have rules for war?

- What problems can you see with the following imaginary press release?

    During a recent action against terrorism, the ground troops called up air support who carried out a targeted strike using smart missiles. Collateral damage was kept to a minimum, with the loss of a few to friendly fire. There were few casualties.

- In July 2003 the sons of Saddam Hussein, Uday and Qusay, were killed by US troops. The US had offered a reward for their capture 'dead or alive'. There was, it seems, no attempt by the US troops involved in the action to try to capture the men alive so that they could be brought to trial.

    What rights were violated here and could this violation be justified?

- Is it right for a state to treat prisoners of war according to how 'evil' that state considers the enemy to be?

REALISM

Realists fully appreciate the horrors of war and so, like others, try to assess its costs, but they also respond to war in terms of its benefits. War sometimes gives a state extra land or resources.

Realists argue that war is a **non-moral activity** – actions such as killing, maiming or stealing may be wrong for individuals, but have no application to nations in times of war. So if a state is thinking of going to war with another state, it does not have to have moral reasons before actually starting a war. Neither can the warring nations be criticised for how they fight the war.

So how can Realists justify this point of view? They give a number of reasons, including:

- There is no real moral authority over nations telling them how to act.
- To survive, a nation has to look after its own interests.
- The threat of war and war itself make it impossible for any nation to do anything but act in its own interest – there is no time to do anything else.

However, even if Realists do not accept moral principles, they can still act in line with them, as it is often more practical to do so (e.g. treat prisoners of war well). In addition, a nation often cannot afford to alienate a nation which does not follow the Just War principles. Realists also say that it is important to protect the state's citizens.

Realists really say that anything is fair when it comes to war, and only self-interest matters. Ethics and war do not mix.

Christian Realism

Christian Realism gives the term a different meaning. According to **Reinhold Niebuhr**, whose Christian Realism was influential in the USA from the late 1930s to the 1960s, it is impossible fully to achieve ethical ideals because sin is present in everyone and in every action, especially self-interest and the desire to control other people. He saw war as evil and the result of human sinfulness, but it may be necessary to prevent greater evils. Niebuhr's views need to be understood within the context of the post-First World War period, and the failure of idealism to prevent that conflict and the conflicts which followed. He saw the importance of justice in society and the importance of creating systems of justice; so Christians sometimes have to support the use of force to restrain evil and prevent greater injustices. He also warned against overestimating our power to do good and the fact that we try to do things without full knowledge and awareness of our limitations. Niebuhr saw the rise of fascism as an evil which demanded the use of force, even by Christians, to get rid of it. Niebuhr thought that although individuals may sometimes rise above self-interest, the same was not true of states, and therefore he opposed pacifism.

Reinhold Niebuhr (1892–1971)

Reinhold Niebuhr was born in Wright City, Missouri, on 21 June 1892. In 1915 he became pastor of the Bethel Evangelical Church of Detroit. From 1928 he taught at the Union Theological Seminary in New York. Niebuhr is best known for his work on the interrelationships between religion, individuals and modern society. He died on 1 June 1971.

PACIFISM

Pacifists reject all war in favour of peace. Conflicts between nations should be settled by international gatherings such as the UN. The use of force is always wrong, even in self-defence, and so pacifism rejects both the Just War theory and Realism.

Pacifism is a broad term and may be roughly divided into Absolute Pacifism, which sees all war as wrong, and Consequentialist or Contingent Pacifism, which sees the costs of fighting the war as always greater than the benefits. However, both forms place great emphasis on the importance of respecting human life, and so reject killing.

Absolute Pacificism

Absolute Pacificism says it is never right to kill another human being, no matter what the consequences of not doing so might be, even loss of life. This may be a religious belief or a secular one. Absolute pacifists see violence as totally unacceptable.

This position is a difficult one to keep in practice, as they would see it as unethical to use violence in any situation, even to rescue an innocent person who is being attacked and may be killed. It is even more difficult to try to persuade others to do likewise. However, once accepted, it does provide a straightforward way of making decisions – there is certainly no need to work through a whole load of criteria like the follower of Just War theory.

Religious Pacifism

In the West, pacifism is rooted in Christianity and was particularly strong in the early Church. It looked to the Gospels, which record that Jesus called his followers not to violence, but to sacrificial love. Jesus taught that we must love our enemies, do good to those who hate us and 'Blessed are the peace-makers' (Matthew 5:9). These themes are rooted in the Jewish prophetic tradition, and followers of Jesus see both his ministry and his sacrificial death as a continuation and a fulfilment of that tradition, which must be carried on by his followers. The early Christians saw Jesus' commands as a prohibition on the bearing of arms, and so they refused to join the Roman army. As explained earlier, a profound change in the Christian attitude to war came at the time of the emperor Constantine, and from this time pacifism has been a minority view within the Christian Church.

However, there have been influential peace churches which continue the original Christian position, such as the Quakers, the Mennonites, the Amish, the Bruderhof Brethren (a community now living in East Sussex) and the Doukhobors (originally from Russia, but now living mainly in Canada). The **Quakers** are the most familiar group in the UK and, having been founded at the time of the civil war, they consider that violence only leads to more violence, and also that it is important that each person actively works to overcome anything which causes conflict between peoples. Most of these pacifist Christian communities were not against state military service, or the idea that a state should be able to defend itself, as they saw the state as a necessary vehicle for social order, but they themselves would not serve in the military. These Christian pacifists follow the teaching of Paul in Romans 13, where he wrote: 'Let every person be subject to the governing authorities; for there is no authority except from God, and those authorities that exist have been instituted by God' (Romans 13:1).

Paul saw those in authority thus: 'It is the servant of God to execute wrath on the wrongdoer' (Romans 13:14b). The state seems permitted to use force, but not the individual Christian. Peace churches see a complete separation between the 'church' and the 'world', and take the stance of *conscientious objectors*, often being persecuted by the authorities who do not share their view.

However, this pacifism does not mean doing nothing, but often encompasses *non-violent direct action*. The most well-known example of this was **Martin Luther King, Jr.**, who used forceful language, non-violent resistance, strikes, peaceful protest and civil disobedience, eventually culminating in his assassination, in the struggle for racial equality in the USA. He was influenced by the campaign for Indian independence led by **Gandhi**, who advocated *ahisma* or non-violence and *satyagraha* or zest for truth. Other examples include the transformation of Polish society by the **Solidarity** movement led by **Lech Wałesa**. However, whether such action will work in a war situation is another question.

Christian pacifism is not, however, limited to small Protestant groups but is followed by many in mainstream Christian denominations. Influential among these was the Catholic monk **Thomas Merton**, who influenced many with his prolific writings. He renounced violence as a way to peace and wrote that the task of the Christian is to work for the total abolition of war.

Merton advocated non-violence as a realistic alternative to violence and killing; the task was to try to win people's minds instead of destroying their bodies. In the Preface of his autobiography he wrote:

Martin Luther King, Jr.

It is my intention to make my entire life a rejection of, a protest against the crimes and the injustices of war and political tyranny which threaten to destroy the whole human race . . . and the world with it. By my monastic life and vows I am saying NO to all the concentration camps, the aerial bombardments, the staged political trials, the judicial murders, the racial injustices, the economic tyrannies and the whole socio-economic apparatus which seems geared for nothing but global destruction in spite of all its fair words in favour of peace.

(*Choosing to Love the World*, 2008, p. 81)

Martin Luther King, Jr. (1929–1968)

Martin Luther King, Jr. was born on 15 January 1929 in Atlanta. He was ordained as a Baptist minister at the age of 18. In 1954 he was appointed pastor of the Dexter Avenue Baptist Church in Montgomery, Alabama. In 1960 he became co-pastor (with his father) of the Ebenezer Baptist Church in Atlanta. In 1963 he led a civil rights campaign in Birmingham, Alabama, working for black voter registration, desegregation, and better education and housing. He led the march on Washington on 28 August 1963 and gave his famous 'I Have a Dream' speech. On 4 April 1968 he was shot and killed in Memphis.

Thomas Merton (1915–1968)

Thomas Merton was born in Prades, France, to American parents. He taught at Columbia University, New York, and then worked in a Roman Catholic centre in Harlem. In 1939 he converted to Roman Catholicism, and in 1941 entered the Trappist monastery of Our Lady of Gethsemane in Kentucky. He died in an accident in 1968 at a Christian–Buddhist conference in Bangkok.

Merton was censored by his superiors, but partly due to him Catholic pacifism is now more common and is even supported by the Vatican as an appropriate faith response to issues of war.

On the mainstream Protestant side, **Walter Wink** criticises Augustine's support of violence to defend the innocent, and the whole Just War theory, as it has led Christians to be one of the most warlike factions on Earth. He says that Christians should be non-violent pacifists who resist evil, but reject any idea of just war.

Contingent Pacifism

Contingent Pacifism is not opposed to war on absolute grounds, but on contingent grounds – war as we know it cannot be waged in a morally acceptable way. In other words, all wars today involve killing of the innocent, and this is morally unjustifiable.

Contingent pacifists accept wars in some circumstances, such as self-defence and defence of others, but the innocent must always be protected. So wars are justifiable in theory, but not in practice. Contingent pacifists need to look at each case to see if there are justifiable ways to fight the war. However, it is not possible to know in advance whether a proposed war will be able to be conducted rightly – without killing the innocent.

Finally, Contingent pacifists are against violence and war in principle, but accept that there may be times when war is the lesser of two evils. **Bertrand Russell** could be considered a Contingent pacifist, although he himself called it 'relative political pacifism', as he believed the Second World War to be a necessary evil to rid the world of Hitler and fascism. This is basically a Utilitarian view: it is bad consequences that make violence and war wrong.

Preferential Pacifism

Preferential Pacifism is a preferential option over violence. Preferential pacifists choose this option partly because war has been so destructive historically. This position in the twentieth century has been linked to economic justice as a basis for peace. In *Populorum Progressio* in 1967, Pope Paul VI wrote: 'To struggle against injustice is to promote the common good. Peace is not just the absence of war.' This was also the basis of the Catholic Workers' Movement and the views of its leaders, such as Dorothy Day, and led to what has become known as 'the preferential option for the poor' – social injustices, inequality and lack of human dignity are seen as militating against social and international peace.

Bertrand Arthur William Russell, 3rd Earl Russell (1872–1970)

Bertrand Russell was born in Trelleck in Wales on 18 May 1872. He studied at Trinity College, Cambridge, and then travelled across Europe and the USA. His specialist fields were logical and mathematical questions but he also had a strong sense of social conscience. In *The Problems of Philosophy* (1912) Russell used sociology, psychology, physics and mathematics to argue against idealism. Russell believed that 'objects perceived by the senses have an inherent reality independent of the mind'.

Sometimes pacifism as a preferential option has to take a back seat to the welfare of the oppressed. This is shown in the actions of the Christian pacifist **Dietrich Bonhoeffer**, who, in spite of his pacifist stance, took part in a failed assassination plot against Hitler and was later hanged at Flossenbürg for his part in the plot.

So, for the Preferential pacifist, pacifism is about how to live life, but sometimes it is either impossible or immoral to maintain a pacifist stance. Pacifism, therefore, is not just one view. There are different sorts and degrees of pacifism, but they all include the view that war and violence are unjustified and that conflicts should be settled in a peaceful way. Pacifism is also seen as more than opposition to violence and war; it must also include the promotion of justice and human rights.

Strengths of pacifism

- Pacifism is clear-cut – it opposes all forms of violence.
- Pacifism follows the teachings of Jesus, which pacifists see as ignored by Just War theory.
- It follows the historical position of the early Christians.
- It promotes the absolute value of human life.

Weaknesses of pacifism

- We do not live in a world based on pacifism and, as **G.E.M. Anscombe** points out, pacifism is wrong because it denies the right of self-defence.
- The state has a duty to protect its citizens.
- Pacifism allows evil to dominate.

APPLYING ETHICAL THEORIES TO ISSUES OF WAR AND PEACE

Utilitarianism

Utilitarianism approaches war not by asking if it goes against moral principles or rules, but by assessing the results it produces. If war produces more happiness or pleasure than unhappiness, then the principle of utility allows it. It depends on whether the loss of life, the number of injured and bereaved, etc. outweigh the benefit.

Utilitarianism is difficult to apply to war, as the results are even more unpredictable than those of many other moral dilemmas. Perhaps it would

> **Dietrich Bonhoeffer (1906–1945)**
>
> Bonhoeffer was born in Breslau on 4 February 1906. He studied theology at Tübingen and Berlin. He became a lecturer in theology in Berlin in 1931. Bonhoeffer was a leading critic of the Nazis and, in 1933, joined the Lutheran Confessing Church which opposed anti-Semitism. After a period in England he returned to Germany as a seminary director for the Confessing Church. He was imprisoned in Berlin in April 1943 and was hanged at the Nazi concentration camp at Flossenbürg on 9 April 1945.

be easier to say that wars should only be fought when it is at least possible that the outcome and the just purpose can be achieved – the Just War criterion of likelihood of success. There are too many 'what ifs?' to be weighed up against each other.

Preference Utilitarianism requires that the preferences of all those involved be taken into account – so in the war in Iraq does an Iraqi count as much as an American or British soldier? What of people in the future – what if in ten years' time Iraq is a free, democratic and prosperous country?

Utilitarians can also oppose war if the loss of human life looks too great, and can reassess their position as events change. Ultimately, though, Utilitarianism approaches issues of war and peace by asking if the end justifies the means.

Kantian Ethics

The many strands of Kantian Ethics can be fruitfully applied to issues of war and peace. Kant's focus on the 'good will' has parallels with Aquinas' contribution to the *jus in bello* condition which requires there to be right intention.

However, applying Kant's categorical imperative is not so straight-forward – it is difficult to find a maxim that could universalise killing, as it is a contradiction *of the will* and the *law of nature.*

Equally, when comparing Kant to Utilitarianism, killing others for a greater good or to reach some ultimate purpose does not meet Kant's requirement to treat people as ends in themselves and not as a means to an end, although a humanitarian intention could be possible.

However, Kant was fairly pessimistic about the human race and believed warfare to be morally permissible in the less than ideal world in which we live. Kant universalises the maxim to preserve one's life, so justifying violence in self-defence. If everyone adopted this maxim and fought only to preserve his or her own life, then Kant's theory of duty would have successfully eliminated war.

Finally, the third part of the categorical imperative, that we should act as though legislating for a Kingdom of Ends, influenced another of his writings, *Perpetual Peace*, written in 1795. Here he recommends a federation of free states, bound together by a covenant prohibiting war – war is a problem which only an international government could solve. This idea was fundamental to the League of Nations (1919–39) and then the more effective United Nations (1949–). However, Kant saw the importance of some sort of world federation – even if it was necessary to wage war to achieve it.

REVIEW QUESTIONS

Look back over the chapter and check that you can answer the following questions:

1   Make brief bullet point notes on each of the following:
    *   *Jus ad bellum*
    *   *Jus in bello*
    *   *Jus post bellum*
2   Make a chart of the strengths and weaknesses of Just War theory.
3   Explain Realism as an approach to war in one short paragraph.
4   List the different types of pacifism and write one or two sentences explaining each.
5   Make a chart of the strengths and weaknesses of pacifism.

Examination Questions Practice

Remember: (a) assesses AO1 and (b) AO2. To help you improve your answers look at the AS Levels of Response. See: http://www.ocr.org.uk/qualifications/as-a-level-gce-religious-studies-h172-h572/.

SAMPLE EXAM STYLE QUESTIONS

a) Explain how war can be considered 'just'. (25 marks)

*   You would need to explain the Just War theory of Thomas Aquinas.
*   You could also explain its origins in Augustine and more modern formulations.
*   You could explain that the conditions for a Just War are divided into *jus ad bellum* and *jus in bello*. You may even include *jus post bellum*.
*   It would be a good idea to consider examples of wars that you consider 'just', such as World War II.

b) How useful is the idea of justice when considering issues of war? (10 marks)

*   You could consider that Just War means that war is a last resort and that both sides should be considered in the conflict.
*   You could also argue that Just War limits the conflict and the number of dead, as well as who can be killed.
*   On the other hand you could look at the question of innocent civilians and ask who is actually innocent.
*   Additionally, you could look at weapons of mass destruction, of faulty intelligence about weapons, and take the realist position that there may not be a simple 'just' cause, but that the war may still be necessary.

SAMPLE AS EXAM STYLE QUESTIONS

a) Explain a Utilitarian approach to war.
b) 'Pacifism is immoral.' Discuss.

a) Explain how the ethics of the religion you have studied would approach the question of going to war.
b) 'Religious believers should be pacifists.' Discuss.

FURTHER READING

Anscombe, G.E.M. 'War and Murder' in *Moral Problems*, Palmer, M., Cambridge, Lutterworth Press, 1991.

Aquinas, Thomas. *Summa Theologiae II–II q.40* (Dominican translation), London, Burns & Oates, 1936.

Coates, A. *The Ethics of War*, Manchester, Manchester University Press, 1997.

Coppieters, B. and Fotion, N. (eds) *Moral Constraints on War*, New York/Oxford, Lexington Books, 2002.

Glover, J. *Humanity: A Moral History of the Twentieth Century*, New Haven, CT, Yale University Press, 2000.

Holmes, R. *On War and Morality*, Princeton, NJ, Princeton University Press, 1989.

Niebuhr, R. *Moral Man and Immoral Societies*, New York, Scribner, 1932.

Norman, R. *Ethics, Killing and War*, Cambridge, Cambridge University Press, 1995.

Rawls, J. *A Theory of Justice*, Harvard, MA, Harvard University Press, 1971.

Wilcockson, M. *Issues of Life and Death*, London, Hodder & Stoughton, 1999.

A2 ETHICS   PART II

11 Meta-ethics
The Language of Ethics

WHAT YOU WILL LEARN ABOUT IN THIS CHAPTER

*   How ethical language is used.
*   What different philosophers think is meant when people use words such as 'good' and 'bad'.
*   Whether morality is a matter of individual feelings or of reason.
*   Whether there are any objective moral truths.
*   The different theories of meta-ethics.
*   Ethical naturalism.
*   Naturalistic fallacy.
*   Intuitionism – G.E. Moore, H.A. Prichard, W.D. Ross.
*   Emotivism – A.J. Ayer, C.L. Stevenson.
*   Prescriptivism – R.M. Hare.

KEY SCHOLARS

*   H.A. Prichard (1871–1947)
*   G.E. Moore (1873–1958)
*   W.D. Ross (1877–1971)
*   C.L. Stevenson (1908–1979)
*   A.J. Ayer (1910–1989)
*   R. M. Hare (1919–2002)

THE OCR CHECKLIST

Candidates should be able to demonstrate knowledge and understanding of:

- the use of ethical language – the ways in which different scholars understand how words like 'good', 'bad', 'right', 'wrong' are used when ethical statements are made;
- how meta-ethics differs from normative ethics;
- the different approaches: cognitive and non-cognitive; ethical naturalism, intuitionism; emotivism and prescriptivism and how these apply to ethical statements.

Candidates should be able to discuss these areas critically and their strengths and weaknesses.

From OCR A Level Religious Studies Specification H572.

WHAT IS META-ETHICS?

Meta-ethics
The analysis of ethical language.

Normative ethics
A term used to describe different moral codes of behaviour; rules by which we make moral decisions (e.g. Utilitarianism, Natural Law, Kantian Ethics, Virtue Ethics).

The word 'meta' in Greek means 'above' or 'beyond'; thus **meta-ethics** goes further than ethical theories to look at what is meant by the terms used in ethics – what does the language mean? Many would say that if we do not know what we are talking about, there is no point to ethical debate.

Meta-ethics differs from **normative ethics**, which decides which things are good and bad and gives us a guide for moral behaviour. The theories of Natural Law, Utilitarianism and Kantian Ethics are examples of normative ethics. Meta-ethics is *about* normative ethics and tries to make sense of the terms and concepts used.

In the twentieth century philosophy was occupied almost totally (in 'analytic' anglophone philosophy at least) with an analysis of language and this dominated ethical discussion to the detriment of practical questions. It was even held that one cannot begin to discuss ethical theories without first understanding the terms used.

You often hear people say something is 'good' or 'bad' or 'right' or 'wrong' – but what do they mean? Are they simply expressing opinions or are they stating matters of fact? Can we really tell right from wrong? Many people would answer this by saying that stating what is believed to be right and wrong is essential for any discussion about our behaviour. If this were not the case then we could never have any *meaningful* discussion about morality. Thus for many people ethical language is about *facts* which are either right or wrong (e.g. 'Abortion is murder' may be seen to be either true or false). However, this may need to be qualified, as ethical language in expressing moral facts about the world is also interconnected with beliefs and feelings which often come before (e.g. 'Abortion is murder for Catholics because they believe in the sanctity of life' or 'Abortion is murder for Catholics because they believe the foetus is a person from conception and so abortion goes against Natural Law').

So we can see that ethical statements are not just about observable facts, but are often statements about what we believe should happen and so are not very easy to establish as true or false, as they may be expressions of points of view that are not shared by everyone. Part of the problem is that words such as 'good', 'bad', 'right', 'wrong', 'ought' are used in everyday life and are often just expressing opinions. In ethics, then, do we know something is good, or do we believe it is good and recognise that our belief is subjective? This is the question that philosophers of meta-ethics try to answer – can our ethical statements have any *meaning*?

Thought Point

What do we understand by 'mean' and 'meaning' when we use it in everyday language?

1   I mean to buy her a Valentine card.
2   I mean to win this race.
3   What is the meaning of life?
4   The convict looked really mean.
5   Those dark clouds mean it is going to rain.
6   Does 'good' mean socially approved?
7   Do you understand what I mean?

So, do ethical statements have meaning? The answers to this question vary. Some are *moral realists* and hold that moral facts are objective facts that are out there in the world. Things are good and bad independently of us. Moral values, such as kind and wicked, are real properties of people in the same way that rough and smooth are properties of physical objects. This view is closely related to **cognitive** language. According to **cognitivists**, moral statements describe the world. If I say that murder is wrong, then I have given to murder the property of wrongness – so my statement is *objectively* either true or false.

Ethical naturalism/ethical cognitivism
A theory that moral values can be derived from sense experience.

Ethical non-naturalism/ethical non-cognitivism
A theory that ethical statements cannot be derived from sense experience.

According to **non-cognitivists**, when someone makes a moral statement they are not describing the world, but expressing their feelings or telling people what to do. As non-cognitivists say that moral statements are not descriptive, they cannot be described as true or false – they are *subjective*.

Meta-ethics is not concerned with what the right or wrong action is in a particular circumstance, but with what it means to be moral.

COGNITIVE THEORIES OF META-ETHICS

Cognitivism is the view that we can have moral knowledge. People who hold cognitive theories about ethical language believe that ethical statements are about facts and can be proved true or false.

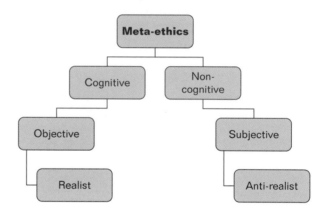

Ethical naturalism

This theory holds that all ethical statements are the same as non-ethical (natural) ones – they are all factual and can, therefore, be verified or falsified. So 'Thomas More was executed for his beliefs in 1535' and 'Thomas More was a good man' can both be proved true or false by looking at the evidence. The first statement is factual, and can be determined by looking at evidence: eyewitness accounts, death certificate and so on. The ethical naturalists would claim that we can do the same for the second statement by establishing if, in his personal behaviour, Thomas More was good, kind, unselfish, caring; or by looking at whether his actions had good consequences. If we find supporting evidence we can conclude that 'Thomas More was a good man' and, if not, then the statement is false. The same holds for any moral issue; if I want to know if euthanasia is right or wrong I simply look at the

Ethical naturalism
- Cognitive and objective
- Ethical and non-ethical statements are the same
- Ethical statements can be verified and falsified

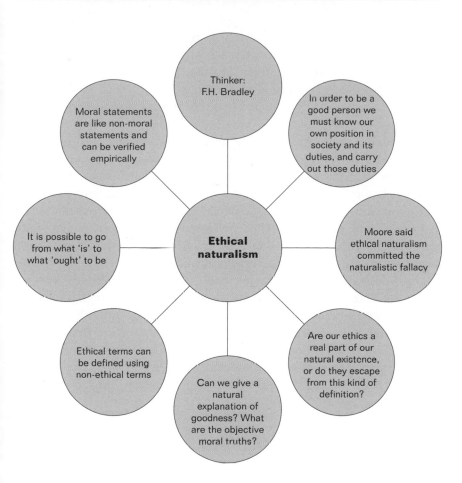

Moral statements are like non-moral statements and can be verified empirically

Thinker: F.H. Bradley

In order to be a good person we must know our own position in society and its duties, and carry out those duties

It is possible to go from what 'is' to what 'ought' to be

Ethical naturalism

Moore said ethical naturalism committed the naturalistic fallacy

Ethical terms can be defined using non-ethical terms

Can we give a natural explanation of goodness? What are the objective moral truths?

Are our ethics a real part of our natural existence, or do they escape from this kind of definition?

evidence so that I can *test* the veracity of the statement. Thus I could argue that euthanasia ends the suffering of an individual; therefore euthanasia is right.

Criticisms of ethical naturalism – the naturalistic fallacy

In *Principia Ethica* (1903) **G.E. Moore** argued against ethical naturalism and called the attempt to identify goodness with a natural quality a mistake. He said that to claim that moral statements can be verified or falsified using evidence is to commit the **naturalistic fallacy**. He based his argument on David Hume, who thinks that to derive an 'ought' from an 'is' is logically invalid:

> I cannot forbear adding to these reasonings an observation, which may, perhaps, be found of some importance. In every system of morality, which I have hitherto met with, I have always remarked, that the author proceeds for some time in the ordinary way of reasoning . . . when of a

Naturalistic fallacy
The claim that good cannot be defined.

sudden I am surpriz'd to find that instead of the usual copulations of propositions, *is* and *is not*, I meet with no proposition that is not connected with an *ought*, or an *ought not*. This change is imperceptible, but is however, of the last consequence.

(Hume, *Treatise of Human Nature*, [1740] 2004)

We cannot, he says, infer from a description of how the world *is* to how the world *ought* to be. Moore used what has become known as the 'open question argument'. For any natural property, it always makes sense to ask 'Is it good?' and the fact that we can even ask this question shows that 'good' and 'bad' cannot be the names of natural properties in the way that 'rough' and 'smooth' are. Thus, for instance, if we claim that happiness is a naturally good thing we could always ask 'Is happiness good?', but if happiness is naturally good this question would make no more sense than asking 'Does happiness make people happy?' However, it does make sense and so we have to conclude that goodness is not a property of happiness. If we say 'Mother Teresa helped the dying' or 'Martin Luther King, Jr. led the civil rights movement' it is still all right to ask 'Were those actions good?' There is still a possibility of people having different opinions, so moving from a factual objective statement to an ethical statement of values does not work because it leaves an open question that has not been answered.

However, Moore himself did believe there were moral properties and his response to this difficulty was to say that goodness is a 'non-natural' property which is indefinable.

Intuitionism – G.E. Moore

G.E. Moore said that good is a simple, unanalysable property, just as a primary colour is. Moore adapted a version of Utilitarianism in that he said that right acts are those that produce the most good, but he said that goodness cannot be identified with some natural property such as pleasure: goodness cannot be defined.

> If I am asked 'What is good?' my answer is that good is good, and that is the end of the matter. Or if I am asked 'How is good to be defined?' my answer is that it cannot be defined, and that is all I have to say about it.
> (Moore, *Principia Ethica*)

Moore said we cannot use our senses to tell whether something is good, but we can use our 'moral intuition' and so we can still say whether a moral statement is true or false. We recognise goodness when we see it – we just

---

G.E. Moore (1873–1958)

Moore was a philosopher and professor whose approach to ethical problems and philosophy made him an important British thinker. His major work was the *Principia Ethica* published in 1903. He was born into an evangelical family but became an agnostic. He was a leading member of the Bloomsbury Group, with John Keynes, Virginia Woolf and E.M. Forster. He believed that 'good' could be understood directly and became known as an 'ethical intuitionist'. He believed that any other attempt to decide what was 'good' failed because of the 'naturalistic fallacy'.

Intuitionism

A theory that moral truths are known by intuition.

A field of yellow sunflowers

know if something is good. Moore called this a 'simple notion' and explained it by saying it is rather like trying to define the colour yellow – just as we cannot explain what 'yellow' is by means of definition, but only by showing someone an example, so likewise we can only explain what goodness is:

> We know what 'yellow' is and can recognise it whenever it is seen, but we cannot actually define yellow. In the same way, we know what good is but we cannot actually define it.
>
> (Moore, *Principia Ethica*)

Intuitionism – H.A. Prichard

Prichard discusses the moral claim 'ought' by saying that no definition can be given to this word, but, like Moore's idea about 'good', we all recognise its properties – everyone recognises when we ought to do a certain action, so moral obligations are obvious. Prichard thought there were two types of thinking – reason and intuition. Reason looks at the facts of a situation and intuition decides what to do. In any situation, Prichard thought that intuition would show which particular action was right and where our moral obligation lay.

He did, however, recognise the problem that people's morals were different, but said this was because some people had developed their moral

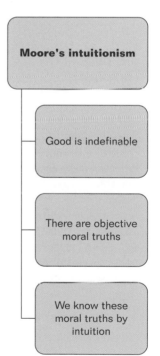

Moore's intuitionism

Good is indefinable

There are objective moral truths

We know these moral truths by intuition

thinking further than others. Prichard does not explain why, nor does he attempt to list any fundamental obligations or moral virtues. Where there is a conflict of obligations he simply says we must look at the situation and decide which obligation is greater. However, according to Prichard, it would seem that intuition would not be something that everyone could use to prove goodness.

Intuitionism – W.D. Ross

Ross fleshed out the bare bones of intuitionism found in Prichard, and, while acknowledging his debt to Moore and Prichard and agreeing that 'right' and 'obligatory' are as indefinable as 'good', he was a deontologist, arguing that it was obvious that certain types of actions, which he called prima facie duties, were right. In any particular situation we would come to recognise certain prima facie duties. Ross listed seven classes of prima facie duties:

1 duties of fidelity (e.g. promise-keeping)
2 duties of reparation – when we have done something wrong
3 duties of gratitude
4 duties of justice
5 duties of beneficence – helping others
6 duties of self-improvement
7 duties of non-maleficence – not harming others.

Ross says that when these prima facie duties conflict, we must follow the one we think is right in the situation, and sometimes one prima facie duty will have to give way to another – that is why Ross called them prima facie duties: they are duties at first sight.

However, Ross still does not tell us how we know what a prima facie duty actually is or how to decide which one to obey in cases of conflict. It seems that Ross would say that this depends on a person's moral maturity – they do not know self-evident truths and intuition has deserted them.

Criticisms of intuitionism

This idea of knowing what is good by intuition and not by any empirical evidence is not proved conclusively by Moore – he says you either agree with him or you have not thought about it properly. However, it would seem that if the naturalistic fallacy shows that you cannot infer value judgements from

---

Prichard's intuitionism

- Obligations are as indefinable as good

- Intuition decides what to do in a situation

- Some people's intuition is better developed than others'

H.A. Prichard (1871–1947)

Prichard was a leading member of the Oxford School of Moral Philosophy. This argued that moral values are ultimate and are known through intuition. His main works were *Kant's Theory of Knowledge* (1909), *Duty and Interest* (1928), *Moral Obligation* (1949), and *Knowledge and Perception* (1950).

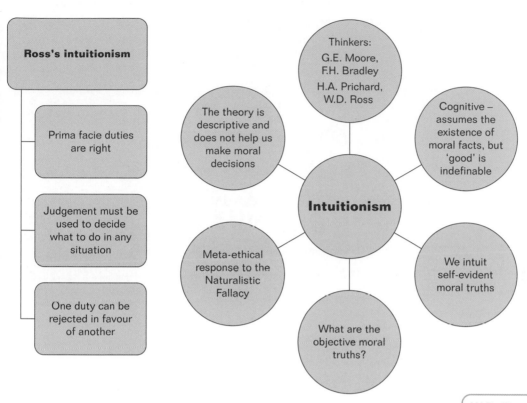

Ross's intuitionism

- Prima facie duties are right
- Judgement must be used to decide what to do in any situation
- One duty can be rejected in favour of another

Thinkers:
G.E. Moore,
F.H. Bradley
H.A. Prichard,
W.D. Ross

The theory is descriptive and does not help us make moral decisions

Intuitionism

Cognitive – assumes the existence of moral facts, but 'good' is indefinable

Meta-ethical response to the Naturalistic Fallacy

We intuit self-evident moral truths

What are the objective moral truths?

natural facts by means of evidence obtained through the senses, then the introduction of 'non-natural' facts and a special 'intuition' simply shrouds the whole issue in mystery. Some recent philosophers, such as virtue ethicists, say it is our emotions and practical wisdom that give us this intuitive knowledge.

In addition, how can we be sure that intuitions are correct, since people may come to different conclusions, whether using intuition or reason to reach their decisions. As sense experience cannot be used, how can we decide between our intuitions? If they contradict each other, both cannot be right, but they will be right for the person whose intuition tells him what to do. We can never know which intuition is true or false, as we do not all recognise goodness intuitively in the same way. Moral intuitions seem to come largely from social conditioning and differ between cultures, so it is hard to see how such intuitions can be a reliable guide to objective ethical truths.

W.D. Ross (1877–1971)

Ross was a Scottish philosopher whose most famous work is *The Right and the Good* (1930). Ross agreed with Moore about the naturalistic fallacy but said that Moore's own theories also failed by the same fallacy. He argued that maximising good was just one of the obligations which led to the moral 'ought' in any particular instance. He said that there could never be one true ethical dilemma because one obligation would always outweigh the others.

Study hint

As you work through this chapter complete the diagram on p. 193 which has been started for you here. Use a large piece of A3 paper and colour-code the different ways of looking at meta-ethics.

Thought Point

1   According to ethical naturalists how do we know what is good?
2   Explain the naturalistic fallacy.
3   Show how Prichard and Ross build on the work of Moore.
4   Use the intuitionism of Prichard and Ross to argue whether one should give money to a man begging in the street.
5   Does intuitionism mean that there is no absolute idea of what is good?
6   Critically examine the strengths and weaknesses of intuitionism.

NON-COGNITIVE THEORIES OF META-ETHICS

Non-cognitivism says that there is no ethical knowledge, because ethical statements are not statements that can be proved true or false. Thus to say 'Euthanasia is wrong' is not a statement about facts, but some other kind of saying. Non-cognitivists make a distinction between facts and values.

Emotivism – A.J. Ayer

Emotivists take a completely different view on moral statements and start from the premise that there is no ethical knowledge because ethical judge-

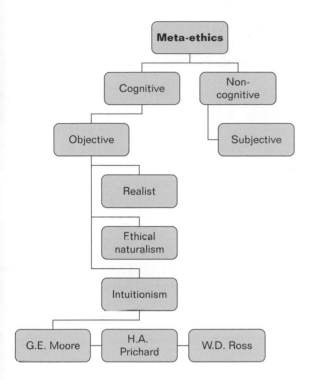

**A.J. Ayer
(1910–1989)**

Ayer first encountered logical positivism while staying in Vienna in 1932. His most important work was *Language, Truth and Logic* (1936). He developed his ideas from the Vienna Circle and also from the work of Hume, Mill and Moore. He argued that empirical truth could only be understood through linguistic analysis, and that unverifiable statements were 'nonsense' and without any philosophical significance.

ments are not the kinds of statements that can be true or false. Emotivism will not tell you how to live a moral life, but simply helps us understand moral statements: as action guiding and as conveying certain attitudes. A.J. Ayer said: 'ethical terms do not serve only to express feelings. They are calculated also to arouse feeling, and so to stimulate action.'

However, this view needs to be examined closely: it says that when we talk about 'good' and 'bad', 'right' and 'wrong', we are simply expressing emotional states of approval and disapproval. Any other interpretation of ethical statements is meaningless. Emotivism has its roots in the *Vienna Circle*, a group of philosophers in the 1920s who developed a theory called **logical positivism** which holds roughly that any truth claim must be tested by sense experience (the *verification principle*). Ethical statements cannot be tested by sense experience, so they are not genuine truth claims and can only express feelings.

A.J. Ayer in his book *Language, Truth and Logic*, published in 1936 when he was just 26 years old, stated briefly that there are only two kinds of meaningful statements:

1   **analytic statements** – the truth or falsity of the statement can be determined simply by understanding the terms that occur in them (e.g. 'all bachelors are unmarried men'). Examples of analytic statements are statements of mathematics or logic.

Logical positivitism
The view that only those things which can be tested are meaningful.

Analytic statements
Statements which are true by definition.

Synthetic statements
Statements that can be true or false and can be tested using experience or senses.

Emotivism
A theory which says that moral statements are just expressions of feelings.

2   **synthetic statements** – the truth or falsity of the statement can be determined by checking to establish the facts either way. Examples of synthetic statements are statements of science, history and ordinary life.

Ethical statements are not verifiable – there are no empirical facts which can be checked to see if any ethical statement is true or false – so they are meaningless. The only way they can be understood is as an expression of feelings. Ayer's theory of ethical language is known as **emotivism**, as it is simply an expression of feeling of approval or disapproval. Emotivism is sometimes known as the *Boo/Hurrah theory* as in saying 'murder is wrong' we are saying 'boo to murder', and in saying 'giving to charity is good' we are saying 'hurrah for giving to charity':

> The presence of an ethical symbol in a proposition adds nothing to its factual content. Thus if I say to someone, 'You acted wrongly in stealing that money,' I am not saying anything more than if I had simply said, 'You stole that money.' In adding that this action is wrong I am not making any further statement about it. I am simply evincing my moral disapproval of it. It is as if I had said, 'You stole that money,' in a peculiar tone of horror, or written it with the addition of some special exclamation marks.
>
> (Ayer, *Language, Truth and Logic*)

A word such as 'steal' invokes feelings about what happened – it is an interpretation of the event.

Emotivism does show how the ethical statements we make can depend on our own attitudes, upbringing and feelings, and this can lead emotivism to be criticised as 'simple subjectivism'. James Rachels said that it can lead to the notion that: 'Where morality is concerned, there are no "facts" and no one is "right".' However, although Ayer does argue that ethical statements have no factual content, he does not believe they have no meaningful function. Emotivism cannot be compared to normative ethical theories, and it does not give any reason why one person's feelings should be any better than another's, or why one person's feelings should stimulate a person to action rather than those of another person. It simply reduces ethical statements to the level of 'I think orange Smarties are best' and so they are simply meaningless.

Emotivism – C.L. Stevenson

C.L. Stevenson gave a more detailed version of emotivism in his book *Ethics and Language* (1944). Stevenson did not use the verification principle, but discussed the emotive meaning of words – many moral terms (e.g. 'honesty',

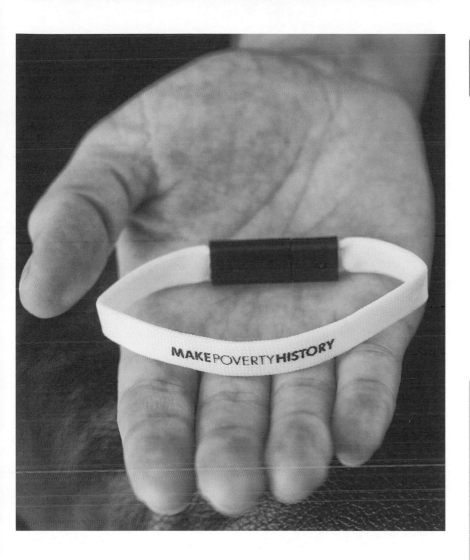

Emotivism – Ayer

Words like 'good' are meaningless

Ethical statements are just expressions of feeling

Ethical statements cannot be validated

C.L. Stevenson (1908–1979)

Stevenson was an American. He was a professor at Yale and then at Michigan. He studied in England with Wittgenstein and G.E. Moore. He developed a theory of emotivism which he used as a foundation for his theory of a persuasive definition. He argued that emotivism as a meta-ethical theory marked out the difference between cognitive, scientific language and non-cognitive language. His defence of emotivism is found in *The Emotive Meaning of Ethical Terms* (1937), *Persuasive Definitions* (1938) and *Ethics and Language* (1944).

'respect', 'steal', 'murder') are both descriptive and emotive, expressing also what we feel about them. So when an individual is making a moral judgement he is not only giving vent to his feelings; he is also trying to influence others' attitudes. Emotivism connects 'caring', 'approving', 'disapproving' with the very meaning of the ethical words. This does mean that ethical statements can be based on emotions; however, these are not merely arbitrary, but rather are based on our experience of the world and how we want it to be.

As Stephenson saw ethical statements as not only expressions of emotion, but also the result of attitudes based on fundamental beliefs, ethical disagreements between people are disagreements about fundamental principles.

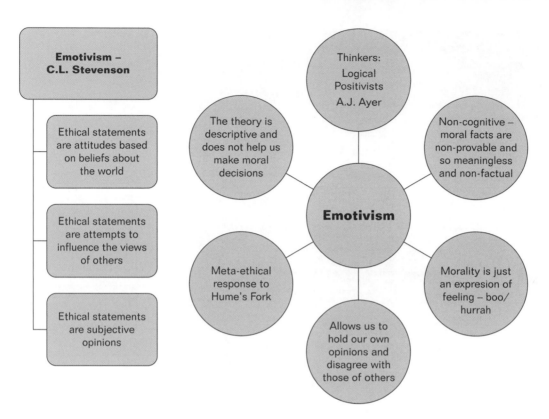

Emotivism – C.L. Stevenson

- Ethical statements are attitudes based on beliefs about the world
- Ethical statements are attempts to influence the views of others
- Ethical statements are subjective opinions

Emotivism

- Thinkers: Logical Positivists A.J. Ayer
- Non-cognitive – moral facts are non-provable and so meaningless and non-factual
- Morality is just an expresion of feeling – boo/ hurrah
- Allows us to hold our own opinions and disagree with those of others
- Meta-ethical response to Hume's Fork
- The theory is descriptive and does not help us make moral decisions

Criticisms of emotivism

When criticising emotivism, it is important to remember that it does not purport to be an ethical theory, but is simply an analysis of the nature and content of ethical language. It starts from the basis of logical positivism and so removes any factual content from ethical language and does not discuss 'ethical facts'.

However, as Rachels points out, moral judgements appeal to reason; they are not just expressions of feeling. So whereas the statement 'I like orange Smarties' needs no reason, moral judgements do, or else they are arbitrary.

Ayer does suggest that ethical statements are more than simply expressions of feeling, but that they have the intention to stimulate others to act in the way they feel is right. This is developed further by Stevenson, who asks: why should one person's feelings about a matter be any better than those of another? All emotivism can do is draw attention to the reasons why people have different views and then let others decide. It has been shown in history that stimulating people to act through powerful and emotive speeches can have some unfortunate results (e.g. Hitler).

Emotivism may be seen as allowing complete freedom of action on the grounds that everyone's opinion is equally valid and so everyone can do as they like.

Prescriptivism – R.M. Hare

Both Ayer and Stevenson based their views on the distinction between facts and values, which Hume (Hume's Fork) had already claimed made it impossible to deduce a prescriptive statement (an 'ought') from a descriptive statement (an 'is'). Hare attacked this distinction and attempted to show that ethical language is essentially **prescriptive**; the role of ethical statements is to say what *ought* to be done and such prescriptions are moral because they are *universal*.

Hare argues that universal prescriptivism gives a better account of the nature of ethical statements than naturalist, intuitionist or emotivist meta-ethical theories. These theories try to explain what we are doing when we make ethical judgements: are we trying to state truths? If so, what kind of truths? Are we just expressing our emotions? Are we suggesting a course of action? Or are we doing something different? All the philosophers we have looked at saw these questions as closely linked to the meanings of ethical terms. Hare says that although these approaches are useful, universal prescriptivism is superior. It says 'You ought to do this', and means that everyone should do the same in similar situations. Ethical statements are prescriptive, which means they do not state facts and are not true or false, but they express our will or wishes; in other words they are like imperatives.

Hare argues that however we use the word 'good', we always do so in relation to a set of standards:

- A good chair is one that supports your back, is comfortable and fit for the purpose.
- A good car again varies, depending on whether it is a family car or a sports car.
- A good person is someone we should try to emulate.

This means that the word 'good' always has a *descriptive* meaning.

If we use the word 'good' in a moral sense, again we are using a set of standards that apply to a person or an action and we commend that person or that action. This means that the word 'good' also has a prescriptive meaning. This can happen with any words that both commend and describe, such as 'steal' and 'murder'. Hare, like the emotivists, is saying that there is a difference between the descriptive meaning and the prescriptive meaning, and when we use words with an ethical meaning we use them prescriptively: 'Stealing is wrong' really means 'You ought not to steal and neither will I.' Prescriptivism holds that, to achieve consistency in moral judgements, when we say that someone else ought to do something, we ought to do it as well. For prescriptivism we are not only saying 'Boo to stealing'; we can say that stealing is wrong as we would not prescribe it for ourselves.

Prescriptivism

A theory that ethical statements have an intrinsic sense so other people should agree with the statement and follow it.

R.M. Hare (1919–2002)

Hare was influenced by A.J. Ayer and C.L. Stevenson, as well as Wittgenstein, Utilitarianism and Kant. He believed that ethical rules should not be based on utility. He used many ideas from Kant, particularly the idea of universalisability; however, his arguments were still consequentialist rather than those of a deontologist. In *The Language of Morals* and *Freedom and Reason*, Hare outlined a theory that he called universal prescriptivism: moral terms such as 'good', 'ought' and 'right' are universalisable and prescriptive. He argued that the combination of universalisability and prescriptivity led to a form of consequentialism, namely Preference Utilitarianism.

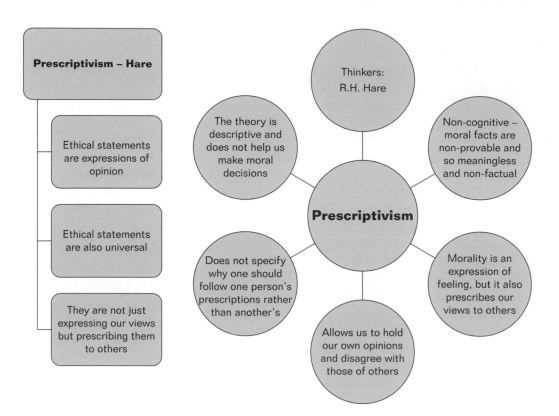

Criticisms of prescriptivism

If moral judgements are founded on prescriptions, this still does not mean that there is a valid reason for following one person's prescriptions rather than another's. It does not necessarily mean that morals are universal, as one person's preferences may be different from those of another. Hare recognised this problem in Chapter 6 of *Freedom and Reason* (1963), where he admitted that the fanatic who prescribed that all people of a certain race be exterminated could be making a moral judgement according to his theory. The only constraint is that one should put oneself 'in another's shoes' before making the judgement and, as the terrorism and suicide bombings of the twenty-first century show, this does not stop the fanatic.

Prescriptivism says that 'ought' judgements are universalisable pre-scriptives or imperatives and not truth claims – they are not objective and there is no moral knowledge or moral truth. This goes against the way people approach ethics in their daily lives – in general people do think it is wrong to steal, lie, kill the innocent, rape and so on. According to Hare, we could just as easily choose the opposite if we wished and we could change our moral principles as we choose or as our circumstances alter.

Thought Point

1   What does it mean to say that ethical language is about feelings, not facts?
2   Why does Ayer reject the idea that good is indefinable?
3   How does Stevenson see moral language as influencing action?
4   What is the difference between descriptive and prescriptive meaning?
5   What are the differences between emotivism and prescriptivism?

REVIEW QUESTIONS

Look back over the chapter and check that you can answer the following questions. (You could also use Harry Gensler's web exercises. The address is given at the end of this chapter under Further reading.)

1   What is meant by the word meta-ethics?
2   Explain one cognitive theory of meta-ethics.
3   Explain the views of G.E. Moore.
4   Explain Ross's intuitionism.
5   Explain one non-cognitive theory of meta-ethics.
6   Explain emotivism.
7   What is prescriptivism?
8   Complete the meta-ethics mind map from memory.

Terminology

Do you know your terminology?

Try to explain the following key words without looking at your books and notes:

- Meta-ethics
- Analytic statements
- Synthetic statements
- Emotivism
- Ethical naturalism
- Intuitionism
- Prescriptivism
- Cognitive
- Non-cognitive

Examination Questions Practice

Remember: each question assesses AO1 and AO2. To help you improve your answers look at the A2 Levels of Response. See: http://www.ocr.org.uk/qualifications/as-a-level-gce-religious-studies-h172-h572/.

SAMPLE EXAM STYLE QUESTION

- **'Ethical language is meaningless.' Discuss.** (35 marks)

- In your answer you would need to consider what is meant by the word meaningless according to the approaches of cognitivists and non-cognitivists, realists and anti-realists.
- You would need to consider whether moral statements can be described as true or false, and whether they are objective or subjective.

- You would then need to analyse the views of the different scholars on this question and whether 'meaning' means the same to all of them. The question could be argued either way, and you may wish to compare ethical language with other forms of language.

SAMPLE A2 EXAM STYLE QUESTIONS

- **To what extent is ethical language meaningful?**
- **'Terms such as "right" and "wrong" are no more than expressions of opinion.' Discuss.**

- **'"Good" always means the same thing.' Discuss.**

FURTHER READING

Ahluwalia, L. *Foundation for the Study of Religion*, London, Hodder & Stoughton Educational, 2001.
Ayer, A.J. *Language, Truth and Logic*, London, Penguin [1936], 2001.
Gensler, H. *Ethics: A Contemporary Introduction*, New York/London, Routledge, 1998.
Gensler, H., Earl, W. and Swindal, J. *Ethics: Contemporary Readings*, New York/London, Routledge, 2004 (see also his website for good multiple-choice exercises to check understanding and knowledge at http://www.harryhiker.com/exercise.htm).
Hare, R.M. *Freedom and Reason*, London, Clarendon Press, 1963.
Hare, R.M. *The Language of Morals*, Oxford, Oxford University Press, 1952.
Palmer, M. *Moral Problems*, Cambridge, Lutterworth Press, 1991 (see the appendix for meta-ethics).
Pojman, L.P. *Ethics: Discovering Right and Wrong*, Toronto, Wadsworth, 2002.
Ross, W.D. *The Right and the Good*, Oxford, Clarendon Press, 1930.
Stevenson, C.L. *Ethics and Language*, Oxford, Oxford University Press, 1945.

12 Virtue Ethics

Essential terminology

Aretaic ethics
Cardinal Virtues
Eudaimonia
Golden Mean
Intellectual virtues
Moral virtues
Phronesis (practical
    wisdom)
Vices
Virtue

WHAT YOU WILL LEARN ABOUT IN THIS CHAPTER

- The principles of Virtue Ethics from Aristotle.
- Modern forms of Virtue theory from Anscombe, Foot, MacIntyre, Hursthouse and Slote.
- Feminism and Virtue Ethics.
- The strengths and weaknesses of Virtue Ethics.
- How to apply Virtue theory to ethical dilemmas.

KEY SCHOLARS

- Plato (428–347 BCE)
- Aristotle (384–322 BCE)
- Thomas Aquinas (1225–1274)
- G.E.M. Anscombe (1919–2001)
- Philippa Foot (1920–2010)
- Julia Annas (1946–)

- Annette Baier (1929–2012)
- Alasdair MacIntyre (1929–)
- Michael Slote (1941–)
- Robert Louden (1953–)
- Rosalind Hursthouse (1943–)

THE OCR CHECKLIST

Candidates should be able to demonstrate knowledge and understanding of:

- the principles of Virtue Ethics from Aristotle;
- the 'agent-centred' nature of Virtue Ethics;

- the concepts of *eudaimonia* and the Golden Mean;
- the importance of practising the virtues and the example of virtuous people;
- more modern approaches to Virtue Ethics.

Candidates should be able to discuss these areas critically and their strengths and weaknesses.

From OCR A Level Religious Studies Specification H572.

WHAT IS VIRTUE ETHICS?

Virtue Ethics goes back to Plato and Aristotle and does not focus on actions being right or wrong, but on how to be a good person. It looks at what makes a good person and the qualities or virtues that make them good. Virtue Ethics *is agent-centred* morality rather than act-centred – it asks 'What sort of person ought I to be?' rather than 'How ought I to act?'

Our word 'virtue' sounds rather old-fashioned and religious, but the Greek word for virtue, *arete*, means excellence. So a virtuous person is one who does things excellently all the time. As we saw in Chapter 3 on Natural Law, a knife has excellence when it cuts sharply – *arete* is not only about people.

Virtue Ethics was re-examined and redeveloped in the twentieth century.

PLATO AND VIRTUE

Plato's moral theory is not one of judging particular actions. It centres around the achievement of man's highest good, which involves the right cultivation of his soul (inner well-being) and the harmonious well-being of his life (***eudaimonia*** or happiness). Happiness must be attained through the pursuit of **virtue** and actions are good when they help to achieve this. Plato seemed to consider certain virtues central: temperance, courage, prudence and justice (later called the **Cardinal Virtues**). Plato thought that when these virtues are in balance a person's actions will be good. However, there was not agreement among the Greek philosophers about which virtues were central, and Aristotle gives a very different account of the virtues.

Virtue Ethics

- Who am I?
- Who ought I to become?
- How do I get there?

Eudaimonia
The final goal of all human activity – happiness, well-being, human flourishing.

Virtue
Habitually doing what is right – being good requires the practice of a certain kind of behaviour.

Cardinal Virtues
Originated in Plato – prudence, justice, temperance, courage. Added to with three theological virtues of faith, hope and charity.

ARISTOTLE AND VIRTUE

Aristotle sought to give an account of the structure of morality and explained that the point of engaging in ethics is to become good:

> For we are enquiring not in order to know what virtue is but in order to become good since otherwise our enquiry would be of no use.
>
> (*Nichomachean Ethics*, Book 1, ch. 2)

Aristotle distinguishes between things which are good as means (for the sake of something else) and things which are good as ends (for their own sake only). He sees one final and overriding end of human activity, one final good – *eudaimonia* or happiness, human flourishing. Aristotle discusses the character traits of a person who is going to achieve *eudaimonia*.

Aristotle's ethical theory is known as **Virtue Ethics** or **Aretaic ethics** because at the centre of his description of the good are the virtues which shape human character and ultimately human behaviour. He suggests that human well-being and human flourishing is a life characterised by the virtues. However, this good human life is one lived in *harmony* and *co-operation* with other people, since Aristotle saw people as not only rational beings but also as social beings. We live in groups (e.g. family, school, village) and he saw the well-being of the group as more important than that of a single member.

Aretaic ethics
Another name for Virtue Ethics, from the Greek word *arete*, which simply means any kind of excellence or virtue.

Acquiring virtues

Aristotle saw two types of virtues:

1 **intellectual virtues** developed by training and education
2 **moral virtues** developed by habit.

Aristotle compares the virtues to skills acquired through *practice* and *habit*. Aristotle writes:

Intellectual virtues
Characteristics of thought and reason – technical skill, scientific knowledge, prudence, intelligence and wisdom.

> We acquire virtues by first doing virtuous acts. We acquire a skill by practising the activities involved in the skill. For example, we become builders by building, we learn to play the harp by playing the harp. In the same way we become just by doing just acts, temperate by doing temperate acts and courageous by doing acts of courage.
>
> (*Nichomachean Ethics*, Book 2, ch.1)

Moral virtues
Qualities of character such as courage, friendliness, truthfulness.

To become virtuous then is rather like playing a musical instrument – it needs teaching and practice before it is possible to play well. We are all

capable of being virtuous and need to get into the habit of acting virtuously from childhood so that we enjoy being virtuous. However, Aristotle believed that while all people have the potential to develop moral and intellectual virtues, only a few will actually achieve this – for Aristotle these were the gentlemen philosophers and today we could say that this depends in part on *social factors*: where we are brought up and the environment in which we live.

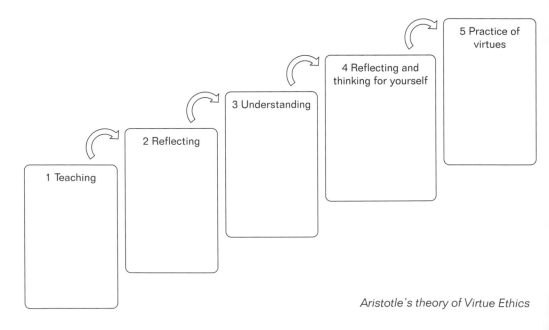

1 Teaching

2 Reflecting

3 Understanding

4 Reflecting and thinking for yourself

5 Practice of virtues

Aristotle's theory of Virtue Ethics

Aristotle saw that a person who achieved *eudaimonia* was someone who used their **reason** well. He saw reason as the supreme human virtue, but by this he did not only mean an ability to think, but also a moral sense – reason included putting into action what you used your reason to judge as good. Reason is *practical* and involves both *understanding* and *responding*.

The Golden Mean (Doctrine of the Mean)

Virtue is to be found in the **Golden Mean**, which involves finding the balance between two means – this is the best way to live in society, as extremes of character are unhelpful (people who are too timid or too assertive can cause problems). Aristotle always said that virtue is to be found between two **vices**, each of which involves either an excess or a deficiency of the true virtue (e.g. courage is the mean – a coward does not have enough courage and the foolhardy just runs into danger).

Vice of deficiency	Virtuous mean	Vice of excess
cowardice	courage	rashness
shamelessness	modesty	shyness
malicious enjoyment	righteous indignation	jealousy
servility	proper self-love	arrogance

Aristotle said that the difference between virtue and vice in both emotions and action was a matter of *balance* and extremes. However, the mean is not the same for everyone and depends on circumstance – you need to apply *phronesis* (practical wisdom) to decide on the right course of action in each situation. *Phronesis* is acquired as we grow up and move away from rules and the demands of authority figures to a more autonomous, person-centred and virtue-centred morality.

The example of virtuous people

As virtue is acquired through *doing,* one way to learn how to be virtuous is to follow the example of virtuous people. Most of us learn how to do things by watching others and imitating them. The lives of Socrates, Jesus, Gandhi, Martin Luther King, Jr., Nelson Mandela and so on give us possible examples of moral excellence. They are not all 'perfect people' but they challenge us to go beyond the minimum, to aspire to 'moral heights' and to see what can be achieved.

Golden Mean
The balance of extremes of virtues and vices. A balance between *excess* (having too much of something) and *deficiency* (having too little of something).

Vices
The direct opposite of virtues – habitual wrong action.

Phronesis
(practical wisdom)
According to Aristotle the virtue most needed for any other virtue to be developed. Balancing self-interest with that of others. Needs to be directed by the moral virtues.

Nelson Mandela

There are many novels and films that show what happens when characters are destructive, such as Darth Vader in *Star Wars* or Dr Octopus in *Spiderman 2*, who sell out to the dark side and warn us of the consequences of losing our own integrity.

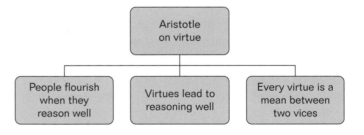

Aristotle on virtue

People flourish when they reason well

Virtues lead to reasoning well

Every virtue is a mean between two vices

Thought Point

1   The following is a list of virtues that lie in the mean between two vices. Write down what you think would be the vice of excess and the vice of deficiency for each one:

- responsible
- honest
- forgiving
- compassionate
- patient

2   What virtues do you think are most important in the world today and what are their corresponding vices?
3   How does Aristotle's approach to ethics differ from other ethical theories you have learnt?
4   Does the Golden Mean imply that Aristotle supports mediocre people who do not take risks?
5   Aristotle implies that being virtuous depends a little on upbringing, environment and so on. Do you agree?

MODERN VIRTUE ETHICS

In the twentieth century there was a revival of interest in Virtue Ethics by philosophers who were unhappy with act-centred ethical theories. Modern versions of Virtue Ethics argue that the assessment of a person's character is an important aspect of our ethical thought and needs to be included in any ethical theory.

G.E.M. Anscombe and Virtue Ethics

In 1958 **G.E.M. Anscombe** published a paper called 'Modern Moral Philosophy' and put forward the idea that modern moral philosophy is misguided, asking if there can be any moral laws if there is no God – what do right and wrong mean without a lawgiver? She suggests an answer in the idea of *eudaimonia,* human flourishing, which does not depend on any God.

Both Kantian Ethics and Utilitarianism do not depend on God, but they are still act-based and ignore the person who acts. She also thought that act-based ethics does not make sense because it ignores a belief people no longer hold, and in stressing the principle of autonomy it neglects the community aspect of morality.

> **G.E.M. Anscombe (1919–2001)**
>
> Anscombe was a close friend of Ludwig Wittgenstein. She taught at Oxford and Chicago, and then took the Chair of Philosophy at Cambridge. She became a Catholic in 1940. In analysing actions she stressed reasons rather than causes and argued for a return to Aristotle's idea of virtue.

Philippa Foot and Virtue Ethics

Philippa Foot attempted to modernise Aristotle's Virtue Ethics while still keeping the Aristotelian understanding of character and virtue. She recognised the importance of the person's own reasoning in the practice of virtue, claimed that virtues benefit the individual by leading to flourishing, and stressed that the virtuous person does far more than conform to the conventions of society. Foot argued that a virtue does not operate as a virtue when turned to a bad end (e.g. when someone needs daring to commit a murder). Virtues are good for us and also help us to correct harmful human passions and temptations.

Alasdair MacIntyre and Virtue Ethics

In his book *After Virtue*, **Alasdair MacIntyre** claims that ethical theories have simply resulted in ethical disagreements. The result of this, he claims, is that people do not think there are any moral truths and consider one opinion to be as good as any other opinion. MacIntyre argues that most people's attitudes today are based on *emotivism* – moral statements are neither true nor false but simply express the feelings and attitudes of the speaker. He says that people often speak and act as if emotivism was true (racism is wrong: 'boo to racism', tolerance is right: 'hurrah for tolerance'). Do you agree with MacIntyre that 'people now think and act as if emotivism were true'?

MacIntyre looked at what has happened to ethical thought through history and concluded that the Age of Enlightenment, which gave rise to theories such as Utilitarianism and Kantianism, had lost sight of the idea of morality being people's achieving their true *telos* – function or purpose. MacIntyre wants to restore the idea that morality should be seen in terms of human purpose, but he thought it would not be possible to restore Aristotle's theory of function and so he attempts to make human function, and so human virtue, depend on community. It is the shared practices of a community which help cultivate virtues. These virtues improve and evolve through time; there is a difference between the Homeric virtues such as strength, courage and honour, the Aristotelian virtues such as courage, justice and temperance, and the Christian virtues outlined by Aquinas. **James Keenan** suggests prudence, justice, fidelity, self-care and mercy. **James Rachels** suggests courage, honesty and loyalty to support friendship. For MacIntyre virtues are 'any virtues which sustain the households and communities in which men and women seek for good together'. MacIntyre opposes much of the individualism of today.

Rosalind Hursthouse and Virtue Ethics

Rosalind Hursthouse has a very Aristotelian framework for her Virtue Ethics, even though she does not agree with all of Aristotle's conclusions. Hursthouse defends a version of Virtue Ethics which claims that virtues are virtues because they help a person achieve *eudaimonia*, and so living a virtuous life is a *good* thing for a human being. Like **Julia Annas** she sees the virtues as shaping the virtuous person's practical reasoning in characteristic ways, and not simply as shaping that person's attitudes or actions. For Hursthouse, being virtuous is the most reliable path to flourishing and she seems to think that no other path is as reliable. She also attempts to address the major criticism of Virtue Ethics that it provides no guidance in moral dilemmas – not in telling us how a virtuous person would act, but by showing how a virtuous person would think about a moral dilemma.

> **Rosalind Hursthouse (1943–)**
>
> Rosalind Hursthouse is Professor of Philosophy at the University of Auckland, New Zealand, and is known for her work in Virtue Ethics. As well as theoretical work on Virtue Ethics, she has also written about the ethical treatment of animals in *Ethics, Humans and Other Animals* (2000).

Michael Slote and Virtue Ethics

Michael Slote describes Virtue Ethics as being mostly based on our common-sense ideas and intuitions about what counts as a virtue, and prefers to use the word 'admirable' to describe an action, rather than 'good' or 'excellent' which need qualifying and explaining. He sees the opposite as a 'deplorable' action, which can mean both foolish and careless and morally blameworthy actions. He describes virtue as 'an inner trait or disposition of the individual', so a virtue is a kind of balanced caring between those who are close to us, namely family and friends, and people in general. He goes on to say that morally admirable caring could, in some way, copy the sort of love we have for those to whom we are close and will always express balanced caring. However, Slote's view does seem to allow a wide range of actions by the person facing a moral dilemma, as a wide range of actions could be fitted into a life that showed balanced caring and does not seem to help very much when having to choose between a family member and strangers.

> **Michael Slote (1941–)**
>
> Michale Slote is Professor of Ethics at the University of Miami. He is a leading figure in the field of Virtue Ethics and argues that, in a particular form (the ethics of caring), it offers advantages over deontology, Utilitarianism and common-sense morality.

Perhaps the major contribution of Slote to the discussion of Virtue Ethics is his explanation of the difference between *agent-focused* and *agent-based* theories. Agent-focused theories understand the moral life in terms of what it is to be a virtuous person, where virtues are inner dispositions – Aristotle's Virtue Ethics is an example of this. On the other hand, agent-based theories evaluate actions according to the inner life and motive of the people who do such actions. He says there are many human traits we find admirable, such as kindness and compassion, and we can identify these by looking at people we admire. Slote focuses on care and concern for others and empathy – he looks at the motives more than the community aspect of virtues.

Thought Point

1   What virtues do you think are important in the twenty-first century? Do you think they will still be important in the future?
2   Do you think Virtue Ethics is worth resurrecting? Why?
3   If we have little control over our personalities, our upbringing or our environment, can we be praised for our virtues or blamed for not possessing virtues?
4   What should someone do when faced with two different possible courses of action, both of which seem to express virtues?
5   How do modern versions of Virtue Ethics differ from the Virtue Ethics of Aristotle?

Feminism and Virtue Ethics

Annette Baier (1929–2012)

Annette Baier was a moral philosopher focusing on Hume's moral psychology. She was a well-known feminist philosopher and was strongly influenced by her colleague Wilfrid Sellars.

Finally, it is worth looking briefly at one more modern version of Virtue Ethics as developed mainly by feminist writers such as **Annette Baier**. They claim that men often think morally in terms of justice and autonomy, which could be seen as 'masculine' traits, whereas women think morally in terms of caring, nurturing and self-sacrifice. Baier advocated a view of ethics that takes account of our natural biases (e.g. the love of a mother for her children and the importance of trust for people in lives and relationships). Writers who discuss the ethics of caring do not always make explicit links with Virtue Ethics, but much in their discussion of specific virtues, their relation to social practices, moral education and so on, is central to Virtue Ethics.

STRENGTHS OF VIRTUE ETHICS

- Virtue Ethics avoids having to use a formula (e.g. 'the greatest good for the greatest number') to work out what we ought to do and focuses instead on the kind of person we ought to be.
- Virtue Ethics understands the need to distinguish good people from legalists – just because one obeys the law and follows the rules does not make one a good person.
- Virtue Ethics stresses the importance of motivating people to want to be good – it stresses the importance of education in showing that good actions are their own reward. It shows how we acquire and learn virtues by imitating others.

- Virtue Ethics tells us how we learn moral principles and involves our entire life, as every moment, even the most mundane, is an opportunity for developing a virtue.
- Virtue Ethics enables us to integrate many aspects of life – our emotions, commitments to others, our friends, social responsibilities – into our ethical reflection; it looks at what makes life worthwhile rather than looking at what is right or wrong in a particular situation or particular moment in our lives. It does not reject our emotions but includes them, and so is more in tune with how people naturally react to an ethical dilemma. It relates our ethical choices to the bigger picture.
- Virtue Ethics sees it as good to be biased in favour of friends and family, unlike Utilitarianism or Kant which see impartiality as important.
- Virtue Ethics does not pretend to be able to tell us what a good person would do in every possible situation but encourages us to be more like such a person so that we will not need an ethical theory to make our decisions for us. It stresses the importance of character – after all, someone who helps the poor out of compassion does seem to be morally superior to someone who does it out of duty.

WEAKNESSES OF VIRTUE ETHICS

- One major difficulty is that of identifying the virtues. Are virtues culturally relative?
- How can Virtue Ethics be applied to moral dilemmas? This is the problem raised by **Robert Louden**: Virtue Ethics does not help people facing a crisis because it does not give any clear rules for action. It is difficult to work out what is the virtuous response to stem-cell research or abortion. Virtue Ethics does not give us any concrete answers and only says it is a matter for the practical wisdom of the person facing the situation.
- Virtue Ethics seems to praise some virtues that we might see as immoral (e.g. soldiers fighting unjust wars may be courageous but that does not make them morally good).
- Louden also points out that it is difficult to decide who is virtuous, as acts that appear virtuous on the outside may not necessarily have good motives and vice versa.
- Virtue Ethics does not seem to have room for basic concepts such as rights and obligations, so as a theory of ethics it seems incapable of dealing with big issues – Virtue Ethics does not always have a view about what makes an act right or wrong.
- Virtue Ethics depends on some final end which gives shape to our lives – there may not be one and being virtuous may not affect it anyway.

Virtue Ethics

Virtue is a disposition to act exercised through practical reasoning

Virtue involves making choices

A virtuous person does the right thing for the right reasons

Virtues are developed like learning a skill

This involves teaching, reflection, understanding and practice

Virtue involves choice and sensitivity to new situations

To predict others' actions we need the same practical reasoning

APPLICATION OF VIRTUE ETHICS TO AN ETHICAL DILEMMA – SEXUAL ETHICS

Virtue Ethics encompasses our entire lives, and sees every moment as a possibility for acquiring or developing a virtue, including sexual relationships. A virtue-based approach to sexual ethics does not give a choice of action from alternatives, nor does it tell us how to respond in a particular situation, such as when a person seems to go against a particular sexual moral norm. However, Virtue Ethics asks how a person acts virtuously over an extended period of time with regard to their sexual relationships. Virtue Ethics is not about decisions, but about the person making those decisions, and the skills and habits that enable the person to act rightly under pressure. As far as sexual ethics is concerned, Virtue Ethics aims to shape what we desire as well as what we do, and so presumes there is a right and wrong in sexual conduct – it is not just private choice.

Virtue Ethics would consider what kind of sexual practices would make a person more virtuous, and would consider that sex expresses human union – a sharing, giving and commitment. It would, therefore see the sexual practices that use others for one's own end, or that harm others as not being virtuous.

Virtue Ethics implies that an action is right if it is what a virtuous person, who exercises the virtues, would characteristically do in a situation. Aristotle talks about practising virtues, and a mature person continually growing in virtues.

One approach to sexual ethics from the point of view of Virtue Ethics might consider the application of certain virtues, such as justice and fairness in sexual ethics, which treats each person with dignity. This could be used to discuss the commercialisation of sex, from prostitution to internet pornography, and the question of the equality of women.

Alternatively, virtue ethicists, such as Michael Slote, emphasise the ethics of care in relationships, and as far as sexual ethics are concerned this requires a sort of three-way balance: care for those who are near to us (intimate care); care for other people in general (humanitarian care); and care for our own well-being (self care). This enables us to balance justice, which asks us to treat all people with impartiality, with fidelity, which asks us to consider our specific interpersonal relationships. Finally, self-care allows one to be accountable for oneself, and not let oneself be taken advantage of in sexual relationships – responsible for ourselves as well as others.

This view implies tolerance towards others' approaches to sexual ethics, while accepting that we are responsible for our character and the choices we make. Virtue Ethics also urges us to rediscover balance in human sexuality and in our sexual relationships.

REVIEW QUESTIONS

Look back over the chapter and check that you can answer the following questions:

1   Where did Virtue Ethics originate?
2   What is the difference between Virtue Ethics and other normative ethical theories?
3   Explain Aristotle's idea of the Golden Mean.
4   How did Aristotle say we acquired virtues?
5   How can Virtue Ethics help us in moral dilemmas?
6   Make a chart of the strengths and weaknesses of Virtue Ethics.

Terminology

Do you know your terminology?

Try to explain the following terms without looking at your books or notes:

*   Aretaic ethics
*   *Eudaimonia*
*   Golden Mean
*   *Phronesis*

Examination Questions Practice

Unless the question specifically asks you about Aristotle's Virtue Ethics, you do not need to limit your answer just to his approach but may consider more modern approaches also. However, you need to remember the constraints on time in the examination.

Remember: each question assesses AO1 and AO2. To help you improve your answers look at the A2 Levels of Response. See: http://www.ocr.org.uk/qualifications/as-a-level-gce-religious-studies-h172-h572/.

SAMPLE EXAM STYLE QUESTION

- **'Virtue Ethics is of little use when dealing with practical ethics.' Discuss.** (35 marks)

- You would need to include the main tenets of Virtue Ethics, e.g. being not doing, Golden Mean, what virtues are, following the examples of virtuous people, etc. and its roots in Aristotle.
- You could also include modern forms of Virtue Ethics such as Anscombe, MacIntyre, etc.
- You would then need to explain what is meant by practical ethics and consider how easy it is to apply Virtue Ethics to practical ethics.

- You could discuss what makes Virtue Ethics so different from other theories, e.g. the fact that it is not rule-based or consequence-based, but looks at the virtuous person.
- You would also need to assess whether other ethical theories are in fact more useful, and compare Virtue Ethics to, for example, Kantian Ethics or Utilitarianism.

SAMPLE A2 EXAM STYLE QUESTIONS

- **'Virtue Ethics is a good approach to the issues surrounding sex and relationships.' Discuss.**
- **'The weaknesses of Virtue Ethics outweigh its strengths.' Discuss.**

- **'Virtue Ethics is of little practical use to someone faced with a moral problem.' Discuss.**

FURTHER READING

Ahluwalia, L. *Foundation for the Study of Religion*, London, Hodder & Stoughton Educational, 2001.

Crisp, R. and Slote, M. *Virtue Ethics*, Oxford/New York, Oxford University Press, 1997.

Hinman, L. 'Ethics Updates' available at http://ethics.sandiego.edu/.

Hursthouse, R. *On Virtue Ethics*, Oxford, Oxford University Press, 1999.

Hursthouse, R. *Ethics, Humans and Other Animals*, London, Routledge, 2000.

Keenan, J. 'Virtue Ethics', in *Christian Ethics: An Introduction*, Hoose, B. (ed.), London, Cassell, 1998.

Lafollette, H. (ed.) *Ethics in Practice – An Anthology*, Oxford, Blackwell, 2002.

MacIntyre, A. *After Virtue*, London, Duckworth, 1985.

Rosenstand, N. *The Moral of the Story* (5th edn), New York, McGraw-Hill, 2006.

Ross, W.D. (trans.) *The Complete Works of Aristotle*, ed. J. Barnes, Princeton, NJ, Princeton University Press, 1984.

Vardy, P. and Grosch, P. *The Puzzle of Ethics*, London, Fount, 1999.

13 Free Will and Determinism

WHAT YOU WILL LEARN ABOUT IN THIS CHAPTER

*   The link between free will and moral responsibility.
*   The ethical theories of hard determinism, libertarianism and soft determinism or compatibilism.
*   The influences of genetics, psychology and social environment on our moral choices.
*   Religious ideas of free will and predestination.
*   The strengths and weaknesses of determinism and free will.
*   The link between free will, determinism and moral responsibility.

KEY SCHOLARS

*   Augustine of Hippo (354–430)
*   John Calvin (1509–1564)
*   John Locke (1632–1704)
*   Baruch Spinoza (1632–1677)
*   Isaac Newton (1642–1727)
*   David Hume (1711–1776)
*   Paul-Henri Thiry (Baron) d'Holbach (1723–1789)
*   Immanuel Kant (1724–1804)
*   Pierre Laplace (1749–1827)
*   Ivan Pavlov (1849–1936)
*   Clarence Darrow (1857–1938)
*   John B. Watson (1878–1958)
*   John Hospers (1918–2010)
*   Richard Dawkins (1941–)
*   Steven Pinker (1954–)
*   Werner Heisenberg (1901–1976)
*   B.F. Skinner (1904–1990)
*   Jean-Paul Sartre (1905–1980)
*   Ted Honderich (1933–)
*   Peter Van Inwagen (1942–)

This chapter contains the views of many scholars and philosophers about which you do not need to know for the OCR examination, but which will add to your understanding of this subject.

THE OCR CHECKLIST

Candidates should be able to demonstrate knowledge and understanding of:

- hard determinism, soft determinism and libertarianism;
- the views of Darrow, Honderich, Hume and Locke;
- theological determinism (predestination) and religious ideas of free will;
- the influences of genetics, psychology, environment or social conditioning on moral choices;
- the implications of these views for moral responsibility;
- the link between free will, determinism and moral responsibility.

Candidates should be able to discuss these areas critically and their strengths and weaknesses.

From OCR A Level Religious Studies Specification H572.

WHAT IS DETERMINISM?

Most people agree that people are morally responsible *only* for the actions they carry out freely and deliberately – actions that are freely chosen. Determinism, however, states that there are laws of nature which govern everything that happens and that all our actions are the result of these scientific laws, and that every choice we make was determined by the situation immediately before it, and that that situation was determined by the situation before it, and so on, as far back as you want to go. Freedom of choice is just an illusion and so personal responsibility is a meaningless concept, as are blame and punishment. This makes it difficult to make any sense of the idea that people are to be held morally and legally responsible *only* for actions carried out freely and deliberately. However, we do feel a sense of responsibility for what we have done even if we did not choose that action; for example, a driver who kills a child who ran out in front of his car would blame himself for the death, even if it was not his fault and he could not have prevented it.

Philosophers have traditionally responded to this problem in different ways:

- **hard determinists** accept determinism and reject freedom and moral responsibility;
- **libertarians** reject determinism and accept freedom and moral responsibility;
- **soft determinists** or **compatibilists** reject the two previous views that free will and determinism are incompatible and argue that freedom is not only compatible with determinism, but actually requires it.

DETERMINISM

Determinism states that everything in the universe has a prior cause, including all human actions and choices. This means that all our decisions, viewpoints and opinions can be best understood when translated into the neutral language of natural science.

This view has a long history and may be seen in the *fatalism* of Greek tragedy, in which people are the helpless victims of circumstances, necessity and the Fates.

Religious determinism

Determinism can also be seen in some versions of Christian **predestination**: the total irrelevance of our actions in this life as God has already decided whether we are saved or not saved. Theological determinism believes that there is a causal chain that can be traced back to an uncaused causer: God.

If God is omniscient and omnipotent then our actions must be pre-determined by Him and we cannot have free will. This poses a problem as in traditional Judaeo-Christianity, humans are autonomous morally responsible beings. In Genesis, God gives humans the responsibility for the world and they are told they may eat any fruit except the fruit of the Tree of the Knowledge of Good and Evil; they eat it and are punished. They must have made a free responsible choice or why would God have punished them? This begs the question of how humans can be free and autonomous if God is

Hard determinism
The belief that people do not have any free will and that all moral actions have prior causes. This means that nobody can be held morally responsible.

Libertarianism
The belief that determinism is false and people are free to make moral choices and so are responsible for their actions.

Soft determinism
The belief that determinism is true in many aspects, but we are still morally responsible for our actions.

Compatibilism
The belief that it is possible to be both free and determined, as some aspects of our nature are determined, but not our ability to make moral decisions.

Determinism
The view that every event has a cause and so, when applied to moral decisions, we do not have free will.

Predestination
The belief that God has decided who will be saved and who will not.

St Augustine of Hippo (354–430)

St Augustine was born on 13 November 354, in Tagaste, Numidia. His father was a pagan but his mother, Monica, worked for Augustine's conversion. From the age of 15 to 30 Augustine lived with a woman from Carthage, and in 372 had a son named Adeodatus, 'the gift of God'. Augustine was ordained in 391. He became Bishop of Hippo in 395.

omniscient, as if He knows our decisions we must be fulfilling some kind of pre-determined plan.

St Paul thought that God chose who would be saved and that he had the right to do this as no one deserves salvation. St Paul saw freedom as no longer being bound by the rules of the Old Testament, but as having the ability to choose to follow God and overcome sin and death through the resurrection of Christ. He saw faith, however, as a gift from God, freely offered to all: humans are free to accept it and may live their lives how they choose, but their final destination is determined by God.

St Augustine built upon this idea and argued that human will is totally corrupt as a result of the Fall and nobody can perform a good action without the grace of God to help. Augustine believed in pre-destination – only the chosen and elected by God will be saved and, as it is not possible to know who has been chosen, all must live good lives. God knows all our choices and the decisions we will make – we will make them freely but it is God who is omnipotent. According to Augustine there are three types of events: those that are caused by chance (in other words we do not know the cause), those caused by God and those that we ourselves cause. Some things we cannot control such as death, but how we live our lives is within our control.

Both the ideas of St Paul and St Augustine are similar to those of soft determinism as they show the difference between the internal and external causes.

Predestination was taken a step further by **John Calvin** who was influenced by the ideas of St Paul and St Augustine. He argued that Paul was in fact preaching predestination: that the destination of everyone is determined by God on the basis of his foreknowledge and that God determines whatever happens in history and that man has only a very limited understanding of God's purposes and plans. This idea is not based on words or particular passages in the Bible but on ideas about revelation, and has to sit side by side with teachings about individual freedom and responsibility. According to Augustine, people need the help of God's grace to do good, and this is a free gift from God, regardless of individual merit. Consequently, God alone determines who will receive the grace that assures salvation.

However, the further idea that while some were predestined to salvation, others were predestined to damnation was rejected. Many Christians, such as **Pelagius**, rejected any deterministic ideas, but determinism was formulated more precisely by John Calvin during the sixteenth century and is still followed by Presbyterian churches today. This belief says that as man is a complete sinner who is incapable of coming to God, and has a sinful free will that is only capable of rejecting God, then predestination must occur or nobody could be saved. God is in total control and people cannot do anything to achieve salvation. According to Calvin, people are not all created with a similar destiny:

John Calvin (1509–1564)

John Calvin was born in Noyon on 10 July 1509. He studied for the priesthood at the Collège de la Marche and the Collège de Montaigue, in Paris. He then studied law at Orléans and Bourges. In 1536 the first edition of his *Christianae Religionis Institutio* (Institutes of the Christian Religion) was published and this work led him to the forefront of Protestantism. He married Idelette de Bure in Strasbourg, but their only child died. In 1541 Calvin moved to Geneva, where he had been invited to modify the constitution in both sacred and secular matters. He wrote a catechism and commentaries on almost all the books of the Bible. He caught quartan fever in 1558 and became very weak. He died on 27 May 1564 and lies in an unmarked grave in Geneva.

eternal life is fore-ordained for some, and eternal damnation for others. Every man, therefore, being created for one or the other of these ends, we say, he is predestined to life or death.

> (Institutes of the Christian Religion, Bk3 Ch21 s5)

This idea suggests that people have no free will as far as their ethical decisions are concerned. It states that God makes his choice about who is to be saved independently of any qualities in the individual – God does not look into a person and recognise something good; nor does he look into the future to see who would choose him, but simply decides who will be saved because he can, and all the rest are left to go their natural way: to hell. So people only do good because God made them that way and put them in a certain environment; and the rest are just limited by their naturally sinful nature and can only choose to be sinful. Logically then, if we have no control over our actions, we have no responsibility for them.

HARD DETERMINISM

> In the Mind there is no absolute, or free, will; but the Mind is determined to will this or that by a cause that is also determined by another, and this again by another, and so to infinity.
>
> (Baruch Spinoza)

Hard determinists are called 'hard' because their position is very strict: according to **hard determinism** all our actions had prior causes – we are neither free nor responsible. Hard determinism is incompatible with free will and moral responsibility, and as all our actions are caused by prior causes we are not free to act in any other way. A person is like a machine, and if a machine is faulty it just needs fixing. The same applies to a person. A person cannot be blamed for their violence; violence either needs 'fixing' or, if this fails, the person needs imprisoning to stop their violence impinging on others. **John Hospers** was a modern hard determinist who advocated this approach; he says that there is always something which compels us both externally and internally to perform an action that we would think was the result of our own free will. He uses several psychoanalytical examples to make his point and concludes: 'It is all a matter of luck.' This is seen most clearly in the film *Clockwork Orange* (1971).

The same position was taken up by **Clarence Darrow** in 1924, when he defended two young men, Nathan Leopold and Richard Loeb, on a charge of murdering a young boy, Bobby Franks. The perfect crime the two men planned went wrong and in the subsequent court case Darrow, their defence lawyer, pleaded for the death penalty to be commuted to life imprisonment, as the two young murderers were the product of their upbringing, their ancestry and their wealthy environment.

> What has this boy to do with it? He was not his own father; he was not his own mother; he was not his own grandparents. All of this was handed to him. He did not surround himself with governesses and wealth. He did not make himself. And yet he is to be compelled to pay.
>
> (Darrow, in *Philosophical Explorations: Freedom, God, and Goodness*, S. Cahn (ed.), 1989)

Baruch Spinoza (1632–1677)

Baruch (or Benedict de) Spinoza was born in 1632 in Amsterdam to a Portuguese-Jewish family. He was one of the most original and radical thinkers of his time. Spinoza had great influence on the Enlightenment and also influenced the development of modern philosophical, political and religious thought.

Clarence Darrow (1857–1938)

Darrow was an American lawyer. In 1924 he defended Richard Loeb and Nathan Leopold on the charge of murdering 14-year-old Robert Franks in Chicago. They were imprisoned, but were saved from the death penalty because of Darrow's defence.

In the Scopes Monkey Trial, heard in Dayton, Tennessee (10–21 July 1925), Darrow defended a teacher who had broken state law by teaching Darwin's theory of evolution.

In the Sweet case in Detroit (1925–6), he successfully defended a black family that had fought against a mob which was trying to expel the family from their home in a white neighbourhood.

Darrow was successful in his plea and the case makes us question whether criminals are morally responsible for what they do:

Punishment as punishment is not admissible unless the offender has the free will to select his course.

(Darrow)

More modern versions of hard determinism point to our genetic heritage, social conditioning or subconscious influences as prior causes. The most extreme modern version of hard determinism is behaviourism.

Psychological behaviourism was first discussed by **John B. Watson**, who suggested that behaviour can be predicted and controlled, as people live and act in a determined universe so that all human behaviour, including ethical decisions, is controlled by prior causes which are, in principle, knowable. Behaviour is influenced, according to Watson, by heredity and environment – nature and nurture. By manipulating the environment people's behaviour can be altered. This idea is called 'conditioning' and was influenced by the work of **Ivan Pavlov**, who conditioned dogs to salivate (as if they were about to be fed) when they heard the sound of a bell. We are all familiar with this, as in schools we are conditioned to act in certain ways when we hear the school bell ring for a lesson change.

However, we are not always conditioned by our environment but will often use it to get what we want – even dogs will eventually go in search of food if no food appears. This sort of behaviour is known as operant

> ### John B. Watson (1878–1958)
>
> John B. Watson was born in Greenville, South Carolina, and studied at the Furman University and the University of Chicago. He is the founder of the school of psychology known as behaviourism.

> ### Ivan Pavlov (1849–1936)
>
> Ivan P. Pavlov was born in Ryazan in Russia. He studied theology and then medicine. He was the first Russian winner of the Nobel Prize for Physiology or Medicine (1904). At the presentation ceremony, Pavlov explained his ideas of 'unconditioned reflexes', 'conditioned reflexes' and reaction to an unrelated external stimulus. His research was published in *Conditioned Reflexes* (1926).

Behaviourism

**B.F. Skinner
(1904–1990)**

B.F. Skinner was born in Susquehanna, Pennsylvania. He studied at Harvard University. Skinner became the leading exponent of the behaviourist school of psychology, explaining human behaviour in terms of physiological responses to external stimuli.

**John Locke
(1632–1704)**

John Locke was born in Somerset on 29 August 1632. He studied at Oxford and lectured in Greek and moral philosophy there from 1661 to 1664. In 1675 Locke moved to France, returning to England in 1679. From 1683 to 1688 he lived in Holland. He returned to England in 1688 after the Glorious Revolution put William III, a Protestant, on the throne. Locke founded the school of empiricism and supported the idea of a social contract. He died at Oates Manor in Essex on 28 October 1704.

conditioning and is most often linked to the work of **B.F. Skinner**, who investigated behaviour modification through reward and punishment. He claimed that, as behavioural science develops and psychologists learn to determine and control human behaviour, it is highly probable that human behaviour is not free but most likely determined. Moral behaviour is about what people ought and ought not to do, but if they could not have done anything else then they had no freedom of choice and cannot be blamed for their actions.

Steven Pinker approached determinism from another angle and looked at the ideas of **Darwin**, developed recently by **Richard Dawkins**, that emotions such as guilt, anger, sympathy and love all have a biological basis. He developed the theory that our moral reasoning is a result of natural selection but he claims that this does not mean the end of moral responsibility. Evolution might, for example, predispose men to violence or to sleeping around, but this does not necessitate or excuse such behaviour – a moral sense is innate in us and so is 'as real for us as if it were decreed by the Almighty or written into the cosmos'.

All theories of determinism are influenced by **Isaac Newton**'s physics, according to which the universe is governed by immutable laws of nature such as motion and gravitation. The world is seen as a mechanism dominated by the law of predictable cause and effect. Followers of Newton, such as **Laplace**, placed such confidence in the all-pervasive power of causality that they thought that the minutest prediction could be made if only we knew the various causal factors involved. This included the actions of people – there is room for neither chance nor choice.

So freedom of choice is just an illusion – we may appear to have moral choices, but we only think we choose freely because we do not know the causes that lie behind our choices. This is illustrated by the philosopher **John Locke**, who describes a sleeping man in a locked room; on awakening he decides to stay where he is, not realising that the door to the room is locked.

The man thinks that he has made a free decision, but in reality he has no choice. So it is with our moral choices – we think we make free decisions simply because we do not know the causes. This view was also taken by **Paul-Henri Thiry (Baron) d'Holbach**, who said that humans and human society and actions can all be understood in terms of cause and effects – freedom is again an illusion:

> You will say that I feel free. This is an illusion, which may be compared to that of the fly in the fable, who, upon the pole of a heavy carriage, applauded himself for directing its course. Man, who thinks himself free, is a fly who imagines he has power to move the universe, while is himself unknowingly carried along by it.
>
> (*Good Sense Without God: Freethoughts Opposed to Supernatural*, 1772)

Ted Honderich also drew the conclusion that, since everything is physically determined, there is no choice and so no personal responsibility; there is not even any 'self' within us that is the origin of our actions – the mind is a by-product of brain activity, and actions are caused by 'psychoneural' events involving both mind and brain. According to Honderich, there is no room for moral blame and no point in punishment for the sake of punishment. For Honderich, each action is an effect, and there is no room for free will.

Evaluating hard determinism

- Hard determinism means we cannot blame or praise people for their actions.
- If hard determinism were true then people would not be morally responsible, and so would not deserve blame for even the most cold-blooded and calmly performed evil actions.
- All choices we make are just illusions – they are determined.
- Hard determinism, therefore, rejects the idea of punishment as retribution, but it does not reject any other views about the justification of punishment; for example, deterrence, self-defence or moral education.
- Classical physics is indeed deterministic, but modern quantum physics is not deterministic and so it makes no sense to worry about determinism in the twenty-first century. Modern physics maintains that the most basic laws of nature are not deterministic but probabilistic.
- If determinism is true then all the horrible things that happen in the world had to happen – this is a very pessimistic view of the world.

LIBERTARIANISM OR INCOMPATIBILISM

The view of those who reject determinism and say we have complete moral responsibility is called libertarianism, or **incompatibilism**, as they believe determinism is false and we have free will. Libertarians say that the ideas of cause and effect cannot be applied to human behaviour and choices; we do have freedom to act and we are morally responsible for our actions. Libertarians do not believe that we are compelled to act by outside forces but that moral actions are the result of the values and character of the individual.

Hard determinism

All human actions have a prior cause

We do not make free moral choices

We are not morally responsible for our actions

Paul-Henri Thiry (Baron) d'Holbach (1723–1789)

Baron d'Holbach was born in December 1723 at Edesheim in the Rhenish Palatinate. He was a French encyclopaedist and philosopher, a celebrated exponent of atheism and materialism. His most famous book was *Système de la nature* (1770), which he wrote under the pseudonym of J.B. Mirabaud. He denounced religion and put forward an atheistic materialism. He died on 21 June 1789 in Paris.

Ted Honderich (1933–)

Honderich is a Canadian from a Mennonite family. He was Grote Professor at the University of London from 1988 until 1998. His book *After the Terror* (2002) caused controversy over the questions he raised about the events of 11 September 2001.

Incompatibilism
The belief that determinism is logically incompatible with free will. Thus some incompatibilists will say that determinism is a fact and so we are not free, but most take the opposite view that free will is a fact and so determinism is false.

This view means that we have free choice and can choose different ways to act, whereas determinism means that we do the only thing we can do and so never really have a choice about anything.

According to **Kant** we do not need to be dominated by the cause and effect of our emotions as we can apply our reason to our decisions, and so we become the originating cause of our actions. Kant argues that the mind exercising reason enables us to make free decisions, whereas if we act from feelings or emotions then we become slaves to our passions. Kant assumed that our will is autonomous and capable of acting from reason and so we are responsible for our actions. Kant argues against Hume who said 'reason is the slave of the passions'.

The most common argument for libertarianism is that it appeals to our *intuitions* – we see ourselves as free agents, able to make moral choices, not as puppets on a string or robots. Unlike puppets or robots we have a mind, and it seems reasonable to conclude that having a mind is necessary in order to have free will. **Peter van Inwagen** uses the analogy of choosing which branch to go down when travelling along a road, whereas determinism is like travelling along a road with no branches – we cannot choose a different way, or reach a different destination.

Libertarians also argue that, unlike **Darrow**'s argument that we do not 'make ourselves', we do 'make our actions' and we could have chosen to do something else. This, they argue, is clear because when asked to defend our actions we blame ourselves, or wonder if we did the right thing – we evaluate our action by asking ourselves whether, at that time, we could have acted differently. We would only blame, criticise or regret, if we believed we had alternative ways of acting. This is a common-sense view of ourselves as choosers and agents with the future open to us in the way the past is not. We know that unforeseen events can alter events in the future – for example, a student may always achieve A grades in practice examination papers, but this does not mean that on the day of the final examination he will do so. His experience may predict that he will do so, but on the day of the examination he may have a bad cold, his dog may have died or he may misread a question – from our observation of the world around us we know that things can always go wrong.

Another answer to the claim of determinism is that it is not the case that all events have a cause: some events are uncaused, and human decisions and choices are an example of such uncaused events. Modern physics is often used to defend this view and especially **Werner Heisenberg**'s uncertainty principle, which says that we cannot know both the location and the momentum of subatomic particles at the same time. He therefore thought it was better to refer to the statistical probabilities rather than formulate general laws. Using this principle as a basis, it seems that determinism is false.

Werner Heisenberg (1901–1976)

Werner Heisenberg was born on 5 December 1901 in Würzburg and studied at the University of Munich. As a physicist and Nobel Laureate he developed a system of quantum mechanics. His uncertainty principle had a profound influence on physics and philosophy.

Many scientists now agree that since the idea of cause does not apply to subatomic particles, not every event in the universe is caused – some are, in principle, unpredictable. **Honderich** rejects the claims of quantum physics, saying that they only apply at the subatomic level; it is certainly not true to think that quantum physics refutes Newtonian mechanics – it is more accurate to say that it qualifies Newton's view and puts his theories in a broader context.

However, using this argument to support libertarianism misses the point. The principle of causality is actually presupposed when considering freedom, as the opposite of causality is *randomness*. A universe in which there are random events is not one in which we have free will. Behaviour caused by a random event is no more freely chosen than behaviour completely determined by the laws of Newtonian physics. Nobody could be held morally responsible for an act that was caused by a random event occurring in his brain. Modern physics seems to maintain that the most basic laws of nature are not deterministic but probabilistic. Einstein said, 'God does not play dice' – but apparently Einstein was wrong.

For free choices to be real, a person must be able to cause the events he chooses. If all human actions take place independently of any cause at all, including the will of the individual, then there is no genuine freedom. I am only *not* free to act if I am forced or compelled.

This idea of freedom is also seen as a goal of moral action – even if our freedom is limited, we show our freedom in our aim to be free and act freely. This is one of the great themes of *existentialism*. For **Jean-Paul Sartre**, freedom is both the goal and the measure of our lives – from nothing man makes himself what he chooses. Freedom here is an end in itself, as it does not matter *what* a person chooses as long as he chooses freely. A person must fill his nothingness with freedom – everything depends on the individual and the meaning he gives to his life. A person may try to avoid this freedom; then he is guilty of *mauvaise foi* and just conforms to what is decided by others. He sees life as ultimately *absurd*, meaningless, and without any reason why an individual exists or chooses to do one thing rather than another. 'To be free is to be condemned to be free.' So freedom is both the underpinning of any morality and it is a goal – to be free is to have a humanly fulfilling life.

Robert Kane is a modern libertarian who argues that we experience deep freedom only at times of struggle when we feel pulled in two equally possible directions and have to exercise our minds and wills to choose a path of self-determination.

Kane believes in five freedoms:

1   Self-realisation
2   Rational self-control
3   Self-perfection

> ### Jean-Paul Sartre (1905–1980)
>
> Jean-Paul Sartre was born in Paris on 21 June 1905. He studied at the École Normale Supérieure, the University of Fribourg, Switzerland, and the French Institute in Berlin. Sartre was a leading existentialist. In his writings he related his philosophical theory to literature, psychology and political action.

4   Self-determination
5   Self-formation

This final freedom allows us to act in a way not determined by our existing character: so we can choose to change. According to Kane, we are only ultimately responsible for those actions by which we 'made ourselves into the kind of persons we are, namely the "will-setting" or "self-forming actions"'.

Now I believe these undetermined self-forming actions or SFAs occur at those difficult times of life when we are torn between competing visions of what we should do or become. Perhaps we are torn between doing the moral thing or acting from ambition, or between powerful present desires and long-term goals, or we are faced with difficult tasks for which we have aversions.

(John Martin Fischer, Robert Kane, Derk Pereboom and Manuel Vargas, *Four Views on Free Will*, p. 26)

Kane claims to be a libertarian, but his libertarian views are certainly limited and are criticised by **Daniel Dennett** who says that these self-forming actions on which Kane says freedom depends may in fact never happen and if they never happen in a person's life then the person does not have any free will.

Libertarianism

- All human actions are free

- We make free moral choices

- We are morally responsible for our actions

Evaluating libertarianism

Autonomous moral agent
Someone who can make a moral decision freely; someone who is totally responsible for their actions.

'Ought implies can'
The idea that someone cannot be blamed for what they could not do, but only for what they were capable of doing but did not do.

- Libertarianism recognises that people have a sense of decision-making, a sense of freedom, a sense of deliberating over their choices in life.
- Personal responsibility underpins our whole system of ethics and law.
- David Hume pointed out that, even if in nature event B consistently follows event A on every observed occasion, to say that event A causes event B is to go beyond observation. It is our way of interpreting the events, not a feature of the events in themselves.
- Libertarians insist that free will is the uncoerced power to choose – but how does a person decide what to do? What criteria does he or she use to make a decision? What about their past experiences, emotions, beliefs and values?

SOFT DETERMINISM OR COMPATIBILISM

Soft determinism or compatibilism says that some of our actions are determined but that we are morally responsible for our actions. Soft determinists argue that there is confusion between determinism and fatalism about what we mean by freedom of choice. Freedom of choice is not compatible with fatalism, 'whatever will be will be', which says that nobody can change the course of events, but it is compatible with determinism, a theory of universal causation, if we include our own values, choices and desires among the choices that determine our actions. Soft determinists agree that all human actions are caused, since if they were not they would be unpredictable and random. They mean that when an individual's actions are free, they are not forced or compelled by any external pressure. Soft determinism claims that human freedom and moral responsibility are far from being incompatible with determinism; rather determinism is incomprehensible without it. The misconception that the two are incompatible comes from a considerable confusion over what we mean when we say we are free. Freedom is incompatible with fatalism, but not with determinism.

- Human freedom cannot be understood *without* determinism because our choice is one of the causal factors.
- Most human choices are a combination of external causes and internal causes.

All actions are controlled by causes, but there are two types of causes:

1   Internal causes which lead to *voluntary* actions of free will, the results of one's own wishes or desires; for example when you leave your country freely because it is your desire to go abroad on holiday.
2   External causes which lead to *involuntary* actions of compulsion, contrary to one's wishes or desires; for example when you leave the country because you are deported by the Government.

According to soft determinists, when we say a person acted freely we mean they did not act under compulsion or external pressure – they acted as free agents, even though their actions were just as much the result of cause as those that are not free. Soft determinists therefore define freedom as the liberty of spontaneity, the freedom to act according to one's nature, which is determined by external factors such as heredity, education and background.

If someone's wishes and desires are counted among the causes of their actions then freedom is also compatible with moral responsibility. If someone could not have acted otherwise because of external constraints then the person is not morally responsible. Also if someone could not have acted otherwise because of internal constraints then the action was a result of their doing and their character, emotions etc. They are not responsible for their action.

This is the view of **David Hume,** who said that every act had to be caused otherwise it was chance not freedom, so freedom and determinism have to go together or everything would just be random. He said that our will is the internal cause, so that freedom is:

> The power of acting or not acting according to the determinations of the will; that is, if we choose to remain at rest, we may; if we choose to move, we also may
>
> (Hume, *Enquiry Concerning Human Understanding*, section 8)

So long as we are not constrained, according to Hume, we are free – just as Locke's man in the locked room voluntarily stays there as he does not know the room is locked. Constraint can be internal, such as addiction, or external, such as being imprisoned. If we are not constrained then we are responsible for our actions.

Soft determinism, however, does not simply combine hard-determinist and libertarian positions, as it doesn't limit free will and it accepts the issue of responsibility and punishment. Although this theory doesn't make clear exactly what in life is determined, it states that we do have free will, and takes account of moral responsibility.

Soft determinism may be seen as the view that determinism is compatible with whatever sort of freedom is necessary for moral responsibility. Linking this to the developments in physics, perhaps we live in an indeterministic universe that is not completely described by modern physics because there are some events (e.g. some human behaviours) that are neither determined nor random. After all, who knows what physics will be like in 25 or 50 years' time?

A clue to solving this argument is given by **Immanuel Kant**, who believed that determinism applied to everything which was the object of knowledge, but not to acts of the will. He said that people work from two different and seemingly incompatible standpoints: the theoretical (pure reason) and the practical (practical reason). Pure reason concerns knowledge, the mind and the way we see the scientifically explicable world; practical reason concerns actions, the will and the way we see ourselves. We cannot look rationally for causes of our actions beyond a genuine act of our will. When we act we always think of ourselves as free. Kant says freedom is a postulate of practical reason. Kant's argument is that our own self-awareness, without which the world would not make sense to us, forces on us the idea that we are free, so we cannot get rid of the idea that we are free without ceasing to see ourselves as the originator of our actions.

Soft determinism, then, is not a position that combines the determinist and libertarian positions; it is not a compromise, it does not limit free will, but is a position taken due to the need to have some accountability and responsibility for human behaviour. Soft determinists clarify what they mean by free: we are not free to fly just using our own bodies to propel us through

Soft determinism

Some aspects of people are determined

But we have free will

So we are morally responsible for our actions

the air – this is to misuse the word 'free' and change it from meaning 'being able to choose' to 'being physically able to do'. According to soft determinists, we are morally responsible for, and can reasonably be punished and praised for, those actions which are caused by our own desires and decisions.

Evaluating soft determinism

- Soft determinism agrees that moral responsibility is important in our society, but that it is not reasonable to hold a person responsible for actions caused by his emotions, beliefs, desires and decisions if he has no choice about having them.
- It is, however, hard for the soft determinist to decide what exactly is determined and what can be freely chosen. The complex nature of people and the roles of physics, genetics and psychology make deciding what exactly is, or is not, a determining factor very hard.
- Soft determinism also allows for creativity in our choices – so not all our choices are the result of existing desires and habits.

Thought Point

- Do we, as Einstein said, 'dance to a mysterious tune, intoned in the distance by an invisible piper'?
- From your own life and experiences, list examples that show we are all determined. Can you think of other explanations for these events?
- Does hard determinism mean there is no point in the moral education of children?
- Does soft determinism overcome the problems of both hard determinism and libertarianism?
- If the future is determined, is God irrelevant?

Activities

Here are some situations in which there is, in principle, freedom of action. Yet how free are we to choose? Consider the problems faced when the influences of the society in which we live are considered:

- The influence of *upbringing* – you need to lie to save a friend's reputation. You know it is the kindest thing to do but you also know that your face will give the game away. What do you do?

continued

- The influence of *common politeness*. You find a lesson really boring and covering material you already know; there are still thirty minutes to go. You are free to walk out but . . .
- The influence of *convention* – you are going to your sixth-form prom. Everyone is dressing up in their ball gowns and dinner suits. You are free to turn up dressed in jeans – or are you?
- The influence of *social pressures* – you visit your boyfriend's/girlfriend's parents and they serve you your least favourite meal and then ask if you enjoyed it. What do you do?

Can you add to this list any situations in which in one sense you are free to act as you like, but in another sense your hands are tied?

REVIEW QUESTIONS

Look back over the chapter and check that you can answer the following questions:

1 Explain the roles of science, society and psychology in determinism.
2 Copy and complete the following revision chart on A3 paper:

Theory	Key scholars	Key ideas	Strengths	Weaknesses	Possible quotations
Hard determinism					
Predestination					
Soft determinism					
Libertarianism					

Examination Questions Practice

Remember: each question assesses AO1 and AO2. To help you improve your answers look at the A2 Levels of Response. See: http://www.ocr.org.uk/ qualifications/as-a-level-gce-religious-studies-h172-h572/.

SAMPLE EXAM STYLE QUESTION

- **'We do not possess any genuine freedom to act ethically.' Discuss.** (35 marks)

- Remember that in A2 questions both the AO1 and the AO2 assessment objectives are assessed together – you need to evaluate and criticise different views as you write your answer. An examination essay must show that you know what the question is about and that you are answering it – it is basically an argument showing your knowledge and that you can use it to justify a point of view. You also need to show that you understand the different viewpoints and all their strengths and weaknesses. Above all you must answer the question set – not the one you would like to have been set.

- In your answer to this question you will need to include the arguments of hard determinists, libertarians and soft determinists, and relate these to what it means to act freely in an ethical way. Be careful not to talk just about acting freely.

- You could explore the implications of being free to act ethically with reference to libertarianism and possibly Kant. You might explain how having no genuine freedom to act ethically implies that it is impossible to blame or praise someone for their ethical decisions and actions. You need to discuss the views of soft determinists that determinism does not rule out free will and so we are free to act ethically.

SAMPLE A2 EXAM STYLE QUESTIONS

- **'Unless we assume that everyone is free to make moral choices, we have no right to punish criminals.' Discuss.**
- **'It is impossible to reconcile any kind of determinism with the concept of free will.' Discuss.**

- **'Our freedom to make ethical choices is an illusion.' Discuss.**

FURTHER READING

Honderich, T. *How Free Are You?*, Oxford, Oxford University Press, 1993.

Macquarrie, J. and Childress, J. *A New Dictionary of Christian Ethics*, London, SCM, 1986.

Palmer, M. *Moral Problems*, Cambridge, Lutterworth Press, 1991.

Van Inwagen, P. *An Essay on Free Will*, Cambridge, Clarendon Press, 1983.

WHAT YOU WILL LEARN ABOUT IN THIS CHAPTER

- Different ideas of what conscience is.
- The views of Jerome, Augustine, Butler, Newman, Freud, Piaget, Kohlberg, Fromm and Dawkins.
- An understanding that conscience requires freedom and knowledge of the good to operate.
- Whether it is right to always follow one's conscience – arguments for and against relying on conscience for making ethical decisions.
- The origins of conscience: society, God or inner feelings?

KEY SCHOLARS

- St Augustine of Hippo (354–430)
- St Jerome (c.347–420)
- Thomas Aquinas (1225–1274)
- Joseph Butler (1692–1752)
- John Henry Newman (1801–1890)
- Sigmund Freud (1856–1939)
- Jean Piaget (1896–1980)
- Erich Fromm (1900–1980)
- Lawrence Kohlberg (1927–1987)
- Richard Gula (1947–)
- Enda McDonagh (1930–)
- Daniel Maguire (1931–)
- Vincent MacNamara
- Jack Mahoney
- Timothy O'Connell
- Vernon Ruland

WHAT IS CONSCIENCE?

Most people probably understand **conscience** as something which tells us right from wrong, but when the issues are considered in more depth the actual nature and function of conscience are harder to establish.

When considering the nature and function of conscience there are four questions to keep in mind:

1   What is conscience?
2   Where does conscience come from?
3   Is conscience innate or acquired?
4   What is its function in ethical decision-making?

Conscience is generally seen as a moral faculty, sense or feeling which compels individuals to believe that particular activities are morally right or wrong. Conscience may also be seen to prompt different people in quite different directions – one person may feel a moral duty to go to war, while another may feel a moral duty to avoid war in all circumstances.

Most of us could make lists of behaviours we could not indulge in, and actions we could not perform, owing to the dictates of our consciences. We consider conscience to be a reliable guide. We could perhaps even agree with Mark Twain when he wrote: 'I have noticed my conscience for many years, and I know it is more trouble and bother to me than anything else I started with.' The last phrase is important, as it implies that conscience is something

Conscience

Our sense of moral right and wrong.

we inherit at birth and remains a fellow traveller with us throughout our lives. Experience seems to tell us, however, that this cannot be so – conscience lacks consistency, whether between people in general or in any particular person. Just think what appalling acts are performed with a clear conscience (just obeying commands) or even in the name of conscience. Even individuals are inconsistent and matters about which we once had conscientious feelings no longer affect us. If conscience is so changeable, how can it be a reliable guide? Does it only represent our views on moral issues as we see them at any given moment?

Views about conscience vary, and different writers will see it in different ways and have different opinions about its role in ethical decision-making.

There are two main types of view that influence which stance is taken:

1   *Religious views*, including biblical teaching, Divine Command theory, the works of Augustine, Aquinas, Butler, Newman, Bonhoeffer, and so on.
2   *Secular views*, including psychological, sociological, humanitarian and authoritarian.

BIBLICAL TEACHING

The word conscience does not appear as such in the Old Testament – the nearest meaning is 'heart':

> Create in me a clean heart, O God, and put a new and right spirit within me.
>
> (Psalm 51:10)

> O that today you would listen to his voice! Do not harden your hearts
>
> (Psalm 95:7b–8a)

> My heart does not reproach me for any of my days
>
> (Job 27:6b)

If this is what is meant by conscience, it seems to make clear the wishes of God to humans.

Jesus also taught his followers to have a pure heart:

> Blessed are the pure in heart, for they will see God
>
> (Matthew 5:8)

It is assumed by some biblical writers and early Christian teachers that our conscience is God-given. This view is put clearly in Paul's letter to the Romans:

When Gentiles, who do not possess the law, do instinctively what the law requires, these, though not having the law, are a law to themselves. They show that what the law requires is written on their hearts.

(Romans 2:1415a)

St Paul uses the Greek word *syneidesis*, which is often translated as conscience or heart but in Greek means 'to know with'. Paul uses it to explain the human ability to know and choose what is good and seems to suggest a moral consciousness that compares an action to a standard. For St Paul conscience seems to show someone's reaction to a past action that does not meet this standard and should be obeyed in the future, but he does not say that it is the only guide and the New Testament writers describe conscience in different ways:

Conscience can be said to be pure:

. . . they must hold fast to the mystery of the faith with a clear conscience.

(I Timothy 3:9)

Conscience can be good:

While Paul was looking intently at the council he said, 'Brothers, up to this day I have lived my life with a clear conscience before God.'

(Acts 23:1)

Pray for us, for we are sure that we have a clear conscience, desiring to act honorably in all things.

(Hebrews 13:18)

However, if the conscience is not active it can be seen as weak or wounded:

For if others see you, who possess knowledge, eating in the temple of an idol, might they not, since their conscience is weak, be encouraged to the point of eating food sacrificed to idols?

(I Corinthians 8:10)

But when you thus sin against members of your family, and wound their conscience when it is weak, you sin against Christ.

(I Corinthians 8:12)

When the conscience is insensitive it is described as 'seared':

Now the Spirit expressly says that in later times some will renounce the faith by paying attention to deceitful spirits and teachings of demons, through the hypocrisy of liars whose consciences are seared with a hot iron. They forbid marriage and demand abstinence from foods, which

God created to be received with thanksgiving by those who believe and know the truth.

(I Timothy 4:1–3)

In I Corinthians 4:4 St Paul wrote, 'I am not aware of anything against myself, but I am not thereby acquitted. It is the Lord who judges me.' In this sentence St Paul uses the word from which the word translated as conscience comes, and, although he says that his conscience does not accuse him and a pure conscience is valuable, it is ultimately Christ who is the final standard against which a person is judged.

Paul's conscience is thus very personal to the individual who possesses it; a direct and personal gift from God to the believer – a view that would become increasingly important in the rise of Protestantism. Yet his conscience also plays a more public and judicial role, adjudicating between various thoughts and, finally, testifying before God at the Day of Judgement.

Traditional Christian teaching is based on this – everyone knows what is right and wrong, as God has given us this ability. It is also implied that by following their conscience, everyone can follow the divine law.

Thought Point

In the following situations are the people acting morally or immorally in following their consciences?

- Anti-abortionists who harass women entering an abortion clinic.
- A soldier who refuses to fight as he believes that a particular war is unjust.
- An environmentalist who tries to stop a by-pass being built through an area of outstanding natural beauty.
- An animal rights activist who breaks into a research centre and sets the animals free.

THE DEVELOPMENT OF CHRISTIAN THOUGHT ON CONSCIENCE

Christian writers in the first centuries CE developed their own idea about conscience and its role in ethical decision-making.

Jerome

St Jerome thought that conscience was intuitive and defined *syneidesis* as 'gleams (or sparks) of conscience by which we discern that we sin'.

Syneidesis

Syneidesis means 'to know with'. St Paul uses it to explain the human ability to know and choose what is good. He seems to suggest a moral consciousness which compares an action to a standard. Used by St Jerome to mean 'gleams (or sparks) of conscience by which we discern that we sin'.

The turning point for the Christian use of conscience was St Jerome's choice of the Latin *conscientia* in his late fourth-century translation of the New Testament from Greek to Latin. In the Greek testament, Paul's Epistles rely upon the term *syneidesis*, a broadly inclusive term which anticipates *conscientia* in its suggestion of mutual knowing, or a knowing by the self 'that knows with itself'. By translating the noun *syneidesis* as *conscientia*, St Jerome was using a term that at the time included the idea of private ethical discernment with public expectation. This meant that from very early on the Christian conscience was seen as serving both the individual and the teachings of the Church.

Augustine

St Augustine of Hippo (354–430) understood conscience as the voice of God speaking to the individual in solitary moments, bringing us closer to God and as a tool that helps us to observe God's laws. When we listen to it, we are really hearing the word of God whispering to us about what is right and what is wrong. Augustine urged all Christians to be concerned about conscience and to consider it most seriously. 'Return to your conscience, question it. . . . Turn inward, brethren, and in everything you do, see God as your witness', he wrote.

According to Augustine, humans have an innate capacity to know the difference between right and wrong. Every person has a conscience, but he believed, however, that this alone is not enough to make a person virtuous: God's grace is needed as well as conscience.

So Augustine's understanding of conscience rested on three main ideas:

1   God implants knowledge of right conduct in humans and this can be known through conscience.
2   A person cannot rightly act (as opposed to knowing what is right) without the grace of God.
3   The motive also has to be right – this is to draw close to God. So, for example, only good acts, such as giving money to charity, where the motive was love of God, were praiseworthy moral acts.

Augustine made the conscience the most important element of moral decision-making, and followers of Augustine have often argued that the conscience is more important than the moral teachings of the Church, e.g. Martin Luther was an Augustinian monk and broke with the Catholic Church, arguing that his conscience would not let him accept the teachings of the Pope. Other writers have placed the conscience above the teachings of the Bible, for example in the late eighteenth and early nineteenth centuries Christians wrestled with the issue of slavery, as St Paul, in his letter to Philemon, supported slavery. Many Christians, such as William Wilberforce,

> **St Jerome**
> **(c.347–420)**
>
> St Jerome (Eusebius Sophronius Hieronymus) was a Christian priest, theologian and historian. He was born in Stridon, on the border of Dalmatia and Pannonia. He travelled extensively across Europe and Asia Minor. From 382 to 405 he translated the Bible into Latin (Vulgate).

struggled with this message, as they believed in the authority of the Bible. In the end, they rejected biblical teaching in favour of their conscience.

However, there are problems with Augustine's view of conscience: it cannot be questioned. It is the voice of God within. Many find this view hard to accept, especially when it goes against the teachings of the Church, and it is not possible to verify whether it is God's voice or self-delusion. It also raises the issue of a God who contradicts himself – what if the conscience of one person leads them to do precisely the opposite of someone else? This led to Augustine's view of conscience being superseded by that of Aquinas.

AQUINAS' APPROACH – REASON SEEKING UNDERSTANDING

Synderesis

Aquinas' idea of what he termed 'right' reason by which a person acquires knowledge of basic moral principles and understands that it is important to do good and avoid evil.

Conscientia

Aquinas called this the actual ethical judgement or decision a person made.

Thomas Aquinas (1225–1274) saw conscience as the natural ability of people to understand the difference between right and wrong. He believed that all people aim for what is good and try to avoid the bad, and he called this the **synderesis** rule (based on the idea that is the nearest Greek word for conscience) and reckoned it was innate to seek the good – sin is a falling-short of God's ideals, seeking what people think is good and is actually bad because these people are not using their powers of reason properly. Aquinas understood that different societies have different views on what is right and what is wrong and, though he says people should always follow their conscience, he does see that people will sometimes get things wrong and make the wrong choices. He argued that conscience 'was the mind of man making moral judgements' and described it as containing two essential parts – *synderesis* and **conscientia**.

Synderesis means the repeated use of what Aquinas termed 'right' reason, by which a person acquires knowledge of basic moral principles and understands that it is important to do good and avoid evil. *Conscientia* is the actual ethical judgement or decision a person makes which leads to a particular course of action based upon these principles. Conscience, therefore, for Aquinas, is being able both to distinguish right from wrong and to make decisions when a person is confronted with difficult moral situations.

Aquinas saw that, although conscience was binding, it could be mistaken. This could be because of a factual mistake where the individual did not know that a general rule applied to a particular situation, and so the individual is not responsible for the wrongdoing. However, when a mistake is due to ignorance of a rule that the individual should have known, then the individual is responsible for the wrongdoing. Conscience is the weighing up of good and bad and coming to the right decision. Aquinas said that a person's conscience could err 'invincibly' – through no fault of their own or 'vincibly' – deliberately.

When Aquinas says it is always right to follow your conscience, he means that it is always right to apply your moral principles to each situation as best you can. He does not mean that if you follow your conscience you are always right – as if your principles are wrong, your conscience will be wrong too.

Aquinas says conscience is reasoning used correctly to find out what God sees is good. It is not just a voice inside us. Do we always use reason in this way? Is reason, always guided by conscience, going to determine what we do, or do we rather use our emotions when making moral choices as **F.C. Copleston** (*Aquinas*, 1955) suggests?

Some Christians would say that Aquinas' rationalistic approach does not consider revelation that comes directly from God.

BUTLER'S APPROACH – CONSCIENCE COMES FROM GOD

The eighteenth-century Anglican priest and philosopher **Joseph Butler** wrote that the most crucial thing which distinguished women and men from the animal world was the possession of the faculty of reflection or conscience. So being human involves being moral. He stated in one of his sermons: 'There is a principle of reflection in men by which they distinguish between approval and disapproval of their own actions . . . this principle in man . . . is conscience.'

Like Aquinas, Butler believed conscience could determine and judge the rightness or wrongness of different actions and thoughts. Conscience, for Butler, also held a powerful position within human decision-making because, as he wrote, it 'magisterially exerts itself' spontaneously 'without being consulted'.

Therefore, there is something authoritative and automatic for Butler about the way conscience works when moral decisions have to be made. He gave to conscience the final say in moral decision-making. Conscience, he said, governed and ordered such aspects and was the final moral authority: 'Had it strength, as it has right; had it power as it has manifest authority, it would absolutely govern the world.'

Butler saw human nature as hierarchical with conscience at the top. At the base are drives, such as the drive for food, which influence us without any thought for the consequences, and above these drives are two general impulses: **self-love** (wanting the well-being of self or enlightened self-interest, not selfishness) and **benevolence** (wanting the well-being of others). Higher than these, and linked closely to the conscience, is the 'principle of reflection' which makes us approve or disapprove of our actions. This is given to us by God and we have to use it to lead a proper, happy life. Conscience has supreme authority, and all moral decisions are decided under the guidance and authority of conscience.

Accept general principles

Apply these principles

with the help of conscience

to particiular situations

Joseph Butler (1692–1752)

Joseph Butler became Dean of St Paul's Cathedral, London, in 1740 and Bishop of Durham in 1750. He is best known for his work *Analogy of Religion* (1736). He argued that belief in natural religion was no more rational than belief in revealed religion. He saw the two as complementary.

Self-love

Butler thought of this as wanting the well-being of self or enlightened self-interest, not selfishness.

Benevolence

Butler saw this as wanting the well-being of others.

An important point made by Butler was that conscience came from God. He believed conscience was a person's God-given guide to right conduct and its demands must therefore always be followed. He does not try to analyse whether conscience is based on reason or feeling or both: he just says that it obviously exists; it comes from God and must be obeyed if a person is to be truly happy.

Butler did not see mistakes made by conscience as a serious problem, as he believed that in any moral dilemma most people will see intuitively what is the right thing to do. However, he considers it wicked to 'blind' one's conscience to clear the way for a wrong action. People can easily convince themselves that all sorts of wrong actions are right and, for Butler, this corruption of conscience by self-deception is worse than the evil action which results from it.

Butler thinks that your conscience will tell you to watch out for the interests of others as far as possible.

Butler has some important ideas which may be applied further:

- The consequence of an action is not what makes it right or wrong, as that has already happened.
- The purpose of conscience is to guide a person into a way of life that will make him happy.
- Conscience will harmonise self-love and benevolence – this may take some sorting out, and so in moral dilemmas we may be uncertain what to do.
- Conscience controls human nature.

NEWMAN'S APPROACH – CONSCIENCE AS THE VOICE OF GOD

Conscience

Principle of reflection

Self-love and benevolence

Basic drives

The nineteenth-century theologian **Cardinal John Henry Newman** also adopted an intuitionist approach to conscience. For example, in his *Letter to the Duke of Norfolk* in 1874, he wrote that when a person follows conscience he is simultaneously, in some mysterious way, following a divine law. Conscience is 'a messenger' of God and it is God speaking to us when we feel this intuitive moral knowledge and make decisions. He argued that, for Christians, conscience is more than simply 'a law of the mind', since it comes from God.

Conscience is an innate ability implanted in us before we have the ability to reason, so his approach is quite different from that of Aquinas or Butler. However, in describing it as a 'law of the mind', Newman does not see it as giving us commandments to follow, but simply a clear indication of what is right. There is no hint of threat, of duty or of dictate. Conscience does not invent the truth, but at its best it detects the truth. Elsewhere in his writings (*The Grammar of Assent*, Chapter 5) Newman says: 'If, as is the case, we feel responsibility, are ashamed, are frightened, at transgressing the voice of conscience, this implies there is One to whom we are responsible, before whom we are ashamed, whose claims upon us we fear.'

Newman believed that conscience could even supersede the Pope, the infallible head of the Catholic Church, but only after serious reflection which may then show that we are not listening to our conscience properly. He wrote 'Conscience is not a long-sighted selfishness nor a desire to be consistent with oneself; but it is a messenger from Him, who both in nature and in grace, speaks to us behind a veil, and teaches and rules us by His representatives. Conscience is the aboriginal Vicar of Christ' (*Letter to the Duke of Norfolk*). This idea of messenger does not set conscience up against the teachings of the Church in Newman's eyes, but if the message is unpalatable or difficult we cannot reinvent it to make it easier, but study it, examine it, try to understand it, especially if we do not agree with it. Conscience for Newman does not just give us an easy way out of ignoring Church teachings that we do not agree with. In his sermon on the Testimony of Conscience, Newman recommends that we should kneel and pray that God 'will lead our weak steps and enlighten our fragile minds'.

Newman's views on conscience were outlined in his *Letter to the Duke of Norfolk* where he outlined the problems that Anglicans faced with Catholic teachings. He believed that there is a distinction between the authority of the Pope, said to be infallible, though Newman questioned this, who gave general propositions and the authority of conscience: 'Certainly, if I am obliged to bring religion into after-dinner toasts, (which indeed does not seem quite the thing) I shall drink – to the Pope, if you please, – still, to Conscience first, and the Pope afterwards' (*Letter to the Duke of Norfolk*).

Newman began with God and wrote: 'God has attributes of justice, truth, wisdom and mercy.' God implanted the law 'which is himself' in the minds of all people – 'this law, as appreciated in the minds of individual men is called conscience'. For Newman the conscience should always be obeyed as it is the voice of God informing the individual's ethical decision-making.

Butler's, Newman's and Augustine's ideas on conscience are much less rationalist than Aquinas' and rely on a more *intuitionist approach*, whereby people are able to sense or intuit what is right and wrong, because God reveals this to them personally.

FREUD'S APPROACH – CONSCIENCE IS GUILT

Sigmund Freud was a psychiatrist who formed a very influential theory of personality. He studied the human mind, and its effects on and reactions

---

John Henry Newman (1801–1890)

John Henry Newman was born on 21 February 1801. He studied at Trinity College, Oxford, and, in 1822, became a Fellow of Oriel College. In 1828 he became vicar of St Mary's, the university church. Newman joined the movement founded by John Keble which called for the Church of England to react against theological liberalism, and to return to the theology and ritual of the time immediately after the Reformation. This became known as the 'Oxford Movement'. He wrote 29 papers for the *Tracts for the Times* (1833–41), which explained the need for this reaction. In 1842 he retired from Oxford to the village of Littlemore, and, three years later, he resigned from the Anglican Church and became a Roman Catholic. In 1846 he became a Catholic priest and entered the Congregation of the Oratory. He published his best-known work, *Apologia pro Vita Sua* (Apology for His Life), in 1864. He was made a cardinal in 1879 and died on 11 August 1890. He was beatified on 19 September 2010 by Pope Benedict XVI.

Sigmund Freud (1856–1939)

Sigmund Freud was born in Freiberg, Moravia, on 6 May 1856. His family were driven out by anti-Semitic riots and moved, via Leipzig, to Vienna. He was inspired by the scientific work of Johann Wolfgang von Goethe and began his medical education in 1873. He studied the central nervous system under Ernst Wilhelm von Brücke. He then worked at the General Hospital in Vienna to gain experience of psychiatry, dermatology and nervous diseases.

Sigmund Freud

with the body. Freud believed there was no such thing as a soul and his view of the mind was essentially mechanistic.

From his work, Freud concluded that the human personality consisted of three areas:

1   The **super-ego** – the set of moral controls given to us by outside influences. It is our moral code or conscience and is often in conflict with the id.
2   *The ego* – the conscious self, the part seen by the outside world.
3   *The id* – the unconscious self, the part of the mind containing basic drives and repressed memories. It is amoral, has no concerns about right and wrong and is only concerned with itself.

For Freud, the conscience is most clearly connected with the sense of guilt we feel when we go against our conscience. Conscience then is simply a construct of the mind – in religious people this would be in response to perceptions of God, and in non-religious people it would be their responses to externally imposed authority. Freud did not believe in any absolute moral law and held that all our moral codes, and thus the content of our consciences, are shaped by our experiences – it is culturally dependent, and this explains the varieties of moral codes that are to be found in different societies.

So if children learn their moral behaviour from their parents, teachers and other authority figures, is any moral choice they may make free? If the super-ego internalises the disapproval of others and creates the guilty

Super-ego

Freud's idea is that the super-ego reinforces ideas of correct behaviour implanted in us when we are young.

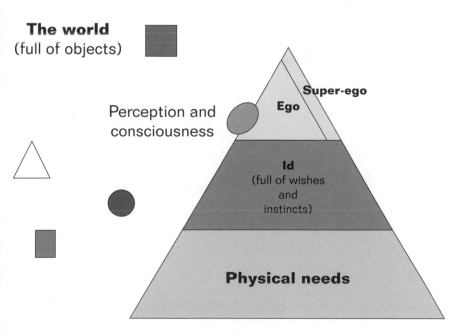

The world
(full of objects)

Perception and
consciousness

Super-ego

Ego

Id
(full of wishes
and
instincts)

Physical needs

conscience that grows into an internal force regardless of any individual rational thought or reflection, is it not just a form of moral control which traps us in its grasp?

PIAGET AND KOHLBERG – THE DEVELOPMENTAL CONSCIENCE

Psychologists since Freud have expanded his ideas to include that of immature and mature consciences which develop as we grow up. This will not necessarily be a continuous development and some people will never reach the stage of having a mature conscience. According to **Jean Piaget** a child's moral development grows and the ability to reason morally depends on cognitive development.

Piaget suggested two stages of moral development:

1   *Heteronomous morality* (between the ages of approximately 5 and 10 years) when the conscience is still immature, rules are not to be broken and punishment is expected if a rule is broken. The consequences of an action will show if it is right or wrong.

2   *Autonomous morality* (approximately ages 10+) when children develop their own rules and understand how rules operate in and help society. The move towards autonomous morality occurs when the child is less dependent on others for moral authority.

Lawrence Kohlberg followed Piaget's ideas and identified six stages of moral development which he believed individuals had to follow in sequence. People move from behaving in socially acceptable ways because they are told to do so by authority figures and want to gain approval, to keeping the law, to caring for others and finally to having respect for universal principles and the demands of an individual conscience. Kohlberg felt that most adults never got beyond keeping the law.

Both Piaget and Kohlberg believed that most moral development and the development of a conscience occur through social interaction.

FROMM'S APPROACH (1) – THE AUTHORITARIAN CONSCIENCE

Erich Fromm believed that all humans are influenced by external authorities – parents, teachers, Church leaders – who apply rules and punishments for breaking them, and that these rules are then internalised by the individual. A guilty conscience is a result of displeasing authority and if that authority is God then the fear of being rejected will have a powerful influence on an individual. Disobedience produces guilt, which in turn weakens our power and makes us more submissive to authority. The way that the Nazi government in Germany in the 1930s manipulated the consciences of its people to feel guilty about helping or not harming Jews is a classic example of the authoritarian conscience. Fromm himself escaped Nazi Germany in 1934.

FROMM'S APPROACH (2) – THE HUMANISTIC CONSCIENCE

Fromm's views changed over time and he obviously saw the humanistic conscience as being much healthier, since it assesses and evaluates our behaviour. We use it to judge how successful we are as people. It is our real self and leads us to realise our potential as far as possible. We use our own discoveries in life, and the teachings and examples of others, to give us personal integrity and moral honesty – quite the opposite of the slavish obedience and conformity of the **authoritarian conscience**.

> **Erich Fromm (1900–1980)**
>
> Erich Fromm was born in Frankfurt-am-Main in Germany, studied at the universities of Heidelberg and Munich, and later at the Psychoanalytic Institute in Berlin. In 1934 he emigrated to America, soon after the Nazis came to power. As a psychoanalyst, Fromm is best known for his application of the theory of psychoanalysis to social and cultural problems.

Authoritarian conscience
Our sense of moral right and wrong formed in us by authority figures whom we want to obey.

Entrance gate to Auschwitz concentration camp

These psychological accounts of conscience may seem to conflict with the religious views of Aquinas, Butler and Newman – but they do not necessarily undermine the possibility of God having some role in our conscience.

MODERN UNDERSTANDINGS OF CONSCIENCE

The Roman Catholic Church at its Second Vatican Council (1962–5) discussed the issue of conscience and agreed that there was a law inside each person which speaks to the individual heart. The emphasis given here was on an understanding of conscience as a personal and inner sense of right and wrong, but which worked like any law, and which held the person to obedience. One Council document, *The Pastoral Constitution of the Church in the Modern World*, stated that this law of the heart is, in fact, 'a law written by God. To obey it is the very dignity of man; according to it he will be judged.'

Modern scholars have attempted to define what conscience is in different ways from earlier thinkers. **Vincent MacNamara**, for example, argues that it is misleading to describe conscience as 'a voice', since this makes it sound like a special faculty or a piece of equipment which human beings possess, a separate thing inside the individual. He says it is much better to see conscience in terms of *an attitude* or *an awareness* people have that there is a moral path to be followed through life and that true human living does not revolve around profit and pleasure. MacNamara argues that the fact that people see that goodness and truth are important is another way of describing conscience; he puts it like this: 'it is not so much that I have a conscience – a special piece of equipment – as that I am a conscience. That is how I am, that is how I find myself. That is a basic truth about life.' This way of describing conscience is based in ideas about the kind of people we are and how we 'see' the world. You could say in a sense that it is linked to Virtue Ethics.

There are similarities in the work of **Richard Gula**, who argues that to consider conscience in terms of a series of laws, even a series of internal laws, is also misleading. He highlights two key terms in respect of the conscience: *vision* and *choice*. This is the ability to act, within a learned framework, through the needs of a Christian community and developed within a Christian understanding. The various communities which form our way of 'seeing' the world also determine the way our conscience works. Therefore, conscience is a way of 'seeing' and then responding, through the choices we make, to the world in which we live. Both MacNamara and Gula focus on a *holistic approach* to conscience.

Vernon Ruland tries to find a *via media* between rationalism and uncritical Divine Command theory and sees a moral decision as reflecting an 'ethics of loyal scrutiny' enriched by many sources of moral and religious wisdom. He explains that the God invoked in our conscience is not the exclusive property of Christians and points out that there are many interlinked sources of what he calls the ways of religious wisdom. Conscience seems to be less the 'voice of God' than our interpretation of that 'voice'.

Timothy O'Connell sees conscience as having three aspects or levels: first, it is our general sense of personal responsibility for who we are and what we become; second, it is our sense of obligation to search out the good, using all the resources of moral reasoning available to us, including the assistance of a moral community such as the Church; and finally it is the concrete judgement a person makes so that good as he sees it must be done. On this final level conscience is infallible and must be followed, but on the second level people can disagree in their conscientious judgements, and wrong judgements can be made. Moral values are discovered by moral reasoning and are imposed by neither external nor internal laws but are discovered by historical human experience of the consequences of action for human fulfilment.

Daniel Maguire agrees with O'Connell, but adds that in discerning what is the correct moral choice we also need to consider the place of creative imagination, humour and the tragic experiences of life, especially great loss, as these open us up to new perceptions of value. Both O'Connell and Maguire see conscience as based on more than human reason; it is also based on the shared experience of the past, the shared experience of a culture and personal experience and affectivity.

DAWKINS – CONSCIENCE AS THE RESULT OF EVOLUTION

Richard Dawkins believes that we have self-promoting genes or selfish genes that are programmed for survival. However, we also have evolved an altruistic (concern for others) gene as part of this survival strategy. Our ancestors found that co-operation is often more successful than competition (as reflected in some ape behaviour today). Dawkins calls this a 'lust to be nice', and says 'we have the capacity to transcend our selfish genes.'

So conscience is biologically programmed into us as a result of millions of years of evolution. Dawkins argues that goodness is innate to humans as we have evolved an innate sense of right and wrong, just as Butler and Newman did – it is just the source that is different.

CONSCIENCE AS A MORAL GUIDE

Crucial questions we need to address when considering conscience are: how important is it as a moral guide, and can it be relied upon? This brings us into discussion of two important areas. First, what authority or status should be given to individual conscience in moral decision-making, and, second, how is a person's conscience formed so that it might be a good basis for making moral choices?

Within the Christian tradition, conscience is given overriding importance in moral decision-making. Conscience must always be followed; a person is obliged to act in accordance with the dictates of conscience.

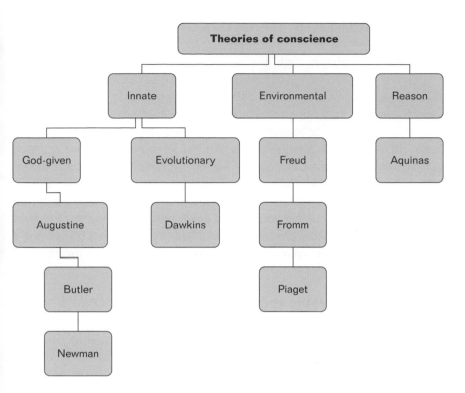

Aquinas gave considerable weight to the role of conscience. He believed that not following the dictates of conscience was always wrong, because by not following it a person was ignoring what he believed to be true. He believed conscience was a deep sense of right and wrong which came from God. Following one's conscience was like following the law of God and, even when conscience was mistaken, Aquinas believed that a person had a duty to follow it.

However, following one's conscience is no guarantee that one is always doing the right thing. It is sometimes possible to be mistaken about what is the right thing to do. This brings us to the second question about the reliability of conscience. For example, many people believe a particular course of action to be right at one time in their lives and then change their minds about that action at a later stage. Aquinas is again helpful in addressing this problem. He argued that it is the duty of everyone to inform and educate one's conscience. However, acting according to conscience, for Aquinas, is not a guarantee that a person is doing what is right; it ensures only that he will be morally blameless.

THE FORMATION OF CONSCIENCE

There are many external guides and pointers which help the individual conscience to make the right decision. To acquire an informed conscience is the responsibility of every person. Most of the approaches to conscience we have considered here think that conscience needs educating and forming.

In using conscience to make moral choices, individuals must ultimately make their own individual decision. No matter how influential external agencies are, following one's conscience always involves a personal evaluation. This is what separates the role of conscience in decision-making from other methods. Following the dictates of conscience demands following what springs from the unique perception and grasp of the situation as perceived by the individual. No one can really be said to be following his conscience if he does not possess the courage to work things out and decide for himself.

PROBLEMS WITH CONSCIENCE

We have stated that for Christians conscience is often regarded as the voice of God. However, this raises some serious questions. If we were always certain that what our conscience told us to do in any moral situation was in fact God's command, it could be argued that we would never err or make mistakes, as God would not tell us things that are wrong. Clearly people do make errors of moral judgement which they regret later. In answer to this, some might reply that God does speak to us, but that we have not built up a sufficiently sensitive conscience to hear God's voice clearly – it is our fault, not God's.

If conscience is defined as being God's voice speaking to us, this implies that we know for certain what God commands of us. In addition, people often have doubts about what is the right thing to do and have difficulty deciding. Besides, even Christian denominations disagree on moral matters such as abortion – deciding what is the right thing to do is not always as clear-cut as 'the voice of God' definition suggests.

Furthermore, many atheists claim that conscience is important to them. Such claims do not rely upon God who, in some sense, regulates the moral order of the universe. For atheists, agnostics and humanists, conscience is part of being human and there is no need to involve God when moral decisions have to be made. Conscience appears to be a universal part of human moral living.

Most people also seem to agree that both reason and the emotions are involved in the workings of conscience and that it is a most natural part of our human make-up, whether we are religious or not. When reason or the heart or both decide what ought to be done, we often feel emotionally drawn towards it, or even emotionally divided, if we partly shrink from doing it. Following one's conscience, therefore, often implies that the whole being, body, mind and heart, is involved, in some way, when making the decision. We may often feel 'pangs of conscience' after doing what we consider to be the wrong thing or experience feelings of approval if we believe we have done the right thing. **Enda McDonagh** says: 'Conscience enables us to judge good and evil, reproaches us when we have done wrong, gives us peace when we have done well.' In this sense, conscience, although a deep part of us, appears to exist simultaneously as a separate entity, often standing over and against us as a judge or a supporter. Finally, conscience implies personal responsiblity, as **Jack Mahoney** wrote:

> And perhaps a little demythologising may be in order, for conscience is not a still small voice, not bells, nor a blind stab in the dark; it is simply me coming to a decision. When I say 'my conscience tells me' all I am really saying is 'I think'.
>
> <div align="right">(<i>Seeking the Spirit</i>, p. 18)</div>

IS CONSCIENCE INNATE OR ACQUIRED?

Conscience needs two things if it is to work successfully – freedom and knowledge of the good. Unless you are free to do something, there is no point in your conscience telling you to do it. Conscience also implies an innate knowledge of what 'good' is. If it is innate we would expect everyone to have a conscience and for it to work more or less the same for everyone. As we have seen, people have different ideas of what is right when faced with a moral situation and they hold different moral principles. Are these principles acquired from parents, teachers, society or religion?

Freud and other psychologists challenge the traditional idea of conscience, but is it the moral principles that are acquired rather than conscience itself? Is conscience more of a skill? As with other skills, does listening to conscience need to be developed? The skill may be innate but the moral principles that guide it are acquired.

Thought Point

- What philosophical problems occur when someone suggests 'Conscience is the voice of God'?
- Is conscience learnt or innate?

continued

- 'It is not so much that I have a conscience – a special piece of equipment – as that I am a conscience.' What do you think MacNamara means by this?
- What is the relationship between conscience and external authority in moral decision-making?

Activities

Form groups of two or three and agree on your own group definition of conscience, giving reasons for your choice.

Choose one recent event in the media which in your opinion demonstrates a courageous decision of conscience. Give reasons for your choice.

REVIEW QUESTIONS

Look back over the chapter and check that you can answer the following questions:

1   Here are the four questions posed at the beginning of the chapter:

- What is conscience?
- Where does conscience come from?
- Is conscience innate or acquired?
- What is its function in ethical decision-making?

    Make brief notes on each of these questions, including the approaches of different philosophers. Mind-mapping would be a good technique to use for this question.
2   Make brief bullet point notes on Freud's approach to conscience.
3   Pick one opposing view to that of Freud and make bullet point notes.
4   List the weaknesses in the statement 'Conscience is the voice of God'.

Examination Questions Practice

Remember: each question assesses AO1 and AO2. To help you improve your answers look at the A2 Levels of Response. See: http://www.ocr.org.uk/qualifications/as-a-level-gce-religious-studies-h172-h572/.

SAMPLE EXAM STYLE QUESTION

- **Assess the view that conscience is not the voice of God, but is learned.** (35 marks)

- In your answer to this question you will need to include the arguments of Aquinas, Butler and Newman, and you may connect these views with the concept of innateness.
- You will need to discuss the opinion that 'the voice of God' can easily become what we mean by 'right' and 'wrong' and can even lead people to indefensible acts, such as the events of 9/11.
- You need to ask whether 'God's voice' would be the same for all, and whether it is the source of values and answerable only to itself – does conscience make the law or does it rather recognise the law and use it to assess the right course of action? The influence of sociologists and psychoanalysts may be introduced to defend the proposition (e.g. Freud and Fromm).

- This question could be argued either way. You could claim that it is God-given but not infallible and requires training. You could relate the idea of conscience as the 'voice of God' to revelation. The idea of *synderesis* may be introduced to defend the case that it is the divine voice. Or alternatively, you may prefer a Freudian or a sociological explanation.

SAMPLE A2 EXAM STYLE QUESTIONS

- **Assess the view that conscience should always be obeyed.**
- **Assess the view that conscience is not a reliable guide to ethical decision-making.**

- **Assess critically the nature and role of the conscience in ethical decision-making.**

FURTHER READING

Baelz, P. *Ethics and Belief*, New York, Seabury Press, 1977.
Bolt, R. *A Man for All Seasons*, London, Methuen, [1960] 1996.
Gill, R. *A Textbook of Christian Ethics*, London/New York, T&T Clark, 1995.
Gula, R. *Reason Informed by Faith*, New Jersey, Paulist Press, 1989.
Hodge, R. *What's Conscience For?*, London, Daughters of St Paul, 1995.
Macquarrie, J. and Childress, J. *A New Dictionary of Christian Ethics*, London, SCM, 1986.
Maguire, D. *The Moral Choice*, New York, HarperCollins, 1979.

Mahoney, J. *Seeking the Spirit: Essays in Moral and Pastoral Theology*, London, Sheen & Ward, 1981.

O'Connell, T. *Principles for a Catholic Morality* (revised edn), New York, HarperCollins, 1990.

Preston, R. 'Conscience', in *A Dictionary of Christian Ethics*, Macquarrie, J. (ed.), London, SCM, 1967.

Rulan, V. *An Ethics of Global Rights and Religious Pluralism*, San Francisco, CA, University of San Francisco Press, 2003.

Singer, P. (ed.) *A Companion to Ethics*, Oxford, Blackwell, 1994.

15 Environmental and Business Ethics

WHAT YOU WILL LEARN ABOUT IN THIS CHAPTER

*   Different ethical approaches to the environment and business, both religious and secular.
*   Rapture and end-time theology.
*   Libertarian extension – deep ecology.
*   Ecologic extension – eco-holism.
*   Conservation ethics – shallow ecology.
*   Humanist theories of the environment – Peter Singer.
*   Shallow ecology versus deep ecology.
*   An understanding of the underlying principles and implications of these different approaches for making decisions about the environment and business.
*   How to assess the different approaches and to evaluate their strengths and weaknesses.
*   The approaches of different ethical theories to the environment and to business ethics.

KEY SCHOLARS

*   St Francis of Assisi (1182–1226)
*   Aldo Leopold (1887–1948)
*   Alan Marshall (1902–1984)
*   Rachel Carson (1907–1964)
*   Aarne Naess (1912–2009)
*   James Lovelock (1919–)
*   Richard Sylvan (Routley) (1935–1996)
*   J. Baird Callicott (1941–)
*   Peter Singer (1946–)

THE OCR CHECKLIST

Candidates should be able to demonstrate knowledge and under-standing of:

*   the issue of how humans should relate to the environment, its resources and species;
*   secular approaches – the Gaia hypothesis;
*   issues in business ethics: the relationship between business and consumers; the relationship between employers and employees;
*   the relationship between business and the environment; business and globalisation;
*   the application and the different approaches of the ethical theories listed below to environmental and business ethics.

The ethical theories:

*   Natural Law;
*   Kantian Ethics;
*   Utilitarianism;
*   Religious Ethics;
*   Virtue Ethics.

Candidates should be able to discuss these areas critically.

From OCR A Level Religious Studies Specification H572.

WHAT IS ENVIRONMENTAL ETHICS?

Environmental ethics considers the ethical relationship between people and the natural world and the kind of decisions people have to make about the environment:

*   Should we continue to cut down the rainforests for the sake of human consumption?
*   Should we continue to manufacture petrol-driven cars when we have the technology to make cars that do not pollute the environment?
*   Should we knowingly cause the extinction of other species?
*   What are our environmental obligations to future generations?
*   Should humans be forced to live a simpler lifestyle in order to protect and preserve the environment?

Most people recognise that our planet is in a bad way and we all seem to have an opinion on environmental issues, such as climate change or the use of four-wheel-drive cars in cities. The importance of environmental ethics is brought home daily by the news of global warming and its effect on our lives, both now and in the future.

There has been a rapid growth in knowledge and technology, so that humans now face choices we have never had to face before that affect the continuation of humanity and the world within which we live.

Environmental ethics has grown in importance in our times because to make no decisions about environmental issues is to decide in favour of the status quo, and that, we are told, is no longer an option.

However, there is no agreed ethics for environmental issues, and no international environmental code. Environmental ethics simply tries to answer the questions of how humans should relate to their environment, how we should use the Earth's resources and how we should treat other species, both plant and animal, but there are also those who are of the opinion that constant change is simply a fact of this planet and the planet will readjust to new conditions as it did in the past. There are differences among scientists as to the exact cause and nature of environmental problems and how to solve them, and so there are differences in the approaches to environmental ethics; some think the traditional forms of ethical thought are good guides and some that these traditional forms (at least in the West) are too human-centred.

There are also the views of Christians and other religious believers who have a particular take on their role and responsibility towards the natural world.

THE RELIGIOUS APPROACH TO ENVIRONMENTAL ETHICS

For the purpose of this book a Christian approach will be followed.

Dominion

The foundation for a Christian approach to the environment is seen by many believers to be the Bible, but as with many ethical issues biblical teaching is not always clear, and the idea that we humans have 'dominion' over the natural world is seen by many as **anthropocentric**. **Peter Singer** criticises this tradition in his book *Practical Ethics*:

> According to the Dominant Western tradition, the natural world exists for the benefit of human beings. God does not care how we treat it.

Anthropocentric

An approach to the environment that places human interests above those of any other species.

Human beings are the only morally important members of this world. Nature itself is of no intrinsic value. . . . Harsh as this tradition is, it does not rule out concern for the preservation of nature, as long as that concern can be related to human well-being.

Singer points out that the teachings of **Aristotle** influenced **Aquinas** and continued to view humans as the only morally important beings – there being no intrinsic value in the natural world.

The value of creation

However, the story of creation, upon which so much of this understanding is based, is itself open to interpretation.

God seems to value the natural world, 'God saw that it was good' (Genesis 1:10a), and the blessing to 'Be fruitful and multiply' (Genesis 1:22a) is given to all creation. Creation is called to praise and glorify God (e.g. Psalm 148:3–10; Isaiah 55:12; Micah 6:1–2).

God is shown as having continuing concern about his creation – not even a sparrow falls without God's knowledge and permission:

> Are not two sparrows sold for a penny? Yet not one of them will fall to the ground apart from your Father. And even the hairs of your head are all counted. So do not be afraid; you are of more value than many sparrows.
>
> (Matthew 10:29)

Intrinsic value

Something's value lies in itself.

If God values creation and creation in return can respond to God, then it seems that the Bible says that all of creation has **intrinsic value**.

This contrasts with the view that God has a special concern for humanity – we are made in God's image:

> So God created humankind in his image, in the image of God he created them; male and female he created them.
>
> (Genesis 1:27)

Dominion

The Judaeo-Christian idea that humans have a special place in the natural world and have responsibility for it.

We are given **dominion** over all creatures:

> Then God said, 'Let us make humankind in our image, according to our likeness; and let them have dominion over the fish of the sea, and over the birds of the air, and over the cattle, and over all the wild animals of the earth, and over every creeping thing that creeps upon the earth.'
>
> (Genesis 1:26)

This surely backs up Singer's view of anthropomorphism and anthropocentrism in the biblical texts. Or are humans, being made in the image of God, also supposed to delight in the intrinsic value of the natural world?

St Francis of Assisi understood that God communicates to us through the natural world – through animals, birds and trees – and that it is a sin to destroy them. In general, his attitude towards the environment was typical of his time: the natural world is inherently good and it is a sign of God's goodness, and so its purpose is to inspire our respect and love. However, he took this a stage further, as he believed that all creatures had the ability and the duty to worship God, all are part of the same creation with the same intrinsic value.

Stewardship

Dominion may be understood as considering that the natural world can be treated however we wish and be tamed for our use. According to **Singer** this is the root cause of our environmental problems, and it is true that the command to 'subdue' the Earth (Genesis 1:28) needs looking at.

When the second creation account in Genesis 2 is compared to the first, we are told that man is put in Eden to protect and preserve it: 'The Lord God took the man and put him in the garden of Eden to till it and keep it' (Genesis 2:15).

Humans may be the peak of creation, but only because we have the role of **stewardship** – we are to care for and conserve creation because it belongs to God: humans are merely caretakers of this property. Humans are co-creators with God and need to use and transform the natural world with care. Creation is made by God and is good, and so must be preserved because it has intrinsic value.

St Francis of Assisi
(1182–1226)

St Francis of Assisi was born in Assisi as Giovanni Francesco Bernardone. He came from a rich family but, after being held prisoner for a year in Perugia, he suffered a severe illness and then changed his way of life. In 1205 he began working with lepers and started to restore damaged churches. He was disinherited by his father and spent three years working with lepers in the woods of Mount Subasio. He then founded the First Order with 12 disciples. In 1212 the Order of the Poor Ladies (later the Poor Clares) was established. After several missionary trips to Spain and Egypt, Francis went to the Holy Land until 1220. On his return to Assisi there were disputes among the friars, and he resigned as Superior and formed the Third Order of Franciscans. In 1224 the marks of Jesus' crucifixion (stigmata) appeared on his body after a period of fasting and prayer. In 1225 he wrote *Canticle of the Creatures*. He was made a saint in 1228 and in 1980 he was proclaimed the Patron Saint of Ecologists.

Stewardship
A way of interpreting the use of dominion, which sees humans as caretakers of the natural world.

Christian environmental ethics

- God created the world and it was good
- The world has intrinsic value
- Humans are the stewards of the world
- Our bad treatment of the world harms our relationship with God, each other and the natural world
- Using creation well and respecting it restores the relationship
- Christians need to reaffirm the importance of environmental ethics

The effect of humanity's sin

The Fall (Genesis 3) is seen by some as the reason for our environmental problems because from this point we became poor stewards of creation:

> The earth dries up and withers, the world languishes and withers; the heavens languish together with the earth. The earth lies polluted under its inhabitants; for they have transgressed laws, violated the statutes, broken the everlasting covenant.
>
> (Isaiah 14:4–5)

Christians teach that we need to use our increasing knowledge to rectify this and re-establish the bond between God and humanity, between God and the natural world. Thus for Christians the environment must be protected, and past mistakes must be used as learning tools and rectified where possible – this will ensure that the Western style of life does not impinge unfairly on the lifestyles of those in poorer nations and on the natural world as a whole.

Christians believe that care for the environment and the avoidance of needless exploitation of the natural world for selfish gain will help bring about peace, harmony and justice. Ultimately, Christian ethics is rooted in the relationship with God, and a Christian's relationship with God depends on how he uses creation and contributes to bringing about the Kingdom of God (I Corinthians 15:21–22; Romans 5:12–21). Love of God and love of one's neighbour are fundamental in Christian ethics and also apply to the environment.

Rapture and end-time theology

However, there are some Christians, especially an influential group of right-wing fundamentalists in the USA, who would follow Singer's interpretation of biblical teaching. They do believe that humans have 'dominion' and that the Genesis creation story teaches that 'man' is superior to nature and can use its resources unchecked. Those who believe in the 'end-time' feel that concern for the Earth and the natural world is irrelevant because they have no future. Destruction of the environment is to be welcomed, and even helped along, as it is a sign of the coming of the Apocalypse and the Second Coming of Christ:

> When he opened the sixth seal, I looked, and there came a great earthquake; the sun became black as sackcloth, the full moon became like blood, and the stars of the sky fell to the earth as the fig tree drops its

winter fruit when shaken by a gale. The sky vanished like a scroll rolling itself up, and every mountain and island was removed from its place.

(Revelation 6:12–14)

Pastor John Hagee from Texas says that the environmental and social crises of today are portents of the Rapture, when born-again Christians living and dead will be taken up into heaven: 'All over the earth, graves will explode as the occupants soar into the heavens', he preaches. Non-believers left behind will have seven years of suffering, culminating in the rise of the Antichrist and the final battle of Armageddon. Once the battle is won, Christ will send the non-believers to hell and re-green the Earth, where he will reign in peace with his followers.

All this may sound totally far-fetched, but this view is powerful in the world and held by many Americans in positions of power – why care about climate change or signing the Kyoto Agreement to limit greenhouse gases if you and those close to you will be rescued in the Rapture?

Thought Point

1 If all life is created by God, show how the teleological argument for the existence of God implies respect for his creative design.
2 Explain how the biblical sources could back up differing approaches to the environment.
3 Explain why it is important that the natural world should have intrinsic value.
4 'Humans should care for their own kind first.' How far do you think Religious Ethics would agree with this?

SECULAR APPROACHES TO ENVIRONMENTAL ETHICS

The modern study of environmental ethics was a response to the work of scientists such as **Rachel Carson** and her influential book *Silent Spring*, which explored the idea of interconnectedness through a study of the use of pesticides and how their effect is felt through the food chain. The fate of one species is linked with that of all other species, including humans.

The Australian writer **Alan Marshall** wrote that over the past 20 years there have been three main ethical approaches to the environment:

1 libertarian extension or **deep ecology**
2 ecologic extension or eco-holism (including the **Gaia hypothesis**)
3 conservation ethics or **shallow ecology**

Biocentric
An approach to the environment that considers the biological nature and diversity of the Earth to be of supreme importance.

Deep ecology
An approach to environmental ethics that sees all life forms as of value and human life as just one part of the biosphere. It rejects anthropomorphism.

Gaia hypothesis
A theory of James Lovelock.

Shallow ecology
The Earth is cared for to make conditions better for humans.

These divisions within the environmental movement are separated by the terms shallow and deep and, when applied to thought, shallow is bad and deep is good, so today they are often referred to as dark green and light green, including all possible shades in between.

Libertarian extension – deep ecology

This really began in 1949 when **Aldo Leopold's** book *Sand County Almanac* was published shortly after his death. This inspired a new approach to the environment and an interest in ecology as a science. The book is a mixture of natural history and philosophy, and calls for a new approach to the environment: 'A thing is right when it tends to preserve the integrity, stability, and beauty of the bionic community. It is wrong when it tends otherwise.'

Leopold stated that we need to develop an ethics to deal with man's relationship to land, animals and plants, and to extend our social conscience from people to land, and that it is not right to see the natural world simply in terms of its economic worth to humans.

In 1973 one of the founding fathers of environmental philosophy, **Aarne Naess**, published a short paper called 'The Shallow and the Deep, Long-Range Ecology Movement'. He basically stated that there are two ecology movements: the first is concerned mostly with pollution, the depletion of natural resources and the usefulness of the Earth for humans (anthro-pocentrism), and the second is concerned with the richness, diversity and intrinsic value of all the natural world – this is deep ecology.

He argued for the intrinsic value and inherent worth of the environment. According to Naess, every being, whether human, animal or vegetable, has an equal right to live and blossom. He called this **ecosophy**, which he defined as follows: 'By an ecosophy I mean a philosophy of ecological harmony or equilibrium' (*The Deep Ecology Movement*, p. 8).

Naess rejected any idea that humans were more important because they had a soul, use reason or have consciousness. So nature does not exist to serve humans; humans are simply a part of nature and all species have a right to exist for their own sake, regardless of their usefulness to humans. This view requires a complete change in how humans relate to the natural world, and Naess actually opposes the Christian view of stewardship as arrogant and depending on the idea of superiority which underlies the thought that humans exist to watch over nature like some sort of middleman between God and his creation.

Naess and the American philosopher **George Sessions** listed an eightfold deep-ecology platform that may be summarised as follows:

Rachel Louise Carson (1907–1964)

Rachel Carson was born in Springdale, Pennsylvania, and studied at the Pennsylvania College for Women and Johns Hopkins University. From 1931 to 1936 she taught zoology at the University of Maryland. She held the post of aquatic biologist at the United States Bureau of Fisheries from 1936 to 1952.

Ecosophy

A word formed by contracting the phrase 'ecological philosophy'. It refers to philosophies which have an ecocentric or biocentric perspective such as deep ecology.

1   All life has value in itself, independently of its usefulness to humans.
2   Richness and diversity contribute to life's well-being and have value in themselves.
3   Humans have no right to reduce this richness and diversity except to satisfy vital needs in a responsible way.
4   The impact of humans in the world is excessive, and rapidly getting worse.
5   Human lifestyles and population are key elements of this impact.
6   The diversity of life, including cultures, can flourish only with reduced human impact.
7   Basic ideological, political, economic and technological structures must therefore change.
8   Those who accept the foregoing points have an obligation to participate in implementing the necessary changes and to do so peacefully and democratically.

Naess proposes therefore that humans should:

- radically reduce the Earth's population
- abandon all goals of economic growth
- conserve diversity of species
- live in small, self-reliant communities
- 'touch the Earth lightly'.

However, many consider these ideas are simply not practical or realistic, especially as the human population is increasing rapidly and humans have just as much right to reproduce as any other species.

As a result of these problems, **Richard Sylvan** developed an alternative approach to deep ecology called *deep green theory,* which involves respect but not reverence for the environment.

Ecologic extension – eco-holism

This emphasises not the rights of humans but the interdependence of all ecosystems and sees the environment as a whole entity, valuable in itself. This is often known as *eco-holism* and its most popular form is **James Lovelock's Gaia hypothesis**.

The Gaia hypothesis challenges the view that humans are the most important species and sees humans as part of a living whole – Gaia. Gaia theory was put forward by James Lovelock in a number of books. The word 'Gaia' was first used by William Golding and comes from the name of the Greek goddess of the Earth. All the life forms of the planet are a part of Gaia

Holistic
An approach to the environment that considers a range of factors, including the importance of balance within the ecosystem.

James Ephraim Lovelock (1919–)

James Lovelock was born on 26 July 1919 in Letchworth. He read chemistry at the University of Manchester and then biophysics in London. He held posts at Harvard Medical School and Yale University.

In 1957 he invented the electron capture detector, which has since been used to study the global atmosphere. His studies of the differences between the atmospheres of the Earth and other planets led to the development of the Gaia theory.

– looking at the Earth from space, Lovelock saw not so much a planet of diverse life-forms as a planet transformed by a self-regulating living system; it was almost a living being.

In his early work Lovelock argued that Gaia is regulated by the living organisms within it to maintain suitable conditions for growth and development – he later rejected this position and saw the regulation as conducted by the whole of Gaia, not just the living organisms. He examined the fossil evidence which showed that climatic change had, in fact, taken place within a very narrow range so that life was never destroyed. Conditions seem to have favoured life; they are not random but intelligently organised – this, he claims, was not carried out by God, as religious believers maintain, but by Gaia herself. However, God could be an explanation for the existence of Gaia and for maintaining her in existence. This theory opposes the Darwinian idea of the survival of the fittest, whereby species evolve to suit the conditions available, and says that the conditions on Earth are actually managed by Gaia herself. The world is not a result of chance but of self-engineering.

According to Lovelock, life could not be destroyed. There are many types of algae that are resistant to ultraviolet radiation, so even if the ozone layer were to be destroyed, life would continue and new life would evolve. On the Bikini atoll where nuclear bombs were tested, life has returned; the same may be said for the site of the Chernobyl disaster. Human life may be wiped out, but humans are just a part of Gaia, and Gaia herself would survive without our presence. This theory challenges humans to change their perceptions and see themselves as part of a whole. If we abuse Gaia then we risk our own survival, as Gaia owes us nothing and we owe her our very existence.

The Earth, then, is a unified, holistic living entity with ethical worth, and in the long run the human race has no particular significance, but we are part of it and all the organisms on Earth are interdependent.

Lovelock's 2006 book, *The Revenge of Gaia*, is more pessimistic about climate change and our reluctance to confront it. He now considers that as the global temperatures rise higher and higher and there are more climatic disasters, the planet may not be able to recover as he previously thought. With a three-degree rise the rainforests will start to die, releasing vast new amounts of carbon dioxide; in the oceans the algae will fail and stop absorbing carbon; there will be floods, crop failures and massive human migrations. Lovelock advocates the rapid expansion of nuclear power to cut fossil fuel emissions. He writes:

> Renewable energy sounds good, but so far it is inefficient and expensive. It has a future, but we have no time now to experiment with visionary energy sources: civilisation is in imminent danger and has to use nuclear energy now, or suffer the pain soon to be inflicted by our outraged planet.

Conservation ethics – shallow ecology

This approach takes a conflicting view to the two previous ones – the only value in animals and plants is their extrinsic, **instrumental value** for humans. They are a means to an end – conservation is important for our welfare and that of future generations.

Conservation ethics looks at the worth of the environment in terms of its utility or usefulness to humans. Conservation is a means to an end and is purely concerned with humanity – so a person chooses to avoid pollution and to reduce, reuse and recycle because these actions seem beneficial to humans in one way or another.

This is the ethic that formed the underlying arguments for the three agreements reached in Rio in 1992 and for the Kyoto summit in 1997. Shallow ecology or light green environmentalism restricts independent moral status to humans – it is anthropocentric. **Biodiversity** should be preserved, as particular species of animals and plants provide us with medicines, food and

Instrumental value
Something's value lies in its usefulness for others.

Conservation ethics
The ethics of the use, allocation, protection and exploitation of the natural world.

Biodiversity
The variety of living things on Earth.

raw materials. So shallow ecology will accept that environmental damage can continue if humans benefit from it. The clearing of rainforests can be justified if it can be shown to benefit humans – making space for people to live or for farming. The preservation of a rainforest may also be the right thing to do provided it can be shown to benefit humans. Neither animals nor plants have rights, and any respect shown to them depends on how humans benefit.

However, for many people contact with the natural world is a part of the good life – part of having a good quality of life – so swimming with dolphins, hill walking or seeing cherry trees in bloom are experiences that are valued for their own sake, not just as an instrumental good.

Looking at this from another angle, **Michael La Bossiere** argues in the *Philosopher's Magazine* (issue 15) that species should be allowed to die out, as this is just part of the natural process of evolution – humans, he says, are a natural species and so any species that becomes extinct due to human activity is simply becoming naturally extinct. Humans have no obligation to prevent natural extinction, but this does not mean that humans should have a free hand in eradicating species, even when it would benefit humanity.

Humanist theories of the environment – Peter Singer

Sentience

The ability to feel pleasure and pain.

Geocentric

An approach to the environment that considers the geological nature and diversity of the Earth to be most important.

Peter Singer used a set of criteria for moral status based on **sentience**. This means that moral worth includes animals – if not, we are guilty of 'speciesism'. Our treatment of all humans and animals should be equal. Singer is a preference Utilitarian, and so believes that animals should receive equal preference. Singer argues that because plants are non-sentient, there is a problem in trying to determine their interests in staying alive. He is not, therefore, convinced by the arguments of deep ecology and admits that, although the argument for the preservation of the environment may be strong, it is difficult to argue for its intrinsic value.

In his book *Practical Ethics*, Singer advocated the preservation of 'world heritage sites', unspoilt parts of the world that acquire 'scarcity value' as they diminish over time. Their preservation ensures their survival for future generations to enjoy. It should be left to future generations to decide whether they prefer unspoilt countryside or urban landscape.

A tropical rainforest would be a good example of a world heritage site, as it is a very specialist ecosystem with vegetation that has taken many thousands of years to evolve. Clearing the rainforest to develop farmland is often pointless due to the soil conditions, and once destroyed the rainforest cannot be replaced.

Shallow ecology versus deep ecology

Shallow ecology	Deep ecology
Natural diversity is valuable as a resource.	Natural diversity has intrinsic value.
Species should be saved as a resource for humans.	Species should be saved for their intrinsic value.
Pollution should be decreased if it threatens economic growth.	Decrease in pollution has priority over economic growth.
Population growth threatens ecological equilibrium.	Human population is excessive today. Overdeveloped countries.
'Resource' means resource for humans.	'Resource' means resource for living things.
Decrease in standard of living is intolerable.	Decrease in quality of life is intolerable.

Destruction of the Amazon rainforest

APPLYING ETHICAL THEORIES TO THE ENVIRONMENT

Utilitarianism

Utilitarianism is not a single theory, but more of a family of theories with different variations. Some Utilitarian approaches are more useful than others when applying them to environmental issues.

As may be seen from the different approaches to the environment examined already in this chapter, many are based to some extent on Utilitarianism. Since it is clear that destroying the environment will bring long-term harm to all species, including humans, Utilitarians will weigh up the long-term harm against the short-term gain made from exploiting natural resources. Quantitative Utilitarianism looks at a situation and weighs up whether the moral course of action is the maximisation of higher pleasures for present and future generations. So, for example, when in the Lake District there was a proposal to impose a 10 mph speed limit on Windermere, a lake that lies within the National Park, a designated area of peace and tranquillity, but which is much used by power-boat enthusiasts and water-skiers, whose activities contribute substantially to the local economy, Bentham would weigh up the amount of pleasure and pain of all those involved. However, the assumption that pleasure is a uniform feature of different types of experience, and simply varies according to how much there is, is questionable. Modern Utilitarians would use a cost-benefit analysis, and this was the approach of David Pearce's *Blueprint for a Green Economy*. Applying this approach to Windermere, it is easy to assess the economic benefit of some of the elements in the situation: power-boating brings money into the area. But how can this be weighed against the loss of tranquillity? Environmental economics would say that tranquillity is also of value and it is simply a case of determining the strength of preferences for it – but is money an appropriate measure of environmental goods? And do people's preferences accurately reflect what is good for them? Should the fate of the environment be dependent on human preferences? In addition, we never know the final result of our actions. What may seem to be to the advantage of the environment now may in the long term prove to be harmful.

It is worth noting the approach of qualitative Utilitarianism; Mill puts the enjoyment and study of nature at the top of his list of higher pleasures – and therefore environmental preservation is imperative.

Preference Utilitarianism considers that the moral course of action is the maximisation of preference satisfaction for the current generation. Assuming that neglecting the environment has no major effect on the current generation, then the case for preserving the environment is weak.

In *Practical Ethics* **Peter Singer** uses the example of building a hydro-electric dam across a gorge that would create employment, stimulate economic growth and provide a cost-effective energy supply but have associated costs. Such costs would include the loss of a beauty spot favoured by walkers and a good place for white-water rafting and the destruction of the habitat of some endangered species and wildlife.

For the preference Utilitarian, the preference satisfaction of a cheap source of electricity would outweigh the preferences of the walkers and the white-water rafters, as well as those of the animals and plants. However, the qualitative Utilitarian would consider the long-term interests of future generations.

Kantian Ethics

Kant's ethical theory is generally seen as anthropocentric, based on the idea that rational nature alone has absolute and conditional value. It may seem that a theory of this kind would allow the exploitation of the natural world; if only rational nature counts as an end in itself, then everything else may be used as a means to an end. However, Kant denies that domestic animals are only to be treated as tools and insists that there are moral limits on how we should use them. Animals should not be worn out and over-worked, nor should they be cast aside once they are too old. Kant thinks it is all right to kill animals for food, but killing for sport he sees as morally wrong. Kant also thinks that we have moral duties regarding the natural world and must not destroy it. This seems at odds with Kant's statements that we only have duties towards rational beings, but he explains that treating animals or the natural world badly makes us into cruel and callous people who will then treat other people badly. People who torment animals are likely to do the same to humans, according to Kant. So cruelty towards animals would not be condemned in its own right, but due to its consequences for humans it should be considered intrinsically wrong. According to Kant, a person cannot have good will unless he shows concern for the welfare of non-rational beings and values the natural world for its own sake.

As well as this approach we can also consider the first formulation of the categorical imperative – that of making a maxim into a universal law. This would forbid much of the exploitation and pollution of the natural world, as it would be illogical to want everyone to be able to act so. The neo-Kantian **Paul Taylor** takes the view that respect for nature is a universal law for all rational beings – but he would not go so far as to accord animals and plants moral rights; instead he suggests giving them legal rights so that they are protected.

Virtue Ethics

Environmental ethics seeks to examine human relationships within the natural world. As we have seen, in the past the emphasis has been on anthropocentric theories based more on duty and consequences, which has led to environmental ethics being somewhat unbalanced. Environmental Virtue Ethics is a new approach which attempts to meet the challenge of a non-anthropocentric theory of values which looks at our relationship with the natural world more objectively.

Environmental Virtue Ethics does not ask why environmental preservation is important for humanity, but what characterises an environmentally good person. It shifts the emphasis from duty and consequences to who we are and how we are to live in the natural world. Environmental Virtue Ethics sees a virtuous life in nature as a necessary condition of human flourishing, *eudaimonia*. Extremes of behaviour are unhelpful both for society and the environment.

Virtue Ethics also looks at examples of virtue to follow and might look at the example of people such as Rachel Carson and Aldo Leopold.

Thought Point

- Read the passage below assigned to your group.
- Summarise the main points.
- Identify the key ethical arguments in the passage.
- Choose one environmental problem (e.g. destruction of the rainforest, saving an endangered species, pollution or global warming) and consider the implications of implementing the environmental ethic from the passage you have read. Look at both positives and negatives.
- Give your own views on the environmental ethic put forward in your passage – as a group or as individuals if there is disagreement.

Reading 1 'The Land Ethic' from Aldo Leopold's *A Sand County Almanac* (pp. 201–4)

There is as yet no ethic dealing with man's relation to land and to the animals and plants that grow upon it. Land, like Odysseus' slave girls, is still property. The land relation is still strictly economic, entailing privileges, but not obligations.

The extension of ethics to this element in human environment is, if I read the evidence correctly, an evolutionary possibility and an ecological necessity . . .

The land ethic simply enlarges the boundaries of the community to include soils, waters, plants, and animals, or collectively: the land.

This sounds simple: do we not already sing our love for obligation to the land of the free and the home of the brave? Yes, but just what and whom do we love? Certainly not the soil, which we are sending helter-skelter downriver. Certainly not the waters, which we assume have no function except to turn turbines, float barges, and carry off sewage.

Certainly not the plants, of which we exterminate whole communities without batting an eye. Certainly not the animals, of which we have already exterminated many of the largest and most beautiful species. A land ethic of course cannot prevent the alteration, management, and use of these 'resources' but it does affirm their right to continued existence, and, at least in spots, their continued existence in a natural state.

In short, a land ethic changes the role of *Homo sapiens* from conqueror of the land-community to plain member and citizen of it. It implies respect for his fellow-members, and also respect for the community as such.

Reading 2 'Utilitarian Environmental Ethics' from Peter Singer's *Practical Ethics* (pp. 56–7)

The argument for extending the principle of equality beyond our own species is simple, so simple that it amounts to no more than a clear understanding of the principle of equal consideration of interests. We have seen that this principle implies that our concern for others ought not to depend on what they are like, or what abilities they possess (although precisely what this concern requires us to do may vary according to the characteristics of those affected by what we do). It is on this basis we are able to say that the fact that some people are not members of our race does not entitle us to exploit them, and similarly the fact that some people are less intelligent than others does not mean their interests may be disregarded. But the principle also implies that the fact that beings are not members of our species does not entitle us to exploit them, and similarly the fact that other animals are less intelligent than we are does not mean that their interests may be disregarded . . . A stone does not have interests because it cannot suffer. Nothing that we can do can possibly make any difference to its welfare. A mouse, on the other hand, does have an interest in not being tormented, because mice will suffer if treated in this way.

Reading 3 'Instrumental Environmental Ethics' from Pearce *et al.*'s *Blue Print for a Green Economy* (pp. 5–7)

One of the central themes of environmental economics, and central to sustainable development thinking also, is the need to place proper values on the services provided by natural environments. The central problem is that many of these services are provided 'free'. They have a zero price simply because no market place exists in which their true values can be

continued

revealed through the acts of buying and selling. Examples might be a fine view, the water purifications and storm protection functions of coastal wetlands, or the biological diversity within a tropical rainforest. The elementary theory of supply and demand tells us that if something is provided at a zero price, more of it will be demanded than if there was a positive price. Very simply, the cheaper it is the more will be demanded. The danger is that this greater level of demand will be unrelated to the capacity of the relevant natural environments to meet the demand. For example, by treating the ozone layer as a resource with zero price there never was any incentive to protect it. Its value to human populations and to the global environment in general did not show up anywhere in a balance sheet of profit or loss, or of costs and benefits. The important principle is that resources and environments serve economic functions and have positive value. To treat them as if they had zero value is seriously to risk overusing the resource . . . We have a sound *a priori* argument for supposing that the environment has been used to excess.

Reading 4 'Deep Ecology' from Devall and Sessions' *Deep Ecology* (p. 70)

Basic Principles:

1   The well-being and flourishing of human and non-human life on Earth have value in themselves (synonyms: intrinsic value, inherent value). These values are independent of the usefulness of the non-human world for human purposes.
2   Richness and diversity of life forms contribute to the realisation of these values and are also values in themselves.
3   Humans have no right to reduce this richness and diversity except to satisfy *vital* needs.
4   The flourishing of human life and cultures is compatible with a substantial decrease of the human population. The flourishing of non-human life requires such a decrease.
5   Present human interference with the non-human world is excessive, and the situation is rapidly worsening.
6   Policies must therefore be changed. These policies affect basic economic, technological, and ideological structures. The resulting state of affairs will be deeply different from the present.
7   The ideological change is mainly that of appreciating *life quality* (dwelling in situations of inherent value) rather than adhering to an

increasingly higher standard of living. There will be a profound awareness of the difference between big and great.

8 Those who subscribe to the foregoing points have an obligation directly or indirectly to try to implement the necessary changes.

REVIEW QUESTIONS

Look back over the chapter and check that you can:

- Explain religious approaches to the environment and Singer's objections.
- Make bullet point notes on the Gaia hypothesis. List reasons for and against it.
- Make a chart comparing deep (dark green) and shallow (light green) ecology.
- List the strengths and weaknesses of a Utilitarian approach to the environment.

Essay question

'Utilitarianism is the best approach to environmental issues.' Discuss. (35 marks)

In your answer to this question you will need to explain the main principles of Utilitarianism and how they might be applied to the environment. It would be better to concentrate on one or two environmental issues such as pollution or global warming or your essay may tend to be too much about environmental issues and not enough about ethical theories.

You will need to examine what is included in the greatest good principle – just humans or also animals and plants? You will need to consider the different forms of Utilitarianism to come to a conclusion about its usefulness.

However, you also need to ask if it is the 'best' approach and this means contrasting it with other approaches (e.g. Religious Ethics, deep ecology, Gaia hypothesis).

WHAT IS BUSINESS ETHICS?

Business ethics considers the ethical relationship between businesses and consumers, between businesses and their employees. It also considers the impact of globalisation on the environment, and on society at large.

Ethicists do not always agree about the purpose of business in society – some see the main purpose of business is to maximise profits for its owners or its shareholders. In this case, only those activities which increase profits are to be encouraged as this is the only way that companies will survive – this was the view of the economist Milton Friedman. Others consider that businesses have moral responsibilities toward their stakeholders, including employees, consumers, the local community and even society as a whole. Other ethicists have adapted social contract theory (based on the ideas of John Rawls in his *A Theory of Justice*) to business, so that employees and other stakeholders are given a voice as to how the business operates. However, this view is criticised as businesses are property, not means of distributing social justice.

Times have changed, however, and ethics in business and corporate social responsibility are becoming crucial. There are many reasons for this, driven by the social, political and economic developments in the world. Consumers have shown their dissatisfaction through taking to the streets, and there have been riots from Genoa to Seattle, bringing together many different types of activists and protesters campaigning on a variety of business-related issues from globalisation and human rights to third world debt. Stakeholders, and especially consumers, are becoming increasingly empowered and vocal, forcing businesses to review their strategies.

Organisations like The Body Shop and The Co-operative Bank have led the way and brought business ethics and social responsibility into the public eye and onto the business agenda, championing key issues such as human and animal rights, fair trade and environmental impact. Consumers now expect businesses to be socially responsible, and businesses are increasingly thinking about what they can achieve by putting the power of their marketing behind some key social issues so that they can help make a positive social difference.

However, business ethics is not as simple as it looks as there is no longer one agreed moral code and multinationals operate in different parts of the world, employing and serving people from different cultures. Profit will still be the main motivating factor for businesses and this affects all the people who work there, generating its own culture with its own standards, so it becomes difficult for individuals to stand up against any attitudes and decisions they disagree with.

Modern technologies also create ethical dilemmas for businesses that never existed until quite recently – such as medical products and gene technologies: should parents be allowed to alter the genetic profile of their unborn child, and should businesses sell products to do this?

All these issues pull businesses in different directions, so that many now set up their own ethical committees. Businesses that get caught acting unethically are publicised in the press, and pressure groups that oppose the activities of certain businesses are better organised, better financed, and so better able to attack such businesses. An extreme example of this is Huntingdon Life Sciences in Cambridgeshire where the Animal Liberation Movement set up a splinter group called SHAC (Stop Huntingdon Animal Cruelty) which started an international campaign to close the company down, often using ethically dubious methods; threatening employees and employees of shareholders and banks. The opponents of this business understand business and its weak points very well as the company nearly went bust; however, the company changed tactics, the public reacted against the extreme methods of SHAC, and in 2007 reported a 5 per cent increase in profits, leading the managing director to plead with the banks to no longer treat the business as 'radioactive' (*Financial Times*, 16 September 2007).

THE RELATIONSHIP BETWEEN BUSINESS AND CONSUMERS

Customer rights – quality, safety, price and customer service – were once the most important ethical concerns in business. Now consumers influence business ethics, and have been instrumental in bringing about change: consumers expect businesses to demonstrate ethical responsibility in its widest sense – affecting the treatment of employees, the community, the environment, working conditions, etc. Some companies have been the focus of consumer criticism and forced to change their practices – Shell over Brent Spar and Ogoniland; Monsanto over GM food; Nike and Gap over child labour. Shell bowed to consumer pressure and did not sink the Brent Spar, and Nike now monitors its factories following the BBC *Panorama* programme.

One of the first ethical businesses was The Body Shop pioneered by the late Anita Roddick. The company became a great success in the mid-1980s following a change in consumer awareness of how beauty products were tested, as it began to look for alternative ways. However, an ethical business does not need to be at the level of The Body Shop as even small gestures like participation in community events or collections for charities can improve a company's appearance to consumers.

Consumer action, therefore, can be very effective, as if enough consumers stop buying from a business then the business will be forced to change or go bust. Ethical business practices will give a better image to the consumer and better sales.

THE RELATIONSHIP BETWEEN EMPLOYERS AND EMPLOYEES

Much of the employer/employee relationship now consists of them working together. In 1978 in the UK the Advisory, Conciliation and Arbitration Service (ACAS) was set up to try to create good and harmonious working relationships. It negotiates in disputes, and has been very successful, as there have been few major employment disputes, and ACAS has been able to suggest guidelines for better relationships in most situations.

For employer/employee relationships to be successful there has to be a balance of interests: the employer wants to plan for the future of the business, make profits and keep employees motivated; the employee wants the best possible conditions and living standards. If employees are unhappy there will often be high turnover of staff, poor time-keeping and much absenteeism – as a result of this discontent, profits will suffer.

However, relationships between employers and employees do not always work out. The internet now allows for rapid sharing of information across the world – and multinationals operate across the world. There are a multitude of websites that publicise and discuss the behaviour of businesses. Whistleblowing is now more acceptable – access to secret information is now better and it is even protected by law in some countries. From 'Deep Throat' (the codename of the informant in the 1972 Watergate Scandal) to Dr David Kelly, whistleblowers have risked their lives to tell what they perceive to be the truth and to make organisations accountable.

The question of whether or not it is ethical for an employee to blow the whistle, especially in the public domain, raises questions of confidentiality and loyalty – there is no simple answer to cover all cases. However, neither confidentiality or loyalty imply that the unethical conduct of others should not simply be reported, especially when product safety or the severe financial hardship of others is concerned. Whistleblowers often risk dismissal and may find it difficult to find similar employment in the future, they may be frozen out or ostracised. There are now organisations to protect whistleblowers such as 'Freedom to Care' which promotes our 'ethical right to accountable behaviour from large organisations' and that employees have an 'ethical right to express serious public concerns' in the workplace and, if necessary, to go public.

Thought Point

1   'Business exists to make a profit.' Is it society's task to protect those who are badly affected in the process?

2   Do you think standards of integrity in business are declining or not? Give reasons and examples.

3   Do you think workers should participate in management?

CASE STUDY

1   There are three area managers in a company: Tom, Steve and Tim. Tom was the latest to join the company and has learnt from Tim and from his own observations that Steve is not to be trusted. Steve seems to have no morals and his only goal seems to be his own advantage. He 'manages upwards', always trying to please the director; he lies to cover up difficulties or shortfalls; he tells his staff to take no notice of established policy – but never in writing and never to more than one person at a time. At the same time Steve gives the impression of being a straight-talking man of the people.

   Tom finds this really hard to deal with but is unsure how to respond. Sinking to Steve's level would not be acceptable, but just putting up

continued

with it like Tim does, and Steve's own staff do, really goes against the grain and all that Tom holds dear. How do you accuse a colleague of dishonesty?

What are the choices facing Tom?

What principles do you think are relevant when dealing with a colleague of this sort?

2   The head of a department in a medium-sized company with a good profit record is 55 years old and has worked for the company for 20 years. He is married with two children at university. His life is his work. However, he is becoming less effective and no longer inspires those who work for him. Several of the brightest young people in his department have left because of the situation.

If you were his boss would you:

a)   Declare him redundant with compensation?

b)   Retire him prematurely on a full pension?

c)   Transfer him to an advisory post?

d)   Take corrective action and leave him in his job?

e)   Transfer him to a new executive position on the same pay until he is 60?

f)   Do nothing or take some other course of action?

3   Why is it important for a business to behave in a socially responsible manner?

THE RELATIONSHIP BETWEEN BUSINESS AND THE ENVIRONMENT

Environmental responsibility is a vital component of a business strategy as it not only helps the environment, but wins the trust of communities and gains the respect of the governments of the countries in which the business operates. All businesses impact on the environment: they emit pollution, they produce waste and use resources. Businesses, however, are continually being encouraged to improve their approach to environmental issues. Every year there is a prestigious award, the Business Commitment to the Environment Award, and in 2007 the Co-operative was one of the winners for its response to global climate change. Some of its efforts for the environment included: the reduction by 86 per cent of its CO_2 emissions, use of 98 per cent green electricity and an ethical investment policy.

However, balancing business growth and environmental quality is always going to be a challenge for business. Businesses are encouraged to have an environmental policy, just as they do for many other issues – again this has often been a reaction to consumer pressure, and also international pressure from organisations such as the World Wide Fund for Nature. UK law and the UN Global Compact also provide minimum standards for how businesses treat the environment, and not only the small but also the large multinational businesses will generally seek to operate within the law to protect their reputation.

Example – The Anglo American Mining Company

Anglo American is one of the 20 largest UK-based companies, heavily involved in mining and quarrying – activities which have an immediate impact on the environment. When Anglo American carries out its mining operations it tries to have a positive effect in three areas:

1   In the area where the mine is located, it carries out its operations with care and tries to improve the lives of local people, e.g. minimising noise and other types of pollution.
2   In the area immediately surrounding the mine, it is active in conservation and improvement.
3   In the wider region around the mine, it contributes financially to local communities and helps generate new businesses.

An example of Anglo American's environmental conservation projects is at Tarmac's Langford Quarry in the UK, where the company has created reed beds in streams and ponds surrounding the quarry. Reed beds are an endangered habitat and local people worked with Tarmac to plant the first 10,000 reeds.

Supermarkets have been one of the businesses where the importance of 'green credentials' has become increasingly important. Concerns about 'food miles' and plastic and packaging are growing among consumers. Supermarkets have realised that they must compete on their environmental ethical credentials as well as price, availability, accessibility, etc., as all these factors influence where consumers shop. Responding to consumer preferences, helping the environment, profitability and corporate social responsibility go hand in hand.

GLOBALISATION

Globalisation means 'the reduction of the difference between one economy and another, so trade all over the world, both within and between different countries, becomes increasingly similar'. This has been going on for a long time, and used to be quite a slow process, but in recent times it has speeded up. The reasons for the increase in the pace of globalisation are:

1   Technological change – especially in communications technology.
2   Transport is both faster and cheaper.
3   Deregulation – an increase in privatisation, and countries now able to own businesses in other countries, e.g. some UK utilities which were once government-owned are now owned by French businesses.
4   Removal of capital exchange controls – money can now be moved easily from one country to another.
5   Free trade – many barriers to trade have been removed, sometimes by grouping countries together such as the EU.
6   Consumer tastes have changed and consumers are now more willing to try foreign products.
7   Emerging markets in developing countries.

All of this means that businesses are now freer to choose where they operate from, and can move to countries where labour is cheaper. This has meant, for example, that much manufacturing has moved to countries such as Indonesia, and many telephone call centres have moved to India.

Indonesian workers
manufacture electronics

National borders are becoming less important as markets stretch across them, and multinationals have taken advantage of this. Consumers are alike, but not the same, in different countries, and businesses have needed to consider local variations.

However, globalisation also brings problems – especially those of justice towards poorer countries. Trade between countries is not totally fair, and some of the richest countries, such as the United States, have very strong trade barriers to protect their national interests. It could be said that globalisation means that the interests of the shareholders are more important than the interests of the employees or the consumers, and it means that the poorest people have just 1.4 per cent of the global income. The disaster at Bhopal in India is a prime example, as the chemical companies concerned continued to deny responsibility for a long time, and some survivors still await compensation. Toxic waste still pollutes the environment.

Anti-globalisation movements campaign against the bad effects of globalisation:

- Amnesty International campaigns for a global human rights framework for business based on the UN Norms for Business.
- The World Council of Churches campaigns for responsible lending and unconditional debt cancellation.
- There are also campaigns for ecological farming practices, and against the imposed privatisation of public services, especially water.

In his book *One World: The Ethics of Globalisation* Peter Singer lists the various global problems that we face and challenges us to develop a system of ethics and justice that can be accepted by all people, regardless of their race, culture or religion.

BENEFITS OF ETHICS FOR BUSINESS

One of the main benefits for a business of behaving ethically is that a better image is given to the world at large, and especially to consumers, resulting in greater profit. It also means that expensive and potentially embarrassing public relations disasters are avoided. As far as employees are concerned, if the business is seen to behave ethically, for example with regard to the environment, it will recruit more highly qualified employees, and this leads to better employee motivation as the employees are proud of their jobs.

PROBLEMS OF ETHICS FOR BUSINESS

Being ethical can increase costs for the business, e.g. they have to pay reasonable wages to all employees. If a business is truly putting its ethics into practice it will have to pass on the same standards down the supply chain and this will mean no longer doing business with suppliers who are not prepared to meet the same standards.

However, businesses are products of the society in which they operate, and if society does not always have clear standards it is not always easy for a business to decide what to do, e.g. some people in our society are completely opposed to experimenting on animals, but others would argue that it is all right for a business to do so if it benefits human health.

Sometimes a business needs to consider that its role is to make a profit, provide jobs and create wealth for society as a whole, and it may consider that ethics are good if they help achieve these aims, and to be ignored if they do not.

Ultimately to really be ethical a business may have to change its whole business practice and organisational culture.

THE RELIGIOUS APPROACH TO BUSINESS ETHICS

For the purpose of this book a Christian approach will be followed.

The Bible gives guidelines that can easily be applied to the ethical issues surrounding business. The Old Testament contains laws and injunctions about the fair treatment of employees, e.g. Leviticus 19:13; about justice, honesty and fairness in business, 'Do not steal'; and laws about just weight, e.g. Deuteronomy 25:13–15, giving the full amount for fair payment. The prophets, especially Amos, spoke out about the unfair treatment of the poor by the rich. People are told to treat others as they would be treated – and in the New Testament Jesus was concerned with not amassing wealth for the sake of it, and sharing with those in need.

In the Middle Ages just price, usury, property and work were the only ethical approaches to business, and it was some time before Christian ethics looked at the real ethical problems facing modern businesses.

Protestant social teaching pulled in two different directions: first, the individualistic approach was concerned with the individual's calling and personal integrity, so a businessman could be praised for his charity; and second, was the concern about the competitive individualism of capitalism and the great social inequalities that it brought about, so social solutions were offered.

Catholic thought was never very individualistic and very early on addressed the problems of modern industrial life. The encyclicals *Rerum Novarum* in 1891, *Laborem Exercens* in 1981 and *Centesimus Annus* in 1991 are fundamental on workers' rights. The idea of the common good, of solidarity, is a basic value in Catholic social teaching and has led the Catholic Church to criticise both communism and free market capitalism which acts against the poor and leads to the selfish pursuit of wealth.

Christian churches, as organisations and as individual Christians within those churches, have increasingly monitored and corrected the harm done by the businesses in which they are shareholders. This has led to changes in behaviour in areas such as environmental impact and marketing practice in the developing world. This role of the ethical investor is not new – in the eighteenth century the Quakers refused to invest in companies that were involved in the slave trade.

APPLYING ETHICAL THEORIES TO BUSINESS ETHICS

Utilitarianism

Utilitarianism considers the majority affected by a certain action – general welfare is important, and this is often seen as good business policy: the general good of the organisation is more important than that of individuals. So, for example, an employee, though qualified for a certain position, will have to give way to another so that the interest of the business as a whole can be preserved. A farmer may have to give up some of his land for a dam project, because it will provide irrigation for lots of farmers and generate electricity for the whole community. However, the best business transactions are the ones in which the best result is achieved, when both business and consumer, employer and employee, shareholders and stakeholders are considered and benefited. This means that when making business decisions all options need considering – no one can just act on intuition if they wish to maximise utility.

Economically, Utilitarianism would seem to be a good ethical approach to business; however, in many cases it is not simple and clear-cut. For example, closing a polluting factory may be good for the environment, but not for the local community who may need the jobs. Whatever the business does it is going to upset one group of people or another. Utilitarianism does not always help here.

Kantian Ethics

Kant believed that morality, in all spheres of human life, including business, should be grounded in reason. His categorical imperative held that people should act only according to maxims that they would be willing to see become universal norms, and that people should never be treated as a means to an end. Kant's theory implies the necessity of trust, adherence to rules, and keeping promises (e.g. contracts). Kant argued that the highest good was the good will – the importance of acting from duty – so, for example, if a merchant is honest in order to gain a good reputation, then these acts of honesty are not genuinely moral. Kant's ethics are ethics of duty rather than consequence: a business behaving morally in order to impress consumers is not truly moral according to Kant. Kant's ethical theory applies well to both employees and consumers as it does not permit people to be treated as means to an end – even if that end is profit. Kantian Ethics would also see a business as a moral community – employers and employees, stakeholders and shareholders, standing in a moral relationship with each other which would influence the way they treat each other. This seems to require that the work that employees are given is meaningful, and that businesses should be organised more democratically.

Kant's universalisation means that business laws would have to be universal, e.g. no bribery or corruption, and this would have a beneficial effect on international business. However, Kantian Ethics has far more to offer to international business ethics as it shows how business can contribute to world peace. **N.E. Bowie** (in *Business Ethics*, 1991) quotes Kant as saying:

> In the end war itself will be seen as not only so artificial, in outcome so uncertain for both sides, in after effects so painful in the form of an ever-growing war debt (a new invention) that cannot be met, that it will be regarded as the most dubious undertaking. The impact of any revolution on all states in our continent, so clearly knit together through commerce will be so obvious that other states, driven by their own danger, but without any legal basis, will offer themselves as arbiters, and thus will prepare the way for distant international government for which there is no precedent in world history.
>
> (Kant, *Idea for a Universal History from a Cosmopolitan Point of View*, 1784)

If business (commerce) brings people together then the chance of peace among nations improves. Bowie considers that Kantian Ethics has rich implications for business ethics.

Virtue Ethics

Virtue Ethics from Aristotle shows that business cannot be separated from society – everyone is part of the larger community, the 'polis', the corporation, the neighbourhood, the city, the country or the world, and our virtues are defined by that larger community. Business is part of that community. Virtue Ethics focuses on the character and motivation of the agent and on the agent's ability to pursue *eudaimonia*. Virtue is also learnt through observation of others' behaviour – as far as business is concerned an individual cannot be ethical in a vacuum, but always as part of the ethical community. This applies to the employers as well as the employees who must show the virtues of character such as honesty, prudence, fairness and courage.

The virtues of co-operation seem to triumph over competition, but does this mean that the virtuous person in business will be the good corporate citizen rather than the high-flier, wheeler-dealer or the entrepreneurial innovator?

Virtue Ethics is interested in the most general traits that make a harmonious society possible, so the traits that make for good business must be the same as those of a good society; the virtues of a successful businessman and those of a good citizen must also be the same. In business, as in society, trustworthiness and co-operation are essential; even the most devious business dealings presuppose an atmosphere of trust, and competition is only possible (as in sport) within a context of general co-operation. Business is an essential part of society, not separate from it, and, as in society, living together is central, and making a profit is just a means.

REVIEW QUESTIONS

Look back over the chapter and check that you can answer the following questions:

- Explain how consumers can influence business ethics.
- Why is environmental responsibility a good business strategy?
- List the benefits and the problems of ethics for businesses.
- List the strengths and weaknesses of a Utilitarian approach to business ethics.
- How does Kant think business can help world peace?

Examination Questions Practice

Remember: each question assesses AO1 and AO2. To help you improve your answers look at the A2 Levels of Response. See: http://www.ocr.org.uk/qualifications/as-a-level-gce-religious-studies-h172-h572/.

SAMPLE EXAM STYLE QUESTION

- **'Kantian Ethics is the best approach to the issues surrounding business.' Discuss.** (35 marks)

- In your answer to this question you will need to explain the main principles of Kantian Ethics – e.g. duty, good will, the categorical and hypothetical imperatives – and how they might be applied to business.
- It would be better to concentrate on one or two business issues, such as relations between business and shareholders, the question of profit and what business methods could be universalised, the relations between employers and employees, and the importance of not treating others as a means to an end, or your essay may tend to be too much about business issues and not enough about ethical theories.
- However, you also need to ask if it is the 'best' approach and this means contrasting it with other approaches (e.g. Religious Ethics, Utilitarianism or Virtue Ethics).

SAMPLE A2 EXAM STYLE QUESTIONS

- **Assess the usefulness of Religious Ethics as an ethical approach to business.**
- **How far would you agree that environmental issues are more of a concern to a religious believer than to a Utilitarian?**
- **'Relativist ethics are the best approach to the environment.' Discuss.**

FURTHER READING

Benson, J. *Environmental Ethics*, London, Routledge, 2000.

Bowie, N.E. *Business Ethics: A Kantian Perspective*, Oxford, Blackwell, 1999.

Chryssides, G. and Kaler, J. *Essentials of Business Ethics*, London, McGraw-Hill, 1996.

Devall, B. and Sessions, G., *Deep Ecology*, Salt Lake City, Gibbs M. Smith, 1987.

Dregson, A. and Inoue, Y. (eds) *The Deep Ecology Movement: An Introductory Anthology*, Berkeley, North Atlantic Books, 1995.

Frederick, R. *A Companion to Business Ethics*, Oxford, Blackwell, 1999.

Leopold, A. *A Sand County Almanac*, Oxford/New York, Oxford University Press, 1968.

Lovelock, J. *Gaia: A New Look at Life on Earth*, Oxford, Oxford University Press, 1979.

Pearce, D., Markandya, A. and Barbier, E.B., *Blue Print for a Green Economy,* London, Earthscan, 1989.

Singer, P. *Practical Ethics*, Cambridge, Cambridge University Press, 1993.

Singer, P. 'All Animals Are Equal' in Sterba, J. (ed.) *Ethics: The Big Questions*, Oxford, Blackwell, 1998.

Singer, P. *One World: The Ethics of Globalization*, Yale, Yale University Press, 2004.

Solomon, R.C. *Ethics and Excellence*, New York, Oxford, Oxford University Press 1993.

Taylor, P. 'The Ethics of Respect for Nature' in Sterba, J. (ed.) *Ethics: The Big Questions*, Oxford, Blackwell, 1998.

Walker, J. *Environmental Ethics*, London, Hodder & Stoughton, 2000.

For those who want to take the topic further than the limitations of A level, I suggest they look at ecological feminism – a good introduction is to be found in Warren, K. 'The Power and Promise of Ecological Feminism' in Sterba, J. (ed.) *Ethics: The Big Questions*, Blackwell, Oxford, 1998.

Essential terminology

Celibacy
Feminism
Gender
Harm principle
Queer theory
Sex

16 Sexual Ethics

WHAT YOU WILL LEARN ABOUT IN THIS CHAPTER

- Different ethical approaches to sexual ethics, both religious and secular.
- Historical views of sex.
- The Old Testament approach to sexual ethics.
- The New Testament approach to sexual ethics: Jesus and Paul.
- Augustine and sexual ethics.
- Thomas Aquinas and sexual ethics.
- Kant and sexual ethics.
- Utilitarianism and sexual ethics.
- Virtue Ethics and sexual ethics.
- Modern influences on sexual ethics.
- Religious Ethics (Christian) and sexual ethics.
- Homosexuality.
- Contraception.
- An understanding of the underlying principles and implications of these different approaches for making decisions about the issues surrounding sexual ethics – premarital and extra-marital sex, contraception and homosexuality.
- How to assess the different approaches and to evaluate their strengths and weaknesses.

KEY SCHOLARS

- Augustine of Hippo (354–430)
- Thomas Aquinas (1225–1274)
- Immanuel Kant (1724–1804)
- Jeremy Bentham (1748–1832)
- John Stuart Mill (1806–1873)
- Sigmund Freud (1856–1939)
- Joseph Fletcher (1905–1991)
- Richard Holloway (1933–)
- Michael Slote (1941–)
- Rosalind Hursthouse (1943–)

THE OCR CHECKLIST

Candidates should be able to demonstrate knowledge and understanding of:

- the issues surrounding sexual ethics – premarital and extra-marital sex, contraception, homosexuality;
- the application and the different approaches of the ethical theories listed below to sexual ethics.

The ethical theories:

- Natural Law;
- Kantian Ethics;
- Utilitarianism;
- Religious Ethics;
- Virtue Ethics.

Candidates should be able to discuss these areas critically.

From OCR A Level Religious Studies Specification H572.

WHAT IS SEXUAL ETHICS?

Sex is an enormously wide term covering a range of issues from homosexuality to marriage, from pornography to prostitution, to the relational dimensions that are expressions of love and pleasure. It is part of being human and involves above all the question of how men and women should treat each other.

In spite of the fact that, or maybe because, sex is so natural to us, we hedge it with rules. As **Richard Holloway** put it: 'Human sexuality is like a runaway car.' It can be destructive or creative, but we are never quite in control of it.

HISTORICAL VIEWS OF SEX

Originally the Greek philosophers saw sex as something weakening to the mind. The Pythagoreans, who influenced Plato, believed that humans should refrain from physical activities and live a more ascetic life. In this way the soul, which is imprisoned in the body, is freed to move to a new form. This

Sex
Biological characteristics that determine whether a person is male or female.

dualism between the physical and the spiritual may be seen in Plato's model of the soul as the charioteer with his two horses: the beautiful white horse that is a model of self-control and responds to the spoken word, and the ugly black horse that needs controlling with a whip. There are in this many levels of interpretation as far as sexual desire/pleasure is concerned – the desire needs controlling but it is allowed to exist; after all, the charioteer needs both of his horses.

The Cynics, on the other hand, saw no point in controlling sexual desire/pleasure and saw no shame attached to the sexual act, even going so far as to perform it in public. The Stoics reacted totally against this and advocated overcoming any emotions that threaten self-control – the Stoics were the original 'stiff upper lips', and sex became linked to reproduction and the continuation of the human race.

So the early history of sex and relationships as far as philosophy was concerned was riddled with contradictions that have continued ever since. The same contradictions may be discerned in early Judaism as found in the Old Testament and later in Christianity. However, for the Greeks sexuality is naturally excessive and so the moral problem is not whether it is right or wrong but how to control it. This did not involve laws which prohibited certain sexual acts, but required individual self-discipline.

THE OLD TESTAMENT APPROACH TO SEXUAL ETHICS

The Old Testament is a reflection of its times and does not seem to have one particular view on sex and relationships. It includes moving love stories, such as the story of Ruth and Boaz; detailed accounts of incest, such as that concerning the two daughters of Lot in Genesis 19, whose incestual relationship with their father has the intention of assuring his line; and there are numerous tales of seduction and sexual revenge. Many of these are recounted in a factual way, without judgement. Sex is even celebrated in the Song of Songs.

In Genesis 1 and 2 there is an understanding that sex is created by God and meant for procreation. However, sex is not seen as wrong but good; yet the contradictions also appear, as sex should not be practised in sinful ways. Sexual involvement with non-Israelites was forbidden, as it would lead away from God (e.g. 1 Kings 11:1–13), and adultery was forbidden, seen as theft and punishable by stoning. This was a society in which women were not equal to men, but had to be part of the household of a man. Women should be virgins on marriage, but this was so the man could be certain that the children were his own and the line was assured.

THE NEW TESTAMENT APPROACH TO SEXUAL ETHICS

Jesus

Jesus himself said very little about sex; in fact he gave very few rules and instructions, but called his followers to live as part of the Kingdom of God, to reflect through their lives God's love for all people and to live justly with each other. As far as sex and relationships are concerned, Jesus seems to have left the issues open. Even in his teachings about marriage and divorce it is not possible to be sure what he said or what he meant. Jesus is quoted as saying: 'Whoever divorces his wife and (*kai*) marries another commits adultery (*porneia*) against her' (Mark 10:11). The wording here is not easy to translate into English; the word '*kai*' could mean 'in order to', not just 'and', and so depending on what the word means, the understanding of what Jesus meant changes. Similarly with the word '*porneia*' – it has three options: it could refer to a woman who was not a virgin on marriage, in which case divorce would follow immediately after marriage; it could mean adultery, in which case a man could divorce his wife for her adultery, but she did not have the same right if he was adulterous; or it could mean 'fornication', which in the Old Testament means chasing after other gods – divorce is allowed if the partner is a non-believer. However, it is clear that Jesus is challenging the view of the wife as the man's property – he is talking more about equality than about sexual relationships. One thing is clear, however, and this is that Jesus is setting out an ideal and divorce falls short of it.

Paul

As we have seen, the New Testament does not have a great deal to say on the subject, and much of Paul's writing is influenced by his expectation of the imminent return of Christ and the end of the world. There was not much point in giving a detailed ethic on sex and relationships, as all human relationships were soon to end. Paul, influenced by Greek thinking, attempted to move the Christian people away from the body towards the soul. So he writes in I Corinthians 6:12–20 that Christians should not let their bodily emotions control them, that sexual activity is to be kept within marriage, that the body is a temple of the Holy Spirit and should be respected.

'All things are lawful for me,' but not all things are beneficial. 'All things are lawful for me,' but I will not be dominated by anything. 'Food is meant for the stomach and the stomach for food,' and God will destroy both one and the other. The body is meant not for fornication but for the Lord, and the Lord for the body. And God raised the Lord and will also raise us by his power. Do you not know that your bodies are members of Christ? Should I therefore take the members of Christ and make them members of a prostitute? Never! Do you not know that whoever is united to a prostitute becomes one body with her? For it is said, 'The two shall be one flesh.' But anyone united to the Lord becomes one spirit with him. Shun fornication! Every sin that a person commits is outside the body; but the fornicator sins against the body itself. Or do you not know that your body is a temple of the Holy Spirit within you, which you have from God, and that you are not your own? For you were bought with a price; therefore glorify God in your body.

This whole passage shows Paul attempting to move people away from bodily pleasures to a more spiritual realm. Marriage was not forbidden, but considered only for those with no self-control.

Paul's views on sex and relationships, marriage and women are also inconsistent. Sometimes he was positive about women – all are equal:

There is no longer Jew or Greek, there is no longer slave or free, there is no longer male and female; for all of you are one in Christ Jesus.

(Galatians 3:28)

Yet elsewhere he argues that women should obey their husbands:

Wives, be subject to your husbands as you are to the Lord. For the husband is the head of the wife just as Christ is the head of the church, the body of which he is the Saviour. Just as the church is subject to Christ, so also wives ought to be, in everything, to their husbands.

(Ephesians 5:22–24)

Thus he returns to the Old Testament view of the wife as the property of the man. When he is positive about marriage and does not just consider it for the weak-willed, he compares marriage with the relationship between Christ and his Church:

Feminism
A way of thinking that seeks to emancipate women in society and give them equal opportunities.

'For this reason a man will leave his father and mother and be joined to his wife, and the two will become one flesh.' This is a great mystery, and I am applying it to Christ and the church.

(Ephesians 5:31–32)

However, this still seems to say that the man is the head of the household, just as Christ is head of the Church.

Paul's views do seem more rigid than the equality message of Jesus, but he was a product of his times, and his focus on the imminent return of Jesus limited his teaching to preparation for that day.

Paul is credited with exerting great influence on the development of Christian thought, but he was also limited by his religious views and the attitudes of the times, especially on the value of **celibacy** and the inferior role of women. However, Platonic dualism and the views of the Greek philosophers were also important, as they stressed the spiritual above the physical – sex and relationships were part of the physical side of us.

Celibacy
Not having sexual relations with another person.

AUGUSTINE AND SEXUAL ETHICS

Augustine of Hippo lived in a world of multiple sects and 'heresies', one of which picked up on and emphasised the dualism of body and soul. This was Gnosticism, a mixture of the Greek traditions, some Judaism and Zoroastrianism. It was from Zoroastrianism that the extreme dualism sprang, along with a pessimistic fatalism. Central to Gnostic teaching was an intense dislike of the body and its needs, a total pessimism about sexuality which infiltrated the early Church. In this world, the views of Augustine were surprisingly liberal, and he considered that, far from abstaining from all sex, it was necessary for procreation, and that, like Paul and the Greeks, sex was a necessary evil. Augustine taught, after his many sexual relationships, that sex was to be restricted to marriage, but it was still 'dangerous'. The devil uses women to lead men away from reason, and pleasure in sex leads men away from reason. For Augustine the problem, and the solution, dated back to creation and the Fall. Adam and Eve, he concluded, must have been made for procreation, though they would not have needed to procreate before the Fall, or at least would have experienced no desire or pleasure. However, God knew that Eve would take the fruit and so he prepared for the consequences. For Augustine, then, sexual desire is a constant reminder of man's rebellion against God – it is our original sin. Augustine, unlike **Pelagius**, believed that we could not control sexual desire – he did not go in for 'muscular Christianity' like Pelagius, who thought that sexual desire could be controlled by the will. So, for Augustine, chastity was the ideal, but sex was allowed, so long as it was not enjoyed, within marriage.

Attitudes such as those of Augustine have had great influence on sexual attitudes and practices in the Western world.

THOMAS AQUINAS AND SEXUAL ETHICS

Thomas Aquinas' views on sexual ethics were accepted as right for Christians until they began to be questioned in modern times.

Aquinas based his thinking about sex and relationships on his understanding of Natural Law, in which he attempted to unite the thinking of Aristotle with Christian theology. Aquinas believed that human life had a purpose or *telos;* good acts developed our human nature and bad acts went against human nature. Aquinas assumed that humans shared a common human nature and so general principles could be applied to everyone, everywhere and at all times. Aquinas concluded that the purpose of the sexual organs and sexual activity was procreation, and any other use of sex was intrinsically wrong. Sex for Aquinas was to take place within the bounds of marriage, and must be open to the possibility of procreation. This became the view of the Catholic Church.

In the *Summa Theologiae*, Aquinas argued that sexual acts can be morally wrong in two different ways:

1   Sex is wrong when 'the act of its nature is incompatible with the purpose of the sex act [procreation]. In so far as generation is blocked, we have unnatural vice, which is any complete sex act from which of its nature generation cannot follow.' Aquinas gives us four examples: 'The sin of self-abuse' (masturbation), 'Intercourse with a thing of another species' (bestiality), acts with a person of the same sex (homosexuality), and acts in which 'the natural style of intercourse is not observed, as regards proper organ or according to other rather beastly and monstrous techniques' (foreplay?)
2   Sexual acts can be morally wrong even if natural; in these cases, 'conflict with right reason may arise from the nature of the act with respect to the other party'; for example, incest, rape or adultery.

Natural Law, however, raises two important questions:

1   Is an 'unnatural act' always wrong, even if it is consummated with mutual and informed voluntary consent?
2   Are there some non-procreative sexual acts that might be natural to human beings? Do we, in fact, share a common nature, but might God have created a variety of human beings with different forms of sexual expression?

KANT AND SEXUAL ETHICS

The categorical imperative causes **Immanuel Kant** to take a conservative attitude to sexual ethics in many ways. A husband who commits adultery cannot want extra-marital sex to be a universal law unless he wants his wife, children, parents and so on to also engage in extra-marital activities. Neither can homosexuality be universalised, since every homosexual is conceived through a heterosexual relationship – although artificial insemination could change this.

According to Kant, the pursuit of sexual pleasure is only allowed when serving more valuable goals, such as marriage, since 'Taken by itself sexual love is a degradation of human nature'. The categorical imperative does not allow people to be treated as a means to an end and so he claims that: 'As soon as a person becomes an object of appetite for another, all motives of moral relationship cease to function, because as an object of appetite for another, a person becomes a thing and can be treated and used as such by everyone.' The Kantian viewpoint seems to be that sexual acts are wrong in themselves, as they involve using another person for one's own pleasure, but this seems to apply to prostitution, not marriage. Kant calls marriage a contract in which two people grant each other reciprocal rights, and so it is not about one person using or abusing another. It seems a rather cold way of putting it, so perhaps it is just as well that he never tried it. However, Kant does not see sex within marriage as wrong, and the purpose of marriage, as he sees it, is not procreation, as in Natural Law, but the union of two people of different sexes. Husband and wife are equal partners in this and sexual enjoyment is a right to be permitted within the partnership.

Thus, Kant emphasises the contractual nature of sexual relationships and seems to find sex morally acceptable as long as one person is not using the other as a means to an end. Using Kant's arguments, it is possible to say that providing sexual services is morally acceptable as long as no coercion is involved. Some forms of prostitution would be allowed, although not if people engage in it against their will, or if they could be harmed mentally or physically by it.

A Kantian would be opposed to pornography because one is taking pleasure in looking at a person in such a way that they are thought of as mere things, mere means of obtaining sexual gratification. However, Kant emphasises the physical side of the 'sex', not the emotional side of the 'relationship'.

UTILITARIANISM AND SEXUAL ETHICS

Utilitarian reasons for having sex are:

- the value of pleasure
- the contribution that shared pleasure makes to the value of a relationship
- that consensual sex creates much good, and, if harm to another person is avoided, provides the greatest happiness for the greatest number of people.

Utilitarians want a happy society and sexual pleasure is an important element of human happiness, so Utilitarians would want to maximise the good things about sex and relationships while minimising their downside. The Utilitarian approach to sex and relationships is often called libertarian, as it allows consenting adults to do what they want and protects their freedom to do so. However, maximisation of sexual pleasure does not mean 'free love', as there are consequences of the latter such as unwanted pregnancies and sexually transmitted diseases like HIV and AIDS, not to mention 'broken hearts'.

Utilitarian arguments will include what many other ethical theories forget – the emotional aspect of a good relationship and the emotional suffering caused by unfaithfulness and deceit. Utilitarianism approaches sex and relationships with something more than the contractarian approach which emphasises the importance of mutual and voluntary informed consent. Under the contractarian approach sex is morally wrong if one or both of those involved lack a knowledgeable consent; for example, the under-aged, the mentally impaired or even the drunk. However, even when a contract is involved, it does not mean that the sexual relationship is necessarily moral. A middle-aged man may have a 'sexual contract' with a 15-year-old illegal immigrant who is desperate for money. He can pay her for having sex with him, and although a 'contract' has taken place, it is not a moral one because the girl, like many prostitutes, may have been forced into prostitution due to her status and poverty.

Jeremy Bentham may allow this kind of sex and 'relationship' as providing the greatest happiness for the greatest number of people. In 'Offences against One's Self: Pederasty', he argued that mutual consent for pleasure cannot make any sex act wrong if both partners are willing. However, he also asked whether such a relationship harmed society and caused unhappiness, either physical or moral (e.g. by undermining marriage, fidelity, family life or causing public offence).

John Stuart Mill also stressed the value of liberty, and in *On Liberty* suggested that this should be a matter of individual choice, without state interference, 'so long as we do not attempt to deprive others of theirs or impede their efforts to obtain it'. However, he also argues that we should seek the 'higher pleasures', and that the goal of ethics is to seek the happiness of all by taking their needs and desires into account.

Utilitarians, therefore, should be tolerant of people with non-traditional sexual orientations, except in cases that do great social harm such as child molesters. Masturbation is permissible, assuming that it really does not make one go blind, although sex and relationships without two people involved may be seen as meaningless, so taking away the greatest amount of happiness for the greatest number of people. Homosexuality and bisexuality can be tolerated, although if homosexuality were the norm, it would be harmful to society.

However, the **harm principle** is important to the Utilitarian, especially in the case of extra-marital affairs, as very often the short-term pleasure they produce is not worth the ultimate pain and misery they can cause.

VIRTUE ETHICS AND SEXUAL ETHICS

Virtue Ethics stands apart from the approaches of most ethical theories and looks at moral choices from the standpoint of the individual and his or her personal qualities, virtues and ideals. Virtue Ethics would consider what kind of sexual practices will tend to make a person more virtuous – those that involve taking pleasure in giving oneself to another and developing intimacy and commitment would make a person more virtuous, whereas those that use others for one's own pleasure would tend to make a person less virtuous. In sex and relationships, Virtue Ethics points to the enduring values of love and commitment, honesty and loyalty, friendship and pleasure, and away from harmful traits such as exploitation and selfishness.

According to **Rosalind Hursthouse**, Virtue Ethics implies that an action is right if it is what a virtuous person, who has and exercises the virtues, would characteristically do in the circumstances. Many modern Virtue ethicists, such as **Michael Slote**, emphasise the ethics of care in relationships, which requires a sort of three-way balance as far as sexual ethics are concerned: care for those who are near to us (intimate care); care for other people in general (humanitarian care); and care for our own well-being (self-care).

This view implies tolerance towards others' approaches to sexual ethics, and it also accepts that we are responsible for our character and the moral choices we make. Virtue Ethics also urges us to rediscover balance in human sexuality and in our relationships.

Gender
Cultural and psychological characteristics that determine whether a person is male or female.

Queer theory
The idea that there can be no fixed rules about what is or is not a legitimate sexual relationship. Being queer is the freedom to define oneself according to one's nature.

Harm principle
The belief that an act or consequence is morally permissible if no harm is done.

MODERN INFLUENCES ON SEXUAL ETHICS

Modern popular thinking, influenced by developments in psychology and sociology, began to question traditional views by asking such questions as: 'Why is sex within marriage for procreation more in accordance with human nature than sex outside marriage for pleasure?' and 'Why cannot sexual relationships be morally right if there is love, loyalty and intimacy?'

According to **Sigmund Freud**, each person's approach to sex and relationships is based on their upbringing and their relationship with their parents. He suggests that sexual personality may be found at the core of moral personality: how we behave towards sexual partners both influences and mirrors how we perceive and interact with people in general. So, the failure to learn to control the pursuit of sexual pleasure undermines the achievement of a virtuous character.

Freud says that we each have a super-ego, which is like an inner voice reminding us of the social norms inculcated in us by our parents and authority figures in society. We need this voice in order to live happily in a law-abiding society. Unlike Aquinas, Freud considers that being moral may not accord with our real natures at all and so it is not possible to base an ethical theory on what we essentially are.

Rules about sex and relationships have existed in every culture, as have disagreements about what is and what is not morally acceptable. Must morally permissible sex have only one function? Must it be heterosexual? Must it be limited to marriage? Does sex require love or just mutual consent? Conditions in the modern world are changing rapidly and, as a result, modern opinions towards sex and relationships are also changing. This has influenced traditional religious teaching also.

RELIGIOUS ETHICS (CHRISTIAN) AND SEXUAL ETHICS

Traditional Christian ethics about sex and relationships is based on the teachings of the Bible, Augustine and Aquinas. Marriage is seen as the norm and the purpose of marriage is seen as fidelity, union and procreation. The unitive role of love is a comparatively modern element, and the role of sex in marriage as an expression of that love is also now recognised. Even sexual pleasure is seen as a gift from God – but only within the context of hetero-sexual marriage.

Jack Dominian argues, and has done for the past 30 years at least, not that sex is dangerous and needs marriage and procreation to protect it; but rather that sex is so powerful and meaningful that justice can only be done to it in a continuous and enduring relationship. He does not see premarital

sex, cohabitation or even one-off adultery as destroying this ideal and even considers that homosexual sex is fine within a permanent loving relationship. He sees society as moving forward and the Church as needing to rethink but not reject its fundamental truths.

HOMOSEXUALITY

One issue that has divided Christianity is that of homosexuality. Every religion is divided between fundamentalists and liberals, between what is revealed and what is discovered. In Christianity, the issue of homosexuality points up that division, with the literal interpretation of the Bible asserting that homosexuality is wrong, and the spirit of the New Testament holding that it is the quality of the relationships which matters. There are many other issues involved, such as homosexuality being not natural, as homosexual sex does not lead to the procreation of children, the question of the 'gay gene', and the actual translation of the words in the Bible.

The two Greek words that have traditionally been translated as homosexual may mean 'loose living' or 'prostitute', so in the New Revised Standard Version of the Bible the word 'homosexual' has been omitted from Paul's letters. The story of Sodom (Genesis 19:4–11) is not about sexuality but hospitality, and so the only references are in the codes of Deuteronomy (Deuteronomy 23:17–18) and Leviticus (Leviticus 20:13). The meaning of these codes was obviously important at the time they were written, but today laws about purity, including the types of animals and fish that could be eaten, which excluded shellfish, and about dress, which outlawed the wearing of garments made from more than one type of yarn, are just irrelevant to many people. One concept underlying the laws was the idea of the pure form of a man and a woman, which led to the prohibition of shaving in men so that they did not look like women, and also of cross-dressing and same-sex relationships. Almost all Christians ignore these prohibitions, except the one about homosexuality. So it seems as though the Bible is being used, as in the possible split in the Anglican Church over the ordination of gay bishops, to reinforce prejudices. As **Richard Holloway** points out, the impetus for social reform comes from society, not from within the Christian Church.

Within the Catholic Church the position is similar – there is no sin involved in having homosexual inclinations, only in putting them into practice. Following Natural Law, any sexual act that is not open to procreation is unnatural and wrong. Again the Catholic Church has done nothing to counteract prejudice against homosexuals.

CONTRACEPTION

A further issue is that of contraception, which in modern times has seen a vast variety of Christian views. Roman Catholic teaching goes back to Augustine's views that marital intercourse was morally justified as procreation was right and necessary and somehow cancelled out all the sinful sexual desire. The story of Onan (Genesis 38:9) was interpreted as teaching that any form of contraception was wrong, whereas Onan's misdeed was his avoidance in producing an heir by his dead brother's wife, not the actual avoidance of pregnancy.

Papal encyclicals stressed that the chief purposes of marriage were procreation and the bringing up of children. *Humanae Vitae*, the encyclical of Pope Paul VI, in 1968 reaffirmed this position, but did allow the use of the 'rhythm method' and other natural methods, as well as periods of sexual abstinence. It considered that the natural end of sexual intercourse was conception and anything that interfered with this was against the precepts of Natural Law and so unlawful.

As recently as 1997 the Vatican's Pontifical Council for the Family said that contraception was an intrinsic evil, 'gravely opposed to marital chastity', as not only did it stop procreation, but harmed true love between the couple and took away from God his role in the transmission of human life.

However, in practice many Catholics have ignored the official Church position. The Canadian Catholic Bishops Conference issued a dissenting document called the Winnipeg Statement, in which they reasserted the primacy of conscience in making ethical decisions. Arguments against the

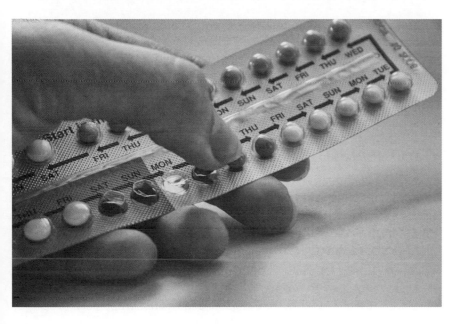

Catholic position include the fact that most acts of intercourse do not lead to procreation and so it cannot be the primary purpose of sex. Also it is argued that the distinctions between natural family planning and contraception have no morally significant differences as both are ways of ensuring that pregnancy does not take place. As the Catholic Church accepts natural family planning, it seems inconsistent in rejecting contraception.

However, the use of condoms to prevent sexually transmitted infections is not addressed by Catholic teaching, and in 2006 a study on the use of condoms within marriage to combat AIDS was ordered by Pope Benedict XVI.

Protestant churches used to have the same view as Catholics on contraception: that it went against God's purpose for marriage. Then in 1930 the Lambeth Conference issued the first statement in favour of birth control, and since then the views of Protestants have steadily changed, so that contraception is no longer regarded as a sin, and that the use or non-use of contraception is up to the individual conscience. Among Protestants, however, there is still ongoing discussion about which forms of contraception are allowed, with many rejecting any form of abortifacient contraception. In general, Protestants allow 'prudent family planning' so as to lead to responsible parenthood where each child is loved and wanted.

Until the 1970s the Eastern Orthodox Church also opposed contraception, but now holds that contraception is acceptable within a Christian marriage if the method of contraception is not abortifacient, it is used with the blessing of a spiritual leader and children are not completely excluded from the marriage.

Most Christian denominations do not accept the use of contraception outside of marriage, as this is seen as simply encouraging or permitting promiscuous behaviour. As far as premarital sex is concerned most Christians see it as wrong, and so abstaining from sex would be morally better than having sex and using birth control.

REVIEW QUESTIONS

Look back over the chapter and check that you can answer the following questions:

- What does the Old Testament say about sex and relationships?
- What does the New Testament say about sex and relationships?
- Why/how did sex become linked with procreation?
- List the strengths and weaknesses of a Utilitarian approach to sex and relationships.

Examination Questions Practice

Remember: each question assesses AO1 and AO2. To help you improve your answers look at the A2 Levels of Response. See: http://www.ocr.org.uk/qualifications/as-a-level-gce-religious-studies-h172-h572/.

SAMPLE EXAM STYLE QUESTION

- **'Natural Law is the most reliable approach when making judgements about sex and relationships.' Discuss.** (35 marks)

- You could start by explaining the main teachings of Natural Law (e.g. purpose, potentiality and actuality, primary and secondary precepts), the deontological and absolute nature of Natural Law and its origins in Aristotle, and how it is a basis for Roman Catholic teaching.

- You could discuss the nature of sexual morality (e.g. sex as procreative, sex within marriage, homosexuality, 'abuses' of sex), and apply Natural Law to sexual ethics. Using examples, you could show how some may see Natural Law as the best approach because, for example, it is universal and God-given, but for others Natural Law may appear out of date and inflexible.

- To really get to grips with this question you need to ask what is meant by 'reliable' and from whose perspective this theory may seem reliable. You may then discuss whether there can be any absolutes in terms of personal relationships or whether some other theories such as Kant, Utilitarianism or Natural Law might be considered more reliable.

SAMPLE A2 EXAM STYLE QUESTIONS

- **Discuss critically the view that in matters of sex we need to follow the dictates of conscience.**

- **'Sex and relationships are matters of personal choice.' Discuss.**

FURTHER READING

Bellioti, R. *Good Sex: Perspectives on Sexual Ethics*, Kansas, University Press of Kansas, 1993.

Blackburn, S. *Lust*, Oxford/New York, Oxford University Press, 2004.

Holloway, R. *Godless Morality*, Edinburgh, Canongate, 1999.

Hursthouse, R. *On Virtue Ethics*, Oxford, Oxford University Press, 1999.

Kant, I. *Lectures on Ethics*, Heath, P. and Schneewind, J.B. (eds), Cambridge, Cambridge University Press, 1997.

Moore, G. 'Sex, Sexuality and Relationships', in *Christian Ethics: An Introduction*, Hoose, B. (ed.), London/New York, Cassell, 1998.

Slote, M. *Morals from Motives*, Oxford/New York, Oxford University Press, 2001.

Vardy, P. *The Puzzle of Sex*, London, Fount, 1997.

Glossary

A posteriori
A statement which is knowable after experience.

A priori
A statement which is knowable without reference to any experience.

Abortion (procured abortion)
The termination of a pregnancy by artificial means.

Absolute
A principle that is universally binding.

Absolutism
An objective moral rule or value that is always true in all situations and for everyone without exception.

Act Utilitarianism
A teleological theory that uses the outcome of an action to determine whether it is good or bad.

Active euthanasia
The intentional premature termination of another person's life.

AI (artificial insemination)
The injection of sperm into a woman.

Analytic statements
Statements which are true by definition.

Anthropocentric
An approach to the environment that places human interests above those of any other species.

Apparent good
Something which seems to be good or the right thing to do but which does not fit the perfect human ideal.

Aretaic ethics
Another name for Virtue Ethics, from the Greek word *arete,* which simply means any kind of excellence or virtue.

Assisted dying/suicide
When a person takes their own life with the assistance of another person. When the other person is a doctor, it is called physician-assisted suicide.

Authoritarian conscience
Our sense of moral right and wrong formed in us by authority figures whom we want to obey.

Autonomous moral agent
Someone who can make a moral decision freely; someone who is totally responsible for their actions.

Autonomy
Self-directed freedom, arriving at moral judgement through reason.

Benevolence
Butler saw this as wanting the well-being of others.

Biocentric
An approach to the environment that considers the biological nature and diversity of the Earth to be of supreme importance.

Biodiversity
The variety of living things on Earth.

Blastocyst
A fertilised egg at about four to five days of development.

Cardinal Virtues
Originated in Plato – prudence, justice, temperance, courage. Added to with three theological virtues of faith, hope and charity.

Categorical imperative
A command to perform actions that are absolute moral obligations without reference to other ends.

Celibacy
Not having sexual relations with another person.

Christian Realism
The belief that Christianity may use violence to bring about the Kingdom of God and secure peace on Earth.

Cloning
A form of genetic engineering by which a plant, an animal or a human is created with the same genetic identity as another.

Compatibilism
The belief that it is possible to be both free and determined, as some aspects of our nature are determined, but not our ability to make moral decisions.

Conscience
Our sense of moral right and wrong.

Conscientia
The actual judgement or decision a person makes which leads to a particular course of action based upon those principles.

Consciousness
Awareness of self as an independent being, the ability to feel pain and pleasure.

Consequentialism
The rightness or wrongness of an act is determined by its consequences.

Consequentialist
Someone who decides whether an action is good or bad by its consequences.

Conservation ethics
The ethics of the use, allocation, protection and exploitation of the natural world.

Copernican Revolution
Belief that the solar system revolves around the sun.

Cultural relativism
What is right or wrong depends on the culture.

Deep ecology
An approach to environmental ethics that sees all life forms as of value and human life as just one part of the biosphere. It rejects anthropomorphism.

Deontological ethics
Ethical systems which consider that the moral act itself has moral value (e.g. telling the truth is always right, even when it may cause pain or harm).

Descriptive relativism
Different cultures and societies have differing ethical systems and so morality is relative.

Determinism
The view that every event has a cause and so, when applied to moral decisions, we do not have free will.

Divine Command theory
Actions are right or wrong depending on whether they follow God's commands or not.

Divine Law
The Bible – this reflects the Eternal Law.

Doctrine of double effect
An action where the main intention is to do good, but which may have a bad side-effect. The good intention makes the action right.

Dominion
The Judaeo-Christian idea that humans have a special place in the natural world and have responsibility for it.

Duty
A motive for acting in a certain way which shows moral quality.

Ecosophy
A word formed by contracting the phrase 'ecological philosophy'. It refers to philosophies which have an ecocentric or biocentric perspective such as deep ecology.

Embryo
The developing bundle of cells in the womb up to eight weeks' gestation.

Emotivism
A theory which says that moral statements are just expressions of feelings.

Ensoulment
The moment when the soul enters the body – in traditional Christian thought this was at forty days for boys and ninety days for girls. The Church now believes that life begins at conception.

Eternal Law
The principles by which God made and controls the universe which are only fully known by God.

Ethical naturalism/ethical cognitivism
A theory that moral values can be derived from sense experience.

Ethical non-naturalism/ethical non-cognitivism
A theory that ethical statements cannot be derived from sense experience.

Eudaimonia
The final goal of all human activity – happiness, well-being, human flourishing.

Euthyphro Dilemma
The dilemma first identified by Plato – is something good because God commands it or does God command it because it is good?

Feminism
A way of thinking that seeks to emancipate women in society and give them equal opportunities.

Foetus
An organism in the womb from nine weeks until birth.

Gaia hypothesis
A theory of James Lovelock.

Gender
Cultural and psychological characteristics which determine whether a person is male or female.

Genetic engineering
The technology involved in cloning, gene therapy and gene manipulation.

Geocentric
An approach to the environment which considers the geological nature and diversity of the Earth to be most important.

Germ line engineering
Changes in the parent's sperm or egg cells with the aim of passing on the changes to their offspring.

Golden Mean
The balance of extremes of virtues and vices. A balance between *excess* (having too much of something) and *deficiency* (having too little of something).

Good will
Making a moral choice expresses a good will.

Hard determinism
The belief that people do not have any free will and that all moral actions have prior causes. This means that nobody can be held morally responsible.

Harm principle
The belief that an act or consequence is morally permissible if no harm is done.

Hedonic calculus
Bentham's method for measuring the good and bad effects of an action.

Hedonism
The view that pleasure is the chief 'good'.

Hippocratic Oath
Written in the fifth century BCE, it became the basis for doctors' ethics. Other promises now replace it, but it is specifically against abortion.

Holistic
An approach to the environment that considers a range of factors, including the importance of balance within the ecosystem.

Human genome
A map of the human genes.

Hypothetical imperative
An action that achieves some goal or end.

Incompatibilism
The belief that determinism is logically incompatible with free will. Thus some incompatibilists will say that determinism is a fact and so we are not free, but most take the opposite view that free will is a fact and so determinism is false.

Instrumental value
Something's value lies in its usefulness for others.

Intellectual virtues
Characteristics of thought and reason – technical skill, scientific knowledge, prudence, intelligence and wisdom.

Intrinsic value
Something's value lies in itself.

Intrinsically good
Something which is good in itself, without reference to the consequences.

Intuitionism
A theory that moral truths are known by intuition.

Involuntary euthanasia
This term is used when someone's life is ended to prevent their suffering, without their consent, even though they are capable of consenting.

IVF (in-vitro fertilisation)
The procedure by which sperm and eggs from a couple are fertilised in a laboratory dish (in vitro = in glass; test-tube babies).

Jus ad bellum
Justice in the decision to wage war.

Jus in bello
Justice in the conduct of war.

Jus post bellum
Justice in the ending of the war.

Just War theory
The belief that war is morally justified if it meets certain criteria.

Kingdom of Ends
A world in which people do not treat others as means but only as ends.

Law
Objective principle, a maxim that can be universalised.

Libertarianism
The belief that determinism is false and people are free to make moral choices and so are responsible for their actions.

Logical positivism
The view that only those things which can be tested are meaningful.

Maxim
A general rule in accordance with which we intend to act.

Meta-ethics
The analysis of ethical language.

Moral absolutism
There is only one correct answer to every moral problem.

Moral objectivism
Truth is objectively real regardless of culture.

Moral relativism
There are no universally valid moral principles and so there is no one true morality.

Moral virtues
Qualities of character such as courage, friendliness, truthfulness.

Natural Moral Law
The theory that an eternal, absolute moral law can be discovered by reason.

Naturalistic fallacy
The claim that good cannot be defined.

Negative Utilitarianism
The principle of minimising pain.

Normative ethics
A term used to describe different moral codes of behaviour; rules by which we make moral decisions (e.g. Utilitarianism, Natural Moral Law, Kantian Ethics, Virtue Ethics).

Ordinary and extraordinary means
According to Natural Law moral duties apply in ordinary situations. A patient may refuse certain treatments on the grounds that they are 'extraordinary' (i.e. over and above the essential).

'Ought implies can'
The idea that someone cannot be blamed for what he could not do, but only for what he was capable of doing but did not do.

Pacifism
The belief that violence is wrong.

Passive euthanasia
Treatment is either withdrawn or not given to the patient in order to hasten death. This could include turning off a life-support machine.

Personhood
Definition of a human being as a person – having consciousness, self-awareness, ability to reason and self-sufficiency.

***Phronesis* (practical wisdom)**
According to Aristotle the virtue most needed for any other virtue to be developed. Balancing self-interest with that of others. Needs to be directed by the moral virtues.

Predestination
The belief that God has decided who will be saved and who will not.

Preference Utilitarianism
Moral actions are right or wrong according to how they fit the preferences of those involved.

Prescriptivism
A theory that ethical statements have an intrinsic sense so other people should agree with the statement and follow it.

Primary precepts
The fundamental principles of Natural Moral Law.

Principle of utility
The theory of usefulness – the greatest happiness for the greatest number.

Proportionality
In war, weapons should be proportionate to the aggression.

Purpose
The idea that the rightness or wrongness of an action can be discovered by looking at whether or not the action agrees with human purpose.

PVS (persistent vegetative state)
When a patient is in this condition, doctors may seek to end their life. The relatives have to agree and usually the patient must be brain-stem dead.

Qualitative
Looking at the quality of the pleasure.

Quality of life
The belief that human life is not valuable in itself; it depends on what kind of life it is.

Quantitative
Looking at the quantity of the happiness.

Queer theory
The idea that there can be no fixed rules about what is or is not a legitimate sexual relationship. Being queer is the freedom to define oneself according to one's nature.

Real good
The right thing to do – it fits the human ideal.

Realism
Normal moral rules cannot be applied to how states act in time of war.

Relativism
Nothing may be said to be objectively right or wrong; it depends on the situation, the culture and so on.

Rule Utilitarianism
Establishing a general rule that follows Utilitarian principles.

Sanctity of life
The belief that human life is valuable in itself.

Secondary precepts
These are worked out from the primary precepts.

Self-love
Butler thought of this as wanting the well-being of self or enlightened self-interest, not selfishness.

Sentience
The ability to feel pleasure and pain.

Sex
Biological characteristics that determine whether a person is male or female.

Shallow ecology
The Earth is cared for to make conditions better for humans.

Situation Ethics
The morally right thing to do is the most loving in the situation.

Slippery slope
This means that when one moral law is broken others will also be gradually broken and there will be no moral absolutes.

Soft determinism
The belief that determinism is true in many aspects, but we are still morally responsible for our actions.

Somatic cell engineering
Changes in somatic (body) cells to cure an otherwise fatal disease. These changes are not passed on to a person's offspring.

Stem cell
A 'master' cell that can become any kind of material.

Stewardship
A way of interpreting the use of dominion, which sees humans as caretakers of the natural world.

Subjectivism
Each person's values are relative to that person and so cannot be judged objectively.

Summum bonum
The supreme good that we pursue through moral acts.

Super-ego
Freud's idea is that the super-ego reinforces ideas of correct behaviour implanted in us when we were young.

Synderesis
Aquinas' idea of what he termed 'right' reason by which a person acquires knowledge of basic moral principles and understands that it is important to do good and avoid evil.

Syneidesis
Syneidesis means 'to know with'. St Paul uses it to explain the human ability to know and choose what is good. He seems to suggest a moral consciousness which compares an action to a standard. Used by St Jerome to mean 'gleams (or sparks) of conscience by which we discern that we sin'.

Synthetic statements
Statements that may be true or false and can be tested using experience or senses.

Teleological
Moral actions are right or wrong according to their outcome or *telos* (end).

Teleological ethics
The morally right or wrong thing to do is determined by the consequences.

Therapeutic cloning
A method of producing stem cells to treat diseases such as Alzheimer's.

Universalisability
If an act is right or wrong for one person in a situation, then it is right or wrong for anyone in that situation.

Utilitarianism
Only pleasure and the absence of pain have utility or intrinsic value.

Viability
Where a foetus is considered capable of sustaining its own life, given the necessary care.

Vices
The direct opposite of virtues – habitual wrong action.

Virtue
Habitually doing what is right – being good requires the practice of a certain kind of behaviour.

Voluntary euthanasia
The intentional premature termination of another person's life at their request.

Zygote
A 'proto-embryo' of the first two weeks after conception – a small collection of identical cells.

Bibliography

PUBLICATIONS

Ahluwalia, L. *Foundation for the Study of Religion*, London, Hodder & Stoughton Educational, 2001.

Anscombe, G.E.M. 'War and Murder', in *Moral Problems*, Palmer, M., Cambridge, Lutterworth Press, 1991.

Aquinas, T. 'Summa Theologiae', in *Basic Writings of Thomas Aquinas*, Pegis, A.C. (ed.), Hackett, IN, Random House, 1997.

Aquinas, T. *Summa Theologiae II–II q.40* (Dominican translation), London, Burns & Oates, 1936.

Aristotle. *Nichomachean Ethics: An Introduction to Aristotle*, McKeon, R. (ed.), Ross, W.D. (trans.), New York, Random House, 1947.

Ayer, A.J. *Language, Truth and Logic,* London, Penguin, [1936] 2001.

Baelz, P. *Ethics and Belief*, New York, Seabury Press, 1977.

Barclay, W. *Ethics in a Permissive Society*, London, Collins, 1971.

Bellioti, R. *Good Sex: Perspectives on Sexual Ethics*, Kansas, University Press of Kansas, 1993.

Benson, J. *Environmental Ethics*, London, Routledge, 2000.

Bentham, J. *Introduction to the Principles of Morals and Legislation*, Harrison W. (ed.), Cambridge, Cambridge University Press, 1948.

Bentham, J. and Mill, J.S. *Utilitarianism and Other Essays*, London, Penguin, 1987.

Blackburn, S. *Being Good: A Short Introduction to Ethics*, Oxford, Oxford Paperbacks, 2002.

Blackburn, S. *Ethics: A Very Short Introduction*, Oxford, Oxford University Press, 2003.

Blackburn, S. *Lust*, Oxford/New York, Oxford University Press, 2004.

Bolt, R. *A Man for All Seasons*, London, Methuen, [1960] 1996.

Bowie, N. E. *Business Ethics: A Kantian Perspective*, Oxford Blackwell, 1999.

Bowie, R. *Ethical Studies* (2nd edn), Cheltenham, Nelson Thornes, 2004.

Butler, J. *1726 Fifteen Sermons*, London, Bell, 1964.

Catechism of the Catholic Church, London, Geoffrey Chapman, 1994.

Coates, A. *The Ethics of War*, Manchester, Manchester University Press, 1997.

Cook, D. *The Moral Maze*, London, SPCK, 1983.

Copleston SJ, F.C. *Aquinas*, New York, Penguin Books, 1955.

Coppieters, B. and Fotion, N. (eds) *Moral Constraints on War*, New York/Oxford, Lexington Books, 2002.

Crisp, R. and Slote, M. *Virtue Ethics*, Oxford/New York, Oxford University Press, 1997.

Davies, B. *Philosophy of Religion: A Guide and Anthology*, Oxford, Oxford University Press, 2000.

Davies, B. *An Introduction to the Philosophy of Religion* (3rd edn), Oxford, Oxford University Press, 2003.

Deane-Drummond, C. (ed.) *Brave New World*, London/New York, T&T Clark, 2003.

Deane-Drummond, C. *Genetics and Christian Ethics*, Cambridge, Cambridge University Press, 2005.

Deidum, T. 'The Bible and Christian Ethics', in *Christian Ethics: An Introduction*, Hoose, B. (ed.), London, Cassell, 1998.

Dominian, J. *Passionate and Compassionate Love: A Vision for Christian Marriage*, London, Darton, Longman & Todd, 1991.

Dregson, A. and Inoue, Y. (eds) *The Deep Ecology Movement: An Introductory Anthology*, Berkeley, CA, North Atlantic Books, 1995.

Fletcher, J. *Situation Ethics*, Philadelphia, PA, Westminster Press, 1963.

Foot, P. *Virtues and Vices*, Oxford, Blackwell, 1978.

Frederick, R. *A Companion to Business Ethics*, Oxford, Blackwell, 1999.

Gensler, H. *Ethics: A Contemporary Introduction*, New York/London, Routledge, 1998.

Gensler, H., Earl, W. and Swindal, J. *Ethics: Contemporary Readings*, New York/London, Routledge, 2004.

Gill, R. *A Textbook of Christian Ethics*, London/New York, T&T Clark, 1995.

Glover, J. *Causing Death and Saving Lives*, London, Penguin, 1990.

Glover, J. *Humanity: A Moral History of the Twentieth Century*, New Haven, CT, Yale University Press, 2000.

Graham, G. *Living the Good Life*, New York, Paragon House, 1990.

Graham, G. *Evil and Christian Ethics*, Cambridge, Cambridge University Press, 2001.

Graham, G. *Eight Theories of Ethics,* London, Routledge, 2004.

Grayling, A.C. *What Is Good? The Search for the Best Way to Live*, London, Phoenix Press, 2004.

Grisez, G. and Boyle, J. 'The Morality of Killing: A Traditional View', in *Bioethics: An Anthology*, Kuhse, H. and Singer, P. (eds), Oxford, Blackwell, 1999.

Gula, R. *Reason Informed by Faith*, New Jersey, Paulist Press, 1989.

Hare, R.M. *The Language of Morals*, Oxford, Oxford University Press, 1952.

Hare, R.M. *Freedom and Reason,* London, Clarendon Press, 1963.

Harman, G. and Jarvis Thomson, J. *Moral Relativism and Moral Objectivity*, Oxford, Blackwell, 1995.

Hinman, L. 'Ethics Updates', available online at http://ethics.sandiego.edu/.

Hodge, R. *What Is Conscience for?*, London, Daughters of St Paul, 1995.

Holloway, R. *Godless Morality*, Edinburgh, Canongate, 1999.

Holmes, R. *On War and Morality*, Princeton, Princeton University Press, 1989.

Holy Bible: New Revised Standard Version (anglicised), Cambridge University Press and Oxford University Press, 1996.

Honderich, T. *How Free Are You?*, Oxford, Oxford University Press, 1993.

Hoose, B. (ed.) *Christian Ethics: An Introduction*, London, Cassell, 1998.

Hope, T. *Medical Ethics: A Very Short Introduction*, Oxford, Oxford University Press, 2004.

Hughes, G. 'Natural Law', in *Christian Ethics: An Introduction*, Hoose, B. (ed.), London, Cassell, 1998.

Hume, D. *Treatise of Human Nature*, London, Penguin, [1740] 2004.

Hume, D. *An Enquiry Concerning Human Understanding and Concerning the Principles of Morals,* Oxford, Oxford University Press, [1748] 1975.

Hume, D. *Dialogues Concerning Natural Religion*, London, Penguin, [1779] 1990.

Hursthouse, R. *On Virtue Ethics*, Oxford, Oxford University Press, 1999.

Hursthouse, R. 'Virtue Theory and Abortion', in *Ethics in Practice: An Anthology*, Lafollette, H. (ed.), Oxford, Blackwell, 2002.

Jarvis Thomson, J. 'A Defense of Abortion', in *Bioethics: An Anthology*, Kuhse, H. and Singer, P. (eds), Oxford, Blackwell, 1999.

Jones, R. 'Peace, Violence and War', in *Christian Ethics: An Introduction*, Hoose, B. (ed.), London, Cassell, 1998.

Kant, I. *Idea for a Universal History from a Cosmopolitan Point of View* (1784) in Kant, 'On History', Beck, L.W. (trans.), New York, Bobbs-Merrill Co., 1963.

Kant, I. *Lectures on Ethics*, Heath, P. and Schneewind, J.B. (eds), Cambridge, Cambridge University Press, 1997.

Kant, I. 'Groundwork of a Metaphysics of Morals', in *The Moral Law*, Paton, H.J. (trans.), London, Routledge, 2005.

Keenan, J. 'Virtue Ethics' in *Christian Ethics: An Introduction*, Hoose, B. (ed.), London, Cassell, 1998.

Kirkwood, R. 'Ethical Theory' in *Dialogue,* Special Issue.

Kuhse, H. 'Why Killing Is Not Always Worse – and Sometimes Better – than Letting Die', in *Bioethics: An Anthology*, Kuhse, H. and Singer P. (eds), Oxford, Blackwell, 1999.

Kuhse, H. and Singer, P. (eds) *Bioethics: An Anthology*, Oxford, Blackwell, 1999.

Lafollette, H. (ed.) *Ethics in Practice: An Anthology*, Oxford, Blackwell, 2002.

Leopold, A. *A Sand County Almanac*, Oxford/New York, Oxford University Press, 1968.

Leopold, A. 'The Land Ethic', in *Ethics in Practice: An Anthology*, Lafollette, H. (ed.), Oxford, Blackwell, 2002.

Louden, R. 'On Some Vices of Virtue Ethics', in *Virtue Ethics*, Crisp, R. and Slote, M. (eds), Oxford, Oxford University Press, 1997.

Lovelock, J. *Gaia: A New Look at Life on Earth*, Oxford, Oxford University Press, 1979.

MacIntyre, A. *A Short History of Ethics*, London, Routledge, 1968.

MacIntyre, A. *After Virtue*, London, Duckworth, 1985.

Mackie, J.L. *Ethics: Inventing Right and Wrong*, London, Penguin, 1990.

Macquarrie, J. and Childress, J. *A New Dictionary of Christian Ethics*, London, SCM, 1986.

Maguire, D. *The Moral Choice,* New York, HarperCollins, 1979.

Maguire, D. *Death by Choice*, New York, Image Books, 1984.

Mahoney, J. *Seeking the Spirit: Essays in Moral and Pastoral Theology*, London, Sheen & Ward, 1981.

Merton, T. *Choosing to Love the World: On Contemplation*, Boulder, CO, Sounds True Inc., 2008.

Mill, J.S. *Utilitarianism*, Indianapolis, Hackett, [1861, 1863], 2002.

Moore, G. 'Sex, Sexuality and Relationships', in *Christian Ethics: An Introduction*, Hoose, B. (ed.), London/New York, Cassell, 1998.

Niebuhr, R. *Moral Man and Immoral Societies*, New York, Scribner, 1932.

Norman, R. *Ethics, Killing and War*, Cambridge, Cambridge University Press, 1995.

Norman, R. *The Moral Philosophers*, Oxford, Oxford University Press, 1998.

O'Connell, T. *Principles for a Catholic Morality* (revised edn), New York, HarperCollins, 1990.

O'Neill, O. *Autonomy and Trust in Bioethics*, Cambridge, Cambridge University Press, 2002.

Palmer, M. *Moral Problems*, Cambridge, Lutterworth Press, 1991.

Palmer, M. *Moral Problems in Medicine,* Cambridge, Lutterworth Press, 1999.

Peters, T. *Playing God? Genetic Determinism and Human Freedom*, London, Routledge, 1997.

Plato. 'Euthyphro', in *The Last Days of Socrates*, Tredennick, H. (trans.), London, Penguin, 1969.

Plato. *The Republic,* Lee, D. (trans.), London, Penguin, 2003.

Pojman, L.P. *Ethical Theory*, Toronto, Wadsworth, 1989.

Pojman, L.P. *Ethics: Discovering Right and Wrong*, Toronto, Wadsworth, 2002.

Preston, R. 'Conscience', in *A Dictionary of Christian Ethics*, Macquarrie, J., London, SCM, 1967.

Rachels, J. 'Active and Passive Euthanasia', in *Bioethics: An Anthology*, Kuhse, H. and Singer, P. (eds), Oxford, Blackwell, 1999.

Rachels, J. and Rachels, S. *The Elements of Moral Philosophy*, New York, McGraw-Hill, 2007.

Ramsay, I. *Christian Ethics and Contemporary Philosophy*, London, SCM, 1966.

Rawls, J. *A Theory of Justice*, Harvard, MA, Harvard University Press, 1971.

Ridley, M. *The Red Queen: Sex and the Evolution of Human Nature*, London, Penguin, 1994.

Ridley, M. *Genome*, London, HarperCollins, 2000.

Robinson, J. *Honest to God*, London, SCM, 1963.

Rosenstand, N. *The Moral of the Story* (5th edn), New York, McGraw-Hill, 2006.

Ross, W.D. *The Right and the Good*, Oxford, Clarendon Press, 1930.

Rulan, V. *An Ethics of Global Rights and Religious Pluralism*, San Francisco, CA, University of San Francisco Press, 2003.

Sacred Congregation for the Doctrine of Faith. 'Declaration on Euthanasia', in *Bioethics: An Anthology*, Kuhse, H. and Singer, P. (eds), Oxford, Blackwell, 1999.

Scruton, R. *Kant*, Oxford, Oxford University Press, 1982.

Sidgwick, H. *Methods of Ethics*, Indianapolis, Hackett, 1981.

Singer, P. *One World: The Ethics of Globalization*, Yale, Yale University Press, 2004.

Singer, P. *Practical Ethics* (3rd edn), Cambridge, Cambridge University Press, 2011.

Singer, P. (ed.) *A Companion to Ethics*, Oxford, Blackwell, 1994.

Singer, P. *Rethinking Life and Death*, Oxford, Oxford University Press, 1994.

Singer, P. 'All Animals Are Equal', in *Ethics: The Big Questions*, Sterba, J. (ed.), Oxford, Blackwell, 1998.

Slote, M. *Morals from Motives*, Oxford/New York, Oxford University Press, 2001.

Smart, J.J.C. and Williams, B. *Utilitarianism: For and against,* Cambridge, Cambridge University Press, 1973.

Solomon, R. C. *Ethics and Excellence*, New York, Oxford, Oxford University Press, 1993.

Song, R. *Human Genetics: Fabricating the Future*, London, Darton, Longman & Todd, 2002.

Spinoza, B. de, *Ethics*, Curley, E. (ed. and trans.), London, Penguin Books, 1996).

Stevenson, C.L. *Ethics and Language*, Oxford, Oxford University Press, 1945.

Stroll, A. *Did My Genes Make Me Do It?* Oxford, Oneworld Publications, 2006.

Taylor, P. 'The Ethics of Respect for Nature', in *Ethics: The Big Questions*, Sterba, J. (ed.), Oxford, Blackwell, 1998.

Thompson, M. *Ethical Theory*, London, Hodder Murray, 2005.

Thompson, M. *Teach Yourself Ethics*, London, Hodder Arnold, 2006.

Van Inwagen, P. *An Essay on Free Will*, Cambridge, Clarendon Press, 1983.

Vardy, P. *The Puzzle of Sex*, London, Fount, 1997.

Vardy, P. and Grosch, P. *The Puzzle of Ethics*, London, Fount, 1999.

Walker, J. *Environmental Ethics*, London, Hodder & Stoughton, 2000.

Ward, K. *The Development of Kant's View of Ethics*, Oxford, Blackwell, 1972.

Warnock, M. *An Intelligent Person's Guide to Ethics*, London, Duckworth, 1999.

Warren, K. 'The Power and Promise of Ecological Feminism', in *Ethics: The Big Questions*, Sterba, J. (ed.), Oxford, Blackwell, 1998.

Warren, M.A. 'Abortion', in *A Companion to Ethics*, Singer, P. (ed.), Oxford, Blackwell, 1991.

Warren, M.A. 'On the Legal and Moral Status of Abortion', in *Ethics in Practice: An Anthology*, LaFollette, H. (ed.), Oxford, Blackwell, 1997.

Wilcockson, M. *Issues of Life and Death*, London, Hodder & Stoughton, 1999.

Wilcockson, M. *Sex and Relationships*, London, Hodder & Stoughton, 2000.

Williams, B. *Morality: An Introduction to Ethics*, Cambridge, Cambridge University Press, 1993.

Williams, B. *Ethics and the Limits of Philosophy*, London, Routledge, 2006.

Wink, W. *Jesus and Nonviolence: A Third Way*, Minneapolis, Abingdon Press US, 2003.

WEBSITES

http://www.newmanreader.org/works/grammar/index.html

http://www.pbs.org/wgbh/questionofgod/ownwords/future2.html

http://www.harryhiker.com/exercise.htm

http://www.angelfire.com/ms/perring/baier.html

http://plato.stanford.edu/

http://www.victorianweb.org/philosophy/utilitarianism.html

http://www.uri.edu/personal/szunjic/philos/util.htm

http://www.utilitarian.org/utility.html

http://www.rep.routledge.com/article/DB047

http://www.nobunaga.demon.co.uk/htm/kant.htm [Kant's works online]

http://www.newadvent.org/

http://www.bbc.co.uk/religion/ethics/

http://www.religioustolerance.org/

http://www.srtp.org.uk/

http://www.justwartheory.com/

http://www.importanceofphilosophy.com

http://en.wikipedia.org/

Index

emotivism 184, 192–6, 208
empathy 70, 72, 209
employer/employee relationship 276
end-times theology 260–1
ensoulment 106
environmental ethics: and business 278–9; Christian approach to 98, 257–60; OCR checklist for 256; and religion 100, 286; secular approaches to 261–2; use of term 256–7
environmental Virtue Ethics 269–70
Epicureans 64–5
equal consideration, principle of 77
Essay on Liberty 131
Eternal Law 29–32, 36
ethical disagreements 195, 208
ethical statements: and emotivism 192–6, 208; meaning of 185–6; and natural statements 186–8; and prescriptivism 197–8; and subjectivism 6; as synthetic 60
ethical theories: normative premises of 7; types of 5
ethics: areas of 4–5; goal of 203; historical change in 14–15; use of term 3
eudaimonia: in Natural Law 27; and Utilitarianism 63–4, 68; and Virtue Ethics 202, 205, 207
Eusebius 157
euthanasia: in hedonic calculus 65–6; and logical fallacies 3–4; OCR checklist for 122–3; and right to life 127–8; use of term 123
Euthyphro Dilemma 36, 92–3
exaggeration 4
examination techniques xiii–xvi
existentialism 225
extinction 266
extra-marital affairs 295, 297; *see also* adultery

fallacies, common 3–4
fatalism 217, 227
fertility treatment 106, 114
fidelity: as duty 57, 190; and sexual ethics 212
Finnis, John 34

Fletcher, Joseph: on assisted reproduction 118; on bioethics 149–50; biography of 17; criticism of 94; development of Situationism 16–17; on love 93; on Utilitarianism 96
flourishing: and eudaimonia 27; in Natural Law 34, 37, 41; and Virtue Ethics 208–9
foetal screening 115–16
foetal stem cells 145
foetus: gene therapy for 144–5; legal protection of 104; in Natural Law 34–5; personhood of 81, 109–13; use of term 102
Foot, Philippa 208
force: as last resort 162; proportional 163
Forms, Plato's theory of 11–12, 21
Formula of End in Itself 52
Formula of a Kingdom of Ends 52–3
Formula of the Law of Nature 50
fornication 291–2
Francis of Assisi 259
free love 296
free will: and Christianity 217, 219; and determinism 220, 223–4, 227–8; and evil 149; OCR checklist for 216; sample exam questions on 231
freedom: and agape 17; and conscience 251; constraints on choice in 229–30; in Kantian Ethics 47, 50, 54; and moral action 225, 227–9
Freud, Sigmund 241–2, 251, 298
Friedman, Milton 274
Fromm, Erich 245

Gaia hypothesis 256, 261, 263–5, 273
Gandhi, Mohandas 174, 205
gender: use of term 297; and Virtue Ethics 210
gene therapy 138–9, 144
generalisation, hasty 4
genetic engineering: and business ethics 274–5; Christian teaching on 149–50; and Kantian Ethics 58–9; OCR checklist for 138; use of term 138–9
genetic screening 142–4, 150

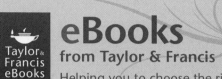

OCR Religious Ethics for AS and A2

Third Edition

Structured directly around the specification, this is a textbook for students of Advanced Subsidiary or Advanced Level courses and is endorsed by OCR for use with the OCR A Level Religious Studies specification. The updated third edition covers all the necessary topics for Religious Ethics in an enjoyable student-friendly fashion. Each chapter includes:

- a list of key issues
- OCR specification checklist
- explanations of key terminology
- overviews of key scholars and theories
- self-test review and exam practice questions.

To maximise students' chances of success, the book contains a section dedicated to answering examination questions. It comes complete with diagrams and tables, lively illustrations, a comprehensive glossary and full bibliography. Additional resources are available via the companion website at www.routledge.com/cw/oliphant.

Jill Oliphant until recently taught Religious Studies at Angley School in Kent. She is also an experienced examiner.

Jon Mayled has been a chief examiner for Religious Studies. He is a freelance writer and editor.